The Bible Speaks Today

Series Editors: J. A. Motyer (OT)
John R. W. Stott (NT)

The Message of Hebrews

Christ above All

Titles in this series

OLD TESTAMENT

The Message of **Genesis 1—11**
David Atkinson

The Message of **Genesis 12—50**
Joyce G. Baldwin

The Message of **Deuteronomy**
Raymond Brown

The Message of **Judges**
Michael Wilcock

The Message of **Ruth**
David Atkinson

The Message of **Chronicles**
Michael Wilcock

The Message of **Job**
David Atkinson

The Message of **Ecclesiastes**
Derek Kidner

The Message of **Jeremiah**
Derek Kidner

The Message of **Daniel**
Ronald S. Wallace

The Message of **Hosea**
Derek Kidner

The Message of **Amos**
J. A. Motyer

NEW TESTAMENT

The Message of the **Sermon on the Mount (Matthew 5—7)**
John R. W. Stott

The Message of **Mark**
Donald English

The Message of **Luke**
Michael Wilcock

The Message of **John**
Bruce Milne

The Message of **Acts**
John R. W. Stott

The Message of **1 Corinthians**
David Prior

The Message of **2 Corinthians**
Paul Barnett

The Message of **Galatians**
John R. W. Stott

The Message of **Ephesians**
John R. W. Stott

The Message of **Philippians**
J. A. Motyer

The Message of **Colossians & Philemon**
R. C. Lucas

The Message of **1 & 2 Thessalonians**
John R. W. Stott

The Message of **2 Timothy**
John R. W. Stott

The Message of **Hebrews**
Raymond Brown

The Message of **James**
J. A. Motyer

The Message of **1 Peter**
Edmund P. Clowney

The Message of **John's Letters**
David Jackman

The Message of **Revelation**
Michael Wilcock

The Message of Hebrews

Christ above All

Raymond Brown

Principal of Spurgeon's College, London

Inter-Varsity Press
Leicester, England
Downers Grove, Illinois, U.S.A.

InterVarsity Press
38 De Montfort Street, Leicester LE1 7GP, England
P.O. Box 1400, Downers Grove, Illinois 60515, U.S.A.

InterVarsity Press®, USA, is the book-publishing division of InterVarsity Christian Fellowship®, a student movement active on campus at hundreds of universities, colleges and schools of nursing in the United States of America, and a member movement of the International Fellowship of Evangelical Students. For information about local and regional activities, write Public Relations Dept., InterVarsity Christian Fellowship, 6400 Schroeder Rd., P.O. Box 7895, Madison, WI 53707-7895.

Inter-Varsity Press, England, is the publishing division of the Universities and Colleges Christian Fellowship (formerly the Inter-Varsity Fellowship), a student movement linking Christian Unions in universities and colleges throughout the United Kingdom and the Republic of Ireland, and a member movement of the International Fellowship of Evangelical Students. For information about local and national activities in Great Britain write to UCCF, 38 De Montfort Street, Leicester LE1 7GP.

USA ISBN 0-87784-289-2
USA ISBN 0-87784-925-0 (set of The Bible Speaks Today)
UK ISBN 0-85110-738-9

Text set in Great Britain
Printed in the United States of America

21 20 19 18 17 16 15 14 13 12 11 10 9 8
05 04 03 02 01 00 99 98 97 96 95 94

General preface

The Bible Speaks Today describes a series of both Old Testament and New Testament expositions, which are characterized by a threefold ideal: to expound the biblical text with accuracy, to relate it to contemporary life, and to be readable.

These books are, therefore, not 'commentaries', for the commentary seeks rather to elucidate the text than to apply it, and tends to be a work rather of reference than of literature. Nor, on the other hand, do they contain the kind of 'sermons' which attempt to be contemporary and readable, without taking Scripture seriously enough.

The contributors to this series are all united in their convictions that God still speaks through what he has spoken, and that nothing is more necessary for the life, health and growth of Christians than that they should hear what the Spirit is saying to them through his ancient—yet ever modern—Word.

J. A. MOTYER
J. R. W. STOTT
Series Editors

Contents

III Our response

Author's preface

At a time in history when thinking people all over the world are troubled about issues such as violence, unemployment, poverty, drug addiction, the arms race, alcoholism, and the breakdown of home and family life, some readers may be tempted to question the relevance of this particular biblical exposition. Many have come to regard the letter to the Hebrews, with its references to animal sacrifices and the like, as one of the most theological and possibly one of the most puzzling of all the New Testament letters. Some of our contemporaries find themselves wondering what contribution is made by its teaching to the serious problems of late twentieth-century society.

For almost nine years I have given a considerable amount of my spare time to the study of this letter and have emerged from the privileged task more than ever convinced of its striking contemporary relevance. Its illustrations are certainly drawn from a different world, but its message is timeless. Far from escaping into the past, it beckons us on to a better future, with its firm assurance that the eternal Son of God is supreme and sufficient. It is the clear, Christocentric message of this letter which makes it an extremely important document for our time. The message of Christ's uniqueness is always relevant. New Testament teaching makes it abundantly clear that nothing is of greater importance for the destiny of mankind, and that theme is certainly the central doctrine of the letter to the Hebrews.

I would like to acknowledge the help I have received from others in the preparation of this book. I have, first of all, been inspired by the work of its most outstanding commentators, notably B. F. Westcott, F. F. Bruce and, more recently, Philip Hughes. Over the years it has also been helpful, for me at least, to attempt an exposition of key passages from the letter at Conferences for Ministers and others, and at Conventions, especially those at Southsea, Frinton and Portstewart. I am grateful to these widely different audiences for their helpful comments and encouragement. I must also express my thanks to the Rev. John R. W. Stott not only for his editorial advice but also for his kind yet firm patience with a slow writer. As one whose main academic discipline is in the field of church history, I benefited a great deal in the initial stages of my work from comments made on a first draft by two of my colleagues on the staff of Spurgeon's College who teach New Testament studies, the Revs. Frank S. Fitzsimmonds and John F. Maile. I shall always be grateful to my former secretary, the late Mrs F. M. Moody, who typed the first draft. I want also to thank Miss Gladys Claydon who later gave me some valuable assistance with the manuscript, and I wish specially to thank my secretary, Mrs Audrey Jones, for typing the entire work in revised form and for giving me so much help in my College work. Finally, I would like to dedicate the book, with gratitude, to my friends in the Senior and Junior Common Rooms of Spurgeon's College. They may not agree with every detail of my interpretation, but they all share my enthusiasm for relevant expository preaching and believe that, whatever the passage of Scripture, the Bible continues to speak today with powerful and persuasive relevance.

RAYMOND BROWN

Chief abbreviations

AG	*A Greek-English Lexicon of the New Testament and Other Early Christian Literature* by William F. Arndt and F. Wilbur Gingrich (University of Chicago Press and Cambridge University Press, 1957).
AV	The Authorized (King James) Version of the Bible, 1611.
JB	The Jerusalem Bible (Darton, Longman & Todd, 1966).
JBP	*The New Testament in Modern English* by J. B. Phillips (Collins, 1958).
LXX	The Old Testament in Greek according to the Septuagint, 3rd century BC.
NEB	The New English Bible (NT 1961, 2nd edition 1970; OT 1970).
NIV	The New International Version of the Bible (Hodder & Stoughton, 1979).
RV	The Revised Version of the Bible (1884).

Commentaries

In order to reduce the number of footnotes, I have not provided a page reference when the quotation cited can be found in the relevant commentary (denoted by the author's name) at the place where the verse in question is discussed.

W. Barclay — *The Letter to the Hebrews* (*Daily Study Bible*, Saint Andrew Press, 1955).

F. F. Bruce — *The Epistle to the Hebrews* (*New London Commentaries*, Marshall, Morgan & Scott, 1965).

J. Calvin — *The Epistle to the Hebrews*, translated by W. B. Johnston (*Calvin's Commentaries*, Oliver & Boyd, 1963).

J. Chrysostom — *Homilies on the Epistle to the Hebrews* (*Library of Nicene and Post-Nicene Fathers*, New York, 1888).

G. F. Hawthorne — Commentary on 'The Letter to the Hebrews' in G. C. D. Howley (editor), *A New Testament Commentary* (Pickering & Inglis, 1969).

J. Héring — *The Epistle to the Hebrews*, translated by A. W. Heathcote and P. J. Allcock (Epworth Press, 1970).

T. Hewitt — *Hebrews: An Introduction and Commentary* (*Tyndale Commentaries*, IVP, 1960).

P E. Hughes	*A Commentary on the Epistle to the Hebrews* (Eerdmans, 1977).
M. Luther	*Lectures on Hebrews* (*Luther's Works* 29, Concordia, 1968).
W. Manson	*The Epistle to the Hebrews* (Hodder & Stoughton, 1951).
J. Moffatt	*A Critical and Exegetical Commentary on the Epistle to the Hebrews* (*International Critical Commentaries*, T. & T. Clark, 1924).
H. W. Montefiore	*A Commentary on the Epistle to the Hebrews* (*Black's New Testament Commentaries*, A. & C. Black, 1964).
A. Nairne	*The Epistle of Priesthood* (T. & T. Clark, 1913).
F. D. V. Narborough	*The Epistle to the Hebrews* (*Clarendon Bible*, Clarendon Press, 1930).
W. Neil	*The Epistle to the Hebrews* (*Torch Bible Commentaries*, SCM Press, 1955).
J. Owen	*An Exposition of the Epistle to the Hebrews* (Edinburgh,^{2} 1812).
A. S. Peake	*The Epistle to the Hebrews* (*Century Bible*, Edinburgh, n.d.).
T. H. Robinson	*The Epistle to the Hebrews* (*Moffatt New Testament Commentaries*, Hodder & Stoughton, 1933).
A. M. Stibbs	'Hebrews', in D. Guthrie and J. A. Motyer (editors), *The New Bible Commentary Revised* (IVP, 1970).
	So Great Salvation (Paternoster, 1970).
B. F. Westcott	*The Epistle to the Hebrews* (Macmillan, 1889).
G. B. Wilson	*Hebrews: A Digest of Reformed Comment* (Banner of Truth, 1970).

Introduction

1. The purpose of the letter

This magnificent letter to the Hebrews was written to a group of first-century Christians who were in danger of giving up. It is clear from even a casual reading of the letter that the times were hard for Jewish Christians especially. Many of them had been exposed to fierce persecution. They had been physically assaulted, their homes had been plundered; some had been cast into prison on account of their faith, others had been ridiculed in public because of their resolute trust in Jesus (10:32–34). Many of these Jewish Christians had accepted all this adversity joyfully. But others had 'shrunk back' from their earlier allegiance to Christ and became apostates. Without going that far, others were in danger of compromise. The letter appeals to all these severely tested believers to keep their faith firmly anchored to the moorings of truth, to maintain their steady confidence in Christ and to press on to mature Christian stability (2:1; 3:6; 6:1).

But how does one encourage such people in critical and adverse times? The author knows they must be urged to 'hold fast', to 'strive to enter', to 'go on to maturity', to 'seize the hope' set before them (3:6; 4:11, 14; 6:1, 18) and so on. Yet he can only make such eloquent and necessary pastoral exhortations because he has already done a far more basic thing. First, as a matter of the utmost importance, he has turned their eyes, not to themselves, hoping for sufficient inward strength, nor to their agonizing troubles, nor to their persecuting contemporaries, but to Christ. No believer can cope with adversity unless Christ fills his horizons, sharpens his priorities and dominates his experience.

This letter's primary exhortation is an appeal for endurance. Familiar with the great personalities of Old Testament times, these Jewish believers are reminded that Abraham 'patiently endured' because God had made a promise to him (6:15). Moses endured because he turned his eyes away from the cruel face of Pharoah and the despondent faces of his Hebrew contemporaries to the face of God. He deliberately looked to the invisible God and was wonderfully upheld (11:27). Most significant of all, Jesus endured. 'The joy set before him' sustained him when sinners opposed him and reviled him (12:2–3). Abraham, Moses and Jesus had all experienced fierce temptation and hostile opposition. Under the pressure of these adversities they might well have given up, but they were not deflected from their course. How could these Jewish Christians endure? What would enable them to stand firm in hazardous times? They must look to Christ.

For this reason, although deeply aware of the problems these believers are facing, the author of this letter does not turn to his necessary pastoral exhortation until he has first reminded them of the uniqueness of Christ. He presents them first of all with an exposition of Christ as prophet (1:1–2), priest (1:3b) and king (1:8–14). Some of their Christian friends had slipped back into Judaism. They had placed their trust not in the work of Christ, but in the works of the law. They had abandoned their faith not only because it was too costly for them to continue, but because they had an inadequate understanding of Christ in the first place. Many of our contemporaries are fascinated by Jesus. We have rock-musicals which present us with an interpretation of Christ's teaching and mission. Commercial films, radio plays and television presentations invite us to look at Christ. But is their portraiture adequate? Nothing is of greater importance in our own time than a reminder of the immense dimensions of the biblical doctrine of Christ.

2. The author of the letter

Ever since early Christian times the writer of this epistle has remained tantalizingly anonymous. Encouraged by the AV title to the letter, many readers have believed it to be the work of the apostle Paul. However, that title does not appear in a single ancient manuscript and, whilst one must obviously agree that Paul *may* have written it, he hardly has any prior claim to the authorship. Indeed, some have argued that the literary style, theological arguments and presentation of the material all indicate the possibility of another early Christian writer with a rather different outlook.

This is not the place to discuss the various theories of authorship. The numerous candidates and appropriate evidence have been well surveyed in the commentaries.[1] Perhaps it is enough here to say that the arguments against Pauline authorship are that he nowhere makes any personal reference to himself (though Timothy is mentioned in 13:23), and that its literary style is quite unlike other undoubtedly Pauline writings. Hebrews is certainly one of the most polished Greek writings in the New Testament, whereas Paul's vigorous letters are marked by occasional 'abruptness, digressions and even disorderliness' (Guthrie). John Calvin certainly entertained no doubts whatever about the un-Pauline character of the epistle and said, 'I can adduce no reason to show that Paul was its author.'[2]

If Paul is to be considered as a possible writer, then one ought also to listen to the arguments of those who ever since Tertullian and Novatian have believed the letter to be the work of Barnabas, the 'good man' of Acts (11:24). Some third-century Christians also suggested that Luke might well have been its author, whereas others throughout Christian history have been convinced that it was written by Clement of Rome. He was certainly well aware of the epistle, as is evident from the quotations and parallel ideas found in his own letter to the Corinthians, probably written about AD 96. Silvanus (1 Pet. 5:12) has also been a candidate for the honour, mainly because of the similarities between Hebrews and 1 Peter. Probably Apollos has more to offer as a likely writer. Martin Luther was reasonably sure in his own mind that the 'eloquent man' from Alexandria, who was 'well

[1] D. Guthrie, *New Testament Introduction* (IVP, [2]1970), pp. 685–698; R. P. Martin, *New Testament Foundations*, 2 (Paternoster, 1978), pp. 348–357; Bruce, pp. xxiii–xxviii; Hughes, pp. 19–30.

[2] Calvin, p. 1.

versed in the scriptures' (Acts 18:24) may well have written Hebrews.

Believing as we do, however, that the gifted, if anonymous, author of this letter was above all else used by God's Spirit as he delivered his 'word of exhortation' (13:22), his precise identity is a secondary matter. Most commentators on Hebrews quote the third-century Christian scholar Origen in any discussion about authorship; he was sure that as to its writer 'only God knows certainly'.

3. The readers of the letter

The traditional Greek title of the letter, *Pros Ebraious*, 'to (the) Hebrews' goes back at least to the late second century. Tertullian's work, *On Modesty*, written at the beginning of the third century, refers to the letter under its Latin title, *ad Hebraeos*, but neither description does much to illuminate the precise destination of this great epistle. Some commentators and interpreters have made the suggestion that the traditional title puts students on the wrong scent in the search for the most likely original readers. They have argued that Gentile readers as well as Jews would be well acquainted with the Old Testament once they became Christian believers, and the fact that the Jerusalem temple is not mentioned in the letter is certainly not so strange if it is addressed to a Gentile audience rather than to a Jewish Christian community.

Many modern writers, however, find themselves convinced that the elusive author of the letter had Jewish Christian readers mainly in mind, and this is certainly the view taken in this exposition. The appeal of some kind of Jewish Christian readership has been enhanced since the discovery of the Dead Sea Scrolls in the late 1940s, and some more recent scholars have suggested that the letter may have been sent initially to a first-century Jewish group which held very similar views to those of the famous Qumran Community which treasured the Scrolls and their teaching. The first readers were well acquainted with the Old Testament in its Greek version, the Septuagint. F. F. Bruce says that they might possibly have belonged to a first-century house church, but were at the same time part of 'the wider fellowship of a city church, and were tending to neglect the bond of fellowship that bound them to other Christians outside their own inner circle'.[3]

As to the precise location of this group or church we cannot be sure. Some have suggested Jerusalem and other places in Palestine have also been named. Alexandria has also been considered as a possible destination, but Rome is the most likely location.

4. The date of the letter

One cannot be absolutely certain about the date of Hebrews but it seems natural to regard 10: 32–34 as a reference to the Neronian persecution (AD 64). Some have insisted that the absence of any reference in the letter to the temple means that it must have been written after the Jerusalem temple's destruction by the Roman armies in AD 70, but such an argument is not specially convincing. The epistle was certainly known by Clement of Rome at the end of the first century for, as we have already observed, there are numerous echoes of Hebrews in Clement's letter to the Corinthian church. It is probably safe to assume that Hebrews was written in the second half of the first century, possibly in the early eighties.

5. The message of the letter

When we come to the teaching of the epistle we are on firmer ground. Hebrews gathers all its leading ideas around two great themes, revelation and redemption, the word of God and the work of Christ. Both these major aspects of Christian preaching are skilfully interwoven in the author's presentation of his message. The word of God certainly dominates the opening and closing chapters (1–6 and 11–13), whilst the work of Christ is given priority of place in the four chapters (7–10) which comprise the highly important central section of the letter.

a. What God has said to us

For the writer of this epistle God's word is of primary significance in the life of every Christian believer. He begins his

[3] Bruce, p. xxx.

exposition by reminding his readers that in Old Testament times it was a *diversified* word (1:1); it came to man through various human channels and in different historical contexts. By 'many and various ways' God revealed himself through his word to sinful and often unteachable mankind. In Christ that essential revelation of God's nature became a *personified* word (1:2–3a); the divine nature, perfect life, vital teaching, unique sacrifice and victorious achievement of Christ are God's greatest and final message to us. The Son is supreme. He is greater than the prophets of Old Testament times (1:1), than the angels (1:36 – 2:18), than Moses (3:1–6) and Joshua (4:1–10). This revelation of God in Christ is a crucial and *decisive* word (2:1–4). It demands a verdict.

It is also an *appealing* word for, although chapter 3 confronts the reader with the seriousness of unbelief (3:12, 19) and disobedience (3:18), two negative responses to the divine message, yet the word of God is presented to us with such compassionate appeal. It is anything but a cold 'take it or leave it' communication. In his love God is begging his people to attend to his voice knowing that eternal issues are at stake: 'Today, when you hear his voice, do not harden your hearts'; 'take care, brethren'; 'exhort one another . . . that none of you may be hardened (3:7–8, 12–13). The word must be received with faith or it is not likely to benefit the hearers, and it must be acknowledged by obedience (4:2, 6, 11). It is, after all, not only persuasive but *powerful*, this 'living' word of God (4:12). It exposes man's inner life, his thoughts, motives, ambitions and sins. 'No creature is hidden' in the presence of a God who speaks to us in Scripture with such devastating honesty and such patient love. Through this revelation of himself in holy Scripture, God searches us out and makes us see ourselves as we really are. It condemns us and convicts us until we acknowledge the seriousness of our sin (4:13) and the immensity of his grace (4:16).

b. What Christ has done for us

This epistle also directs our attention to the work of Christ, and this theme is interpreted with both imagination and practical application in chapters 7 – 10. In this central section of the letter our author presents his rich doctrine of Christ's work with the aid of a number of vivid contrast pictures. The priesthood of the old covenant was temporary, but Christ 'holds his priesthood permanently' (7:24). Those priests of Old Testament times were themselves 'beset with weakness' and constantly exposed to the same sinful tendencies as those who came to them for help, but Christ was sinless (5:2; 7:26). The priests of former days offered the blood of goats and bulls, but Christ offered himself (9:13; 7:27). Their sacrifices could effect only a partial cleansing, nothing more than 'the purification of the flesh', whereas the sacrifice of Christ purifies man's disturbed and guilty conscience (9:9, 13–14; 10:22). The Old Testament sacrifices were a necessary reminder of the seriousness of sin (10:3), but by Christ's offering our sins can be taken away (9:26; 10:11–12). Constant repetition was an essential feature of the Old Testament sacrificial system, but Christ's sacrifice was offered 'once for all' (10:11–12).

In this letter the great themes of revelation and redemption are persuasively expounded and applied. Man is ignorant and he needs God's word in Scripture. Man is also guilty and he needs Christ's work, that redemptive sacrifice by which alone we are forgiven (9:22; 10:18–22). Through the work of Christ, the person who is cleansed and liberated is dedicated to God. 'Sanctification' is an important theme in this letter (2:11; 10:10, 14, 29; 13:12). Through the offering of Christ's sinless body on the cross we have been 'set apart' for the work of God in the world. No longer do we obey the dictates of our selfish natures, alienated from God. In Christ our lives have been surrendered to his use and we belong to him.

In order to obtain for us 'such a great salvation' (2:1), Jesus came into this world as the perfect revelation of God's mind and message (1:2–3). He came from God determined to pursue the Father's will (10:5–7). Although addressed in this letter clearly as 'God' (1:8), the humanity of our Lord is a theme which pervades the whole letter. 'Nowhere in the New Testament is the humanity of Christ set forth so movingly.'[4] Jesus came from the tribe of Judah. He was 'made like his brethren' (7:14; 2:17). He knew the force and sinister power

[4] H. R. Mackintosh, *The Doctrine of the Person of Christ* (Edinburgh, 1937), p. 79.

of temptation, but overcame these pressures and remained sinless and undefiled (2:18; 4:15; 7:26). In life's hazardous experiences he often suffered, but through it all he 'learned obedience' (2:10; 5:8). In the garden of Gethsemane, towards the close of his earthly ministry, he prayed 'with loud cries and tears', deeply aware of the cost of that sacrifice which was to be offered (5:7; 9:14). He went out from that garden to be arrested, mocked and crucified. At his 'trial' he was humiliated by fierce 'opposition from sinful men' (12:3 NIV). But he 'suffered outside the city gate' (13:12 NIV) and 'endured the cross, scorning its shame' (12:2 NIV) because he knew it to be the will of God for him and the only way he could 'take away sins' and make us holy (10:10, 11, 14). Christ was raised from the dead by 'the God of peace' (13:20). He lives for ever (7:24), and is now exalted at the Father's right hand (7:26; 8:1; 10:12), where he appears for us in the presence of God (9:24). In that holy place (6:19; 9:12) he intercedes for us (7:25) and will certainly appear a second time to bring salvation, in the ultimate sense, 'to those who are waiting for him' (9:28).

Hebrews expounds the finished word of God, found in both Old and New Testaments and brought to completion and finality in Christ (1:2). It also expounds the finished work of Christ who fulfils God's purposes not only in what he says but in how he lived and died. His saving work is complete and effective. What he achieved on the cross 'once for all' effects the salvation of all who believe (4:3; 10:39), obey (5:9) and continue (3:6, 14).

6. The relevance of the letter

If this epistle is read hastily or superficially, one might be tempted to imagine that its themes are antiquated, irrelevant, or even esoteric. The young Charles Haddon Spurgeon found it difficult to understand. With typical humour he recalled his teenage feelings about the letter: 'I have a very lively, or rather deadly, recollection of a certain series of discourses on the Hebrews, which made a deep impression on my mind of the most undesirable kind. I wished frequently that the Hebrews had kept the Epistle to themselves, for it sadly bored a poor Gentile lad.'[5] The reaction of young Spurgeon is understandable enough, but many older people have also confessed to a sense of bewilderment concerning the teaching of Hebrews. It takes them into a world of ceremonial and sacrifice, priestly observances and traditional religious customs. Old and honoured patriarchal figures rub shoulders with devout priests constantly involved in the ceaseless round of animal offerings and sacrificial gifts.

Yet although the letter's illustrative material may not always belong to our thought world, its leading ideas have a striking relevance, and many of its most outstanding themes and practical teaching are of immense importance to late-twentieth-century man. We have already seen that the letter makes important assertions on two doctrinal issues which have come increasingly to the fore in contemporary theological debate; the doctrines of revelation and the deity of Christ. Its teaching in chapter 2 about the creation of man has particular relevance in the present ecology debate and, at a time when the idea of 'liberation' is theologically fashionable, the same chapter reminds us that even if man is politically free there are greater tyrannies to oppress him and from which he can be delivered.

It is important also to emphasize that in an age of religious pluralism this letter is a constant reminder of the necessity of God's salvation in Christ. However sensitive one chooses to be to the claims of other world religions, it is impossible for any serious student of the New Testament to escape what has been called 'the scandal of particularity'. By this phrase we refer to those clear and uncompromising assertions of New Testament Scripture that the only way we can come to God the Father is through Jesus Christ his Son (Jn. 14:6). Other religions testify most eloquently to man's basic spiritual needs, but the Christian gospel asserts that only in Christ can those needs be met (Acts 4:12). In a day when many people may try to discern some form of acceptable syncretism, whereby Christ and his gospel become merely one expression among others of the idea of salvation, Hebrews directs us to the uniqueness of Christ's redemptive work. In this letter the Old Testament priest, who stands day after day performing his religious duties, typifies the futility of any religious system

[5] C. H. Spurgeon, *The Early Years* (Banner of Truth, 1962), p. 48.

which ignores the supremacy of Christ's work.

One does not need to turn to other religions to find expressions of belief where Jesus is ignored or given a special place among religious equals. As we shall see, the danger can be found in some expressions of Christianity, to say nothing of the various sects such as Jehovah's Witnesses and others which refuse to give prominence to the deity of Christ and the finality of his perfect work. This central doctrine of the atoning work of Christ has been exposed to the attack of some contemporary theologians. One writer explains the death of Christ in these terms: 'Jesus' death is in fact but the crown of his life . . . Luther King could bring civil rights to the blacks of America, similarly only by risking his life. Not only must he be prepared to be roughed up by southern policemen; he must risk assassination – and the greater his success, the more likely did the assassination become. And so with Jesus. To live the life of love, to teach love, and to found the community of love *entailed* the likelihood of the cross.'[6] But this letter asserts that Jesus did not die simply as a willing martyr for a good cause. It teaches not the 'likelihood' of the cross but its absolute necessity. He died in our place and without the shedding of his blood 'there is no forgiveness of sins' (8:22). Good men though they undoubtedly were, people like Martin Luther King cannot possibly be set alongside Christ; Christ's death was a saving sacrifice, essential for man's redemption.

The importance of this letter is to be discerned not only in the way it expounds a number of theological issues of contemporary significance, but also in its interpretation of basic human problems, relevant in every generation. The letter's opening paragraph explains that by his death Jesus 'provided purification for sins' (1:3 NIV), and that phrase forms the substance of the letter's argument in its central section. The issue of human guilt is as old as time itself, but, for all man's sophistication and the elaborate psychological escape routes he has provided for himself to evade the responsibility for his sin, men and women still suffer because of this powerful malevolent force, the enemy within. This sinister tyrant has the persuasive ability to make us do the things which, in our

[6] J. Hick (editor), *The Myth of God Incarnate* (SCM Press, 1977), p. 58.

better moments, we would despise, or say the things we would hate other people to say to us, or feed on thoughts which, if given verbal expression in company, would scarcely allow us to hold up our heads for shame. There is a timelessness about the message of Hebrews. It addresses its clear message of forgiveness and hope to every man or woman weighed down by a sense of guilt.

Moreover, man does not only need to be forgiven. Many of our thinking contemporaries are overwhelmed by a sense of frustration and bewilderment and a general loss of direction in life. They ask about the purpose of living. Do we exist merely in order to eat, drink, sleep, work, and die? Or is there a meaning to life? What is man? Why is he here in this world? Skilfully using a well-known passage in Psalm 8, our author reminds his readers that man is not as he was meant to be (2:8). But the perfect man has come in order that 'by the grace of God' he might do something for alienated, rebellious and enslaved man which he could not possibly do for himself. Jesus became like us (2:9, 14) that we might become like him. In him alone can we attain our true destiny. He delivers us from selfishness and makes us 'holy' men and women who are surrendered to God's purposes in the world. He identifies with us and calls us his brothers. We belong to him as God's children and he leads us to glory (2:10–13).

Another issue of perennial significance is the matter of death and the life to come. Modern man does everything to hide from the reality of death, but we cannot evade it. We can only move day by day closer to it. It is the great inescapable reality and this letter addresses itself to the human anguish of lives that are 'held in slavery by their fear of death' (2:15 NIV). The teaching of Hebrews is that Christ has effected an eternal deliverance. He not only came into this world as a baby at Bethlehem (2:14; 10:5–9), but he voluntarily exposed himself to the experience of death that he might enter fully into our human anguish. He suffered death and tasted death (2:9) for everyone. He knew that it was the great enemy of mankind, the devil, who had the ability to tyrannize man with the fear of death and the uncertain beyond. Jesus passed through that experience victoriously, conquering the powers of sin, death and the devil, and emerged as one brought back from the dead by the God who procures and inspires peace

(13:20) in the hearts and lives of all those who believe in him. Those who take seriously the teaching of this letter can look death in the face and bless God that, delivered from fear, they have peace and hope.

A further perpetually relevant theme in Hebrews is focused in the letter's vigorous doctrine of the Christian life. Throughout Christian history believers have been saddened by the defection of people who were once close partners in Christian work and zealous workers in the cause of Christ. Every church of whatever denomination has known the experience of receiving new members with immense spiritual potential, who were later to drift away from the fellowship of Christ's people and even make a deliberate point of rejecting the faith which at one time they believed with such conviction and shared with such effectiveness. Hebrews chapters 3 and 4, and other related passages, deal with this sad circumstance within the context of first-century apostasy. The author is deeply persuaded that a personal relationship with Christ expressed in repentance and faith determines the believer's salvation (5:9). But in the teaching of the letter salvation is clearly portrayed as an ongoing process. It is in no sense a static event locked away in the past, an isolated item in a believer's spiritual autobiography. Obviously what has been done in the past is of immense importance, both what has been achieved for us and what has been effected in us. We have been made holy (10:10). But salvation is a continuing process; we are being made holy (10:14). The writer of Hebrews glories in the present and future aspects of salvation. He saves now (7:25) and he will appear a second time to bring salvation to those who are waiting for him (9:28). The letter insists that these first-century Christians clearly recognize their responsibility not only to believe in Jesus but to go on with him.

Hebrews is a distinct challenge to any superficial or undemanding interpretations of the gospel. It reminds us of Christ's teaching about discipleship, that if any man will follow him he needs to take up his cross, and that without some experience of denial and self-crucifixion he cannot possibly belong to the followers of Jesus. In the past some forms of well-intentioned evangelism have suffered because they have presented the Christian life as the way to happiness, fulfilment, or peace, without also explaining that it is the way of the cross which is also the way to glory. Jesus reverently submitted himself to God's will (5:7) and in the experience of suffering 'learned obedience' (5:8) and was 'made perfect' (5:9). We do no justice to the New Testament gospel if we rob it of its sacrificial dimension and merely emphasize the benefits of the Christian life to the total exclusion of its cost.

Hebrews recognizes that if a believer is to pay this price, there will be times when he may feel socially isolated or opposed by his contemporaries. The letter portrays Jesus as the sympathetic priest with an answer to the problem of loneliness. Because of his own experience of hardship, adversity and rejection, he is able to enter into 'our weaknesses'. Although he is now the ascended Lord who has gone into heaven (4:14–15), the majestic Son of God, he is also the compassionate Son of man who has been through the experience of temptation and emerged as a victor. Hebrews emphasizes the truth that there is a man in heaven. In the harsh experiences of his lifetime he endured opposition and he knows how we feel. Hebrews reminds us that we are never alone, that the Lord who lived on this earth has the same compassion and strength, and that he is our changeless friend, alongside us in the experiences of everyday life and determined to stay with his people for ever (13:8).

It is possible that the closing chapters of Hebrews have brought more comfort to despondent Christians than almost any other part of New Testament Scripture. From 10:19 onwards we find ourselves in the company of first-century Christians exposed to the threat of persecution. We imagine ourselves alongside them in a Christian meeting (10:25) listening to the warm pastoral exhortation given by the writer as he reminds his readers of their fellow believers who suffered in earlier days, and of the Old Testament heroes and their spiritual successors who lived valiantly for God in difficult times. Every generation of Christians values encouragement of this kind, and the reason Hebrews chapter 11 has become so popular is that from time to time we all need a renewed summons to courageous living and, much more, to renewed confidence in a God who is faithful (11:11). When believers encounter hard times they need not only a reminder of the past (11:1–40), but also a vision of the future (12:22–29), of the city of the living God to which they belong and of the kingdom which cannot be shaken. This letter's concluding exhortations, for all their disjointed appearance, have a marked contemporary relevance. They remind us that our homes must be used for the work of Christ, that some of our fellow Christians are 'prisoners of conscience', that marriage is to be honoured and its special relationship kept pure. The materialist is rebuked, the church leader encouraged, and the believer warned about 'strange teachings', a sad feature even more characteristic of our own time than of the first century.

Far from being preoccupied with antiquated issues, Hebrews is a New Testament letter with arresting contemporary application. We must turn now to its opening paragraph where, in unforgettable language, we are reminded of our writer's favourite theme, the centrality and supremacy of Christ.

PART I
GOD'S SON

1:1–3
1. The majestic Christ

We live in a society which recognizes the necessity of good communication. In the world of commerce millions are spent on persuasive advertising; it has become a highly developed technique and one of recognized financial importance. Politicians know how vital it is to communicate effectively. Diplomats recognize the immense dangers that can arise in international affairs when there occurs a serious 'breakdown in communications'. Stresses in family life frequently arise in situations when the partners in a marriage merely talk to each other but fail to communicate.

The letter to the Hebrews begins by asserting the greatest single fact of the Christian revelation: God has spoken to man through his word in the Bible and through his Son, Jesus. In Christ God has closed the greatest communication gap of all time, that which exists between a holy God and sinful mankind.

In many and various ways God spoke of old to our fathers by
the prophets; 2*but in these last days he has spoken to us by a*
Son, whom he appointed the heir of all things, through whom
also he created the world. 3*He reflects the glory of God and*
bears the very stamp of his nature, upholding the universe by
his word of power. When he had made purification for sins,
he sat down at the right hand of the Majesty on high.

Some first-century Jewish Christians had abandoned their faith because they no longer recognized Christ's deity and equality with God. The author's first task is to expound and exalt God's Son. He reminds them of eight things about Jesus.

1. Jesus is God's prophetic voice

It is naturally important in these circumstances for the author to emphasize the continuity of the Old and New Testaments. Christ does not break with the great Jewish past. He comes to bring it to fulfilment. Without him the Old Testament revelation is partial, fragmentary, preparatory and incomplete. God spoke at different times by different means. He used *many and various ways.* But in Christ he spoke fully, decisively, finally and perfectly. The first-century Christians must listen to him, the greatest prophet of all times. Ezekiel portrayed the *glory* of God,[1] but Christ reflected it (1:3). Isaiah expounded the *nature* of God as holy, righteous and merciful,[2] but Christ manifested it (1:3). Jeremiah described the *power* of God,[3] but Christ displayed it (1:3). He far surpassed the best of prophets of earlier times, and these wavering Christians must listen to his voice.

Although we are glad to acknowledge that something essential, new and eternally effective has been accomplished by Christ, we are not to set one Testament against the other, but recognize that 'all Scripture is God-breathed'.[4] The way in which this letter unites both Testaments is a persuasive reminder of the authority of Scripture, a truth which is just as much exposed to attack now as in previous generations. The early Christian communities found themselves harassed by a number of zealots who wanted to discard the Old Testament revelation, and the problem is certainly not confined to antiquity. In our day, those who take seriously the message of the Old Testament as well as the New, and who are determined to submit themselves to its teaching, are hastily dismissed in some circles as unintelligent obscurantists or unthinking fundamentalists. A commitment to Scripture demands that we grapple honestly with any difficulties our contemporaries have about the biblical narratives, but the teaching of this letter encourages us to reaffirm our confidence in the God who has spoken clearly to mankind in Scripture and in his Son.

[1] Ezk. 1:28; 3:23. [2] Is. 1:4, 18; 11:4.
[3] Je. 1:18–19; 10:12–13. [4] 2 Tim. 3:16 NIV.

'Attending to the word' is a key theme in Hebrews, especially in the opening and closing sections of the letter. These Christians cannot hope to press on to mature spiritual experience if they ignore, minimize or despise it.[5] Christ is God's greatest prophet with a distinctive message for *these last days*. His coming inaugurated a new era. In him the last days have most certainly begun; the phrase conveys the superiority of the message and the urgency of the times.

2. Jesus is God's Son

Those Jewish Christians whose faith in Christ was faltering may have come to regard him merely as a good man, a captivating teacher, or an impressive leader. He was all that, but much more. He is the Son of God. The theme of Sonship is a recurrent one in this letter. We are here reminded of the message of the Son (1:2). Later passages discuss the superiority of the Son, his reign, mission, achievement, obedience, nature and perfection.[6] One interpreter of the letter's teaching entitles his commentary *Sonship and Salvation*.[7] It is an excellent reminder of this epistle's leading ideas. Because these two ideas are inseparably united, apostasy is so serious and disastrous. Without the work of the Son there is no salvation. Those who deliberately and persistently spurn the Son of God (10:29) are inevitably exposed to spiritual atrophy. How can they possibly be brought to repentance when there is no salvation outside Christ?[8] They have refused to walk in the only way ordained by God. They have opposed the truth revealed by God. They have despised the life approved by God. How can man hope to be saved if he rejects the Saviour?

3. Jesus is God's appointed heir

Christ was appointed *heir of all things*. Possibly this idea of the inheritance of Christ is drawn from Psalm 2:8, later to be used in the unfolding argument: 'I will make the nations your heritage.' But surely by describing Christ as 'heir of *all*

[5] Heb. 2:1–3; 12:25. [6] Heb. 1:5, 8; 3:6; 4:14; 5:8; 7:3, 28.
[7] J. Scott Lidgett, *Sonship and Salvation: A Study of the Epistle to the Hebrews* (London, 1921).
[8] Jn. 14:6.

things', he intends to convey to us the idea that the Lord Jesus will inherit not only this earth but the entire universe. The Son obviously comes into a rich inheritance. Moreover, in other contexts the New Testament says that believers share this inheritance.[9] The seventeenth-century commentator John Trapp says, 'Be married to this heir and have all.'

4. Jesus is God's creative agent

The author takes his readers directly from Christ's destiny in the future to his role in the beginning of creation. He is at pains to emphasize that the Lord we have trusted was no mere Galilean preacher. He shared actively in the creative work of Almighty God. It is all closely linked with the idea of inheritance; in other words, 'what the Son was to possess he had been instrumental in making' (Moffatt). Surely a Christ whose hands had shaped the universe and summoned the galaxy of stars into being could hold these Jewish Christians in days of testing and guide their steps through times of adversity. If the chaos before creation[10] could be overcome, surely he could control their destiny and provide their immediate needs.

5. Jesus is God's personified glory

For the Hebrew people the *glory of God* was a visible and outward expression of the majestic presence of God. When the law was given at Sinai 'the glory of the Lord' settled on the mountain. Likewise, the glory of God became manifest at 'the tent of meeting'; it was a visible sign to God's people of his continuing presence.[11] Later, when the ark of the covenant was captured, the Hebrew people lamented, 'The glory has departed.'[12] Now, says the author of this letter, in these last days this same glory has been seen in the person of Christ who *reflects* or is 'the radiance of God's glory' (NIV). The word used (*apaugasma*) can mean either 'radiation out from' or 'reflection back'. These early Christians knew only too well that their non-Christian Jewish neighbours refused to acknowledge the deity of Christ. Wistfully, they recalled the

[9] Rom. 8:17. [10] Gn. 1:2.
[11] Ex. 24:15–17; 33:18–23; Lv. 9:5–6, 23. [12] 1 Sa. 4:21–22.

great moments of their history when God's glory had been manifest. Some may even have thought with pride about the Jerusalem temple, doomed to destruction in AD 70; surely the glory of God was manifest there in its ceaseless ritual and sacrificial cultus! But the author of this letter reminds his readers that nowhere has the glory of God been more perfectly manifest than in the person of God's Son. In Christ all the majesty of God's splendour is fully revealed.

6. Jesus is God's perfect revelation

How can this writer impress upon his readers the message of Christ's person? He insists that Jesus bears the very stamp of God's nature. All the attributes of God became visible in him. The *stamp* vividly presents the picture of an image or superscription on a coin or medal. It exactly and perfectly matches the picture on the die. The verbal form of the word used here (*charaktēr*) means 'to engrave'. In other words, if man wants to see God he must look to Christ. How could the first-century Jews, who were opposing these Jewish Christians, hope to know God if they were turning their backs upon Christ in whom God is perfectly revealed? The terms used in this great introductory passage of the letter clearly expound the unity of Christ's nature with the Father and yet maintain the distinction of his person. The word translated 'nature' (*hypostasis*) here describes the very essence and actual being of God. As Hughes points out, 'the radiant light of God's glory' suggest 'the oneness of the Son with the Father' while 'the perfect copy of his nature' maintains 'the distinctness of the Son from the Father' though, as this commentator observes 'oneness and distinctiveness are implied in each'.

7. Jesus is God's cosmic sustainer

This letter's introductory exposition of the superiority and adequacy of Christ moves on to its dramatic climax as mention is made of Christ's present work in the universe. He keeps the planets in orbit by his authoritative and effective word of power. It is the author's compelling way of emphasizing Christ's equality with God. Every Jew passionately believed that Almighty God kept the entire universe in the hollow of his hand.[13] He is not only creator but sustainer. Quite deliberately this is described as part of Christ's present role. The word of authority which has been proclaimed by the Lord as prophet is the same word which holds the universe in order.[14] It is important for the writer to emphasize that Christ's word is powerful and able to do what he determines. He speaks in the universe and what he commands is done. He has spoken in their hearts and what he demands can most certainly be accomplished whatever opposition and persecution they may encounter. In the strong hands of such a Christ they are eternally secure.

Possibly our vision of Christ is limited. We are in danger of confining him to our restricted experience or limited knowledge. We need a vision of Christ with these immense cosmic dimensions, a Christ who transcends all our noblest thoughts about him and all our best experience of him. These first-century readers would be less likely to turn from him in adversity if they had looked to him in adoration. The opening sentences of the letter are designed to bring them and us to our knees; only then can we hope to stand firmly on our feet.

8. Jesus is God's unique sacrifice

In presenting this impressive opening exposition of God's Son, the author rightly emphasizes Christ's work in redemption as well as creation. This is to become a central theme in his later exposition. At this point our attention is turned from who Christ is to what he did. Philip Hughes reminds us that there is a contrast here which ought not to be missed. Jesus is *ceaselessly* 'the radiant light of God's glory and the perfect copy of his nature' (JB). He *continously* upholds 'the universe by his word of power'. But when he gave himself up on the cross Jesus shed his blood *once for all* at a single point in time. No repetition of this saving act will ever be necessary, nor can anything that we do serve to procure our own salvation. Christ is God's unrepeatable sacrificial provision for the greatest problem of mankind – sin. Our author explains that Christ's saving death on that first Good Friday was a finished work.

[13] Is. 40:12–26. [14] Col. 1:17.

This cosmic Christ effected such purification entirely alone. Some manuscripts emphasize this aspect of his sacrificial work with the words 'by himself'. Whether this reading is original or not, the truth is certainly supported in a host of different contexts through the epistle. In his own person he did for sinful man what man could never achieve for himself. The law said, 'Do this.' It demanded man's work. But Christ came and effected by his saving death man's purification from sin. His message was, 'Trust this.' Man was urged to believe in Christ's work, not his own. It was not to be achieved by the multiplicity of good works, but by Christ's work.

When this eternal work of purification was brought to its triumphant conclusion in the death and resurrection of Christ, our Lord *sat down at the right hand of the Majesty on high* (1:3). The first readers of this letter were not likely to miss the implication of this statement and, if they did, its author was to press home its meaning in a later passage (10:11–12). The Old Testament priest's cultic work had constantly to be repeated because it was only temporarily beneficial. But Christ 'offered for all time a single sacrifice for sins'. The priest stood because his task was never complete. He could never hope to bring it to the moment of final achievement. Only Christ's sacrifice could be eternally effective. He *sat down* to indicate that the work was finished. On that day when he bore our sins in his own body, he cried, 'It is finished.'[15]

This letter's introductory exposition of the supremacy of Christ has already indicated that he is unique in his teaching (1:2), nature (1:2–3) and work. This chapter goes on to assert that he is unique in his status. He is superior to angels (1:4). He has ascended to the throne of God. The *right hand* is the place of special honour. This sacrificial, saving work is recognized and authenticated by God. He is given the seat of distinctive privilege. The Son who was humiliated on earth (12:3) is enthroned in heaven.

The first few sentences of Hebrews confront the reader with one of the most important issues in the contemporary theological debate, the doctrine of the person of Christ. It seems that in every generation some different aspect of biblical

[15] Jn. 19:30.

teaching is exposed to rigorous scrutiny and fresh examination. In the present century people have questioned the doctrine of God, and the 'God is dead' theologians have had their say. Man is said to have 'come of age' intellectually and no longer to stand in need of his earlier religious props and ecclesiastical supports. In the sixties *Honest to God* was a distillation of ideas which had been the preoccupation of some theologians for a decade or two, but it took the English-speaking world by storm and, like most storms, caused considerable havoc and damage. More recently, however, possibly in the wake of earlier doctrinal aridity, cynicism, and even unbelief, the biblical doctrine of Christ has been exposed to severely critical treatment and the incarnation declared by some radical theologians as an unacceptable doctrinal idea.

This letter's lofty teaching about the person and work of Christ, expounded with the aid of arresting titles[16] of Jesus, is a stark challenge to modern humanitarian Christologies, most of which tend to reduce Jesus to an inspired man with a unique sense of religious destiny, or an outstanding example of benevolent concern and altruistic service, or a fervent zealot with a passion for liberation, usually interpreted in political terms. Whilst preserving the important truth of Christ's essential humanity, this letter presents its readers with a revelation of Jesus in his matchless deity. He is the enthroned Lord, worthy of all our honour and worship.

In contrast to this clear uncompromising teaching, the contributors to *The Myth of God Incarnate*[17] are generally dismissive about the New Testament assertions concerning the deity of Christ, arguing that, whilst such ideas were perfectly appropriate in their first-century context, there is no reason why twentieth-century believers need accept them. Don Cupitt has written further on the subject, maintaining, for example, that the title 'Son of God' does not imply that Christ

[16] Son (1:2, 5, 8; 2:6; 5:8; 7:28), the radiance of God's glory (1:3), the image of God (1:3), the first-born (1:6), God (1:8), the Lord (2:3), the pioneer of our salvation (2:10), a merciful and faithful high priest (2:17), high priest (4:14; 5:5; 6:20; 7:26; 8:1; 9:11), apostle and high priest (3:1), the Son of God (4:14; 6:6; 10:29), the guarantor of a better covenant (7:22), mediator (8:6; 9:15; 12:24), pioneer and perfecter of our faith (12:2), the great shepherd of the sheep (13:20).

[17] J. Hick (editor), *The Myth of God Incarnate*.

was divine.[18] He begins by asserting that 'everything in our historical knowledge is relative and merely probable, and nothing is certain' and then goes on to ask what possible 'evidence could there be which could oblige us to admit that a certain historical figure though in every observable respect human was really more than human – was even co-equal with God?'[19] But Hebrews introduces us to a Christ whose perfect sinless nature is a *unique revelation*, whose *sacrifice* is alone effective for our salvation, and whose *authority* in heaven and on earth is without rival. As we are about to see in the succeeding verses, the angels worship the exalted Christ because they recognize his deity. We believers hasten to offer our adoration because, in addition, we have personally experienced his salvation. No wonder that, throughout the centuries, Christians have taken upon their lips the confession of a transformed doubter, released from his cynicism: 'My Lord and my God.'[20]

[18] D. Cupitt, *Jesus and the Gospel of God* (Lutterworth, 1979), p. 8.
[19] *Ibid.*, pp. 13–14. [20] Jn. 20:28.

1:4–14

2. Superior to the angels

Before turning to the next section, it is necessary to comment on a theme which is of great significance in Hebrews, its author's approach to the Old Testament. In the verses which follow we have an example of his use of Old Testament Scripture and in every other chapter of the letter he continues to make extensive reference to Old Testament sayings, incidents, personalities and concepts. Unless we understand his view of the Old Testament, we may occasionally find ourselves puzzled by his quotations. Take, for example, two instances in the passage we are about to consider. In these verses he uses a number of sayings to support his firm conviction that Christ is greater than the angels. In one verse (1:8) he takes a saying from Psalm 45:6, initially addressed to an Old Testament king, and utilizes it to provide a clear assertion about the deity of Christ. In another verse (1:10) he quotes from Psalm 102:25–26 about God's creative activity to support his conviction, already expressed in the letter's opening verses, that Christ participated in the work of creation. We may ask whether it is appropriate to use two verses originally addressed in one instance to a human king and in the other to almighty God to justify his view about Jesus. Several things need to be understood.

It is, first of all, his profound conviction that the Old Testament is a Christ-centred book. Its writers frequently look beyond their immediate scene to a day when their predictions would be fulfilled, and their impressive language describes greater realities than those apparent in their immediate circumstances. This is in no sense an outlook confined to the author of Hebrews. When the Old Testament prophet depicted the sufferings of the Servant of the Lord in the famous Servant Songs in Isaiah, several people in Old Testament times may have been considered as possible candidates for this particularly costly office and mission. It may have portrayed the prophet himself, or a trusted colleague, or a coming hero, or the nation of Israel, or a remnant of the people. But when the Ethiopian eunuch asked for guidance about the *precise* identity of the Servant in Isaiah 53, Philip told him that the prophecy was fulfilled in Christ.[1] When the writer of Hebrews chapter 1 comes to the two psalms we have mentioned, he looks beyond their initial meaning and, without denying the validity of that original context, extracts a further and more important message from the words. It is not that he superimposes on the text a meaning it was not intended to convey; he brings out a truth already there. He believes that Christ is everywhere present in the Old Testament, though that might not necessarily have been discerned by the original writers and readers.

With this deeper perception the author of Hebrews shows us that the Old Testament describes Christ's superiority over the angels in chapter 1, his unity with his people in chapter 2, his appointment by God to his priestly ministry in chapter 5, its indestructible character in chapter 7 and his obedience to the Father in chapter 10. With the further aid of Old Testament imagery he explains Christ's eternal work in terms of priesthood and sacrifice, and Christ's present blessings in terms of covenant and promise. It is important for us to recognize that this was not only our author's view of the Old Testament; it was Christ's own approach to it as well. When Jesus talked with those two despondent travellers on the road to Emmaus, he pointed out how slow they had been to grasp what the Old Testament writers had said about the coming Messiah: 'And beginning with Moses and all the prophets, he interpreted to them in all the scriptures the things concerning himself.'[2]

Furthermore, the author of this letter was deeply persuaded that in addition to its Christocentric character the Old Testament is a book with abiding relevance. Its message was not

[1] Acts 8:34–35. [2] Lk. 24:27.

locked away in remote antiquity, providing merely an historical account of God's dealings with Israel. Its teaching about ceremonial and sacrifice is richly fulfilled in Christ. Its message to the covenant community about God's reliability, faithfulness and love was as relevant to those first-century Christians as when the promises were first made in Old Testament times.

The author opened this letter by affirming the variety and validity of the Old Testament revelation. Now he demonstrates the depth of his conviction by citing a series of Old Testament texts to assert the superiority of Christ. Deeply aware of the infinite distance between man and God, the Jewish people had placed their hope in mediators. At critical times in their history God had sent angels to reveal his will.[3] These first-century readers knew only too well that Jesus was more than a good man, yet their Jewish contemporaries would not acknowledge his deity. Under religious pressure and social ostracism, some of these Jewish Christians were in danger of compromising their faith. Possibly they said, 'He was something other than man, but not quite God.' Perhaps they might argue, 'He was the greatest of the angels, and even created by God as a perfect angel for a special assignment among men.' The writer of the epistle uses a number of verses from the Septuagint, the Greek version of the Old Testament, to show the untenable nature of such a view. Christ is the Son of God and as such he is infinitely superior to the most dignified member of the angelic host.

. . . He sat down at the right hand of the Majesty on high,
4having become as much superior to angels as the name he has obtained is more excellent than theirs.
5For to what angel did God ever say,
'Thou art my Son,
today I have begotten thee'?
Or again,
'I will be to him a father,
and he shall be to me a son'?
6And again, when he brings the first-born into the world, he says,

[3] Gn. 18:1–8; 19:1–23; Acts 7:53; Gal. 3:19.

'Let all God's angels worship him.'
7*Of the angels he says,*
'Who makes his angels winds,
and his servants flames of fire.'
8*But of the Son he says,*
'Thy throne, O God, is for ever and ever,
the righteous sceptre is the sceptre of thy kingdom.
9*Thou hast loved righteousness and hated lawlessness;*
therefore God, thy God, has anointed thee
with the oil of gladness beyond thy comrades.'
10*And,*
'Thou, Lord, didst found the earth in the beginning,
and the heavens are the work of thy hands;
11*they will perish, but thou remainest;*
they will all grow old like a garment,
12*like a mantle thou wilt roll them up,*
and they will be changed.
But thou art the same,
and thy years will never end.'
13*But to what angel has he ever said,*
'Sit at my right hand,
till I make thy enemies
a stool for thy feet'?
14*Are they not all ministering spirits sent forth to serve, for the sake of those who are to obtain salvation?*

1. His superior name (1:4–5)

Christ cannot be relegated to the rank of angel because *the name he has obtained is more excellent than theirs.* Their name means 'messenger', and nobody will deny that at times they were wonderfully used as God's heralds. They were prominent not only in Old Testament Scripture but also in New Testament experience. Jesus was strengthened by angels, both in the wilderness at the beginning of his earthly ministry, and in the garden of Gethsemane at its close.[4] They did not only come alongside the Lord Jesus in moments of crisis as messengers of God's love and strength, but they also came to the help of Christ's people when they entered the hostile

[4] Lk. 1:19, 26–37; 2:13–14; Mt. 4:11; Lk. 22:43.

realms of adversity and peril. They were sent by God to release prisoners, to instruct preachers, to encourage believers, to judge blasphemers and to help travellers.[5] But, inspiring as all these events were, the angels concerned were but messengers; that was their name and that was their function. Christ has a name superior to the best of angels. He is far more than a mere messenger. He is the Son of God.[6]

2. His superior dignity (1:6)

The angels were messengers, but he is the Son. The angels were worshippers, but he is the One they adore. At the incarnation they united in worship and did so because God had demanded it: *Let all God's angels worship him*, which is a rendering of Deuteronomy 32:43 in the Septuagint: 'Let the sons of God worship him . . . and let all the angels of God ascribe strength to him.' It is also a Septuagint quotation of Psalm 97:7: 'Worship him, all his angels.' In other words, the writer is saying: 'It is the angels' task to exalt the Son.' He is obviously of far superior honour to those who, at God's command, offer him their constant and adoring praise.

3. His superior nature (1:7)

Angels worship Christ because they recognize him as of a totally different and far superior nature to theirs. They are the servants, the winds and the flames of God's purposes,[7] but Christ is clearly addressed in terms of incomparable deity and in contrast to the angels: *Of the angels he says . . . But of the Son he says, 'Thy throne, O God, is for ever and ever'* (1:7–8). Moreover, the deity of Christ is here portrayed as eternal in character and not merely temporary. The title 'Son' is not a mere name in honour of his work on earth; it defines a relationship which is of eternal quality. It is *for ever and ever.* In the teaching of this letter Christ is vividly expounded in terms of his human tenderness, but never at the expense of his essential deity. The first-century Christians were thus

[5] Acts 5:19; 8:26; 10:3; 12:23; 27:23–25.
[6] Heb. 1:5, quoting Ps. 2:7; 2 Sa. 7:14.
[7] Ps. 104:4 (LXX Ps. 103:4).

warned in unmistakable terms that to turn their back on Christ was to forsake God.

4. His superior role (1:8a)

Of the Son he says, 'Thy throne, O God, is for ever and ever.' So far in the opening chapter of the letter we have been told that Christ has spoken (1:1) and that he is seated (1:3), his purifying work complete. Now we are assured that Christ is sovereign. He is not only the prophet who speaks, and the priest who saves, but also the king who rules. Don Cupitt, the Cambridge radical theologian to whom we have already referred, includes this saying among the New Testament statements about Christ's deity which he chooses to discard. He points out that in the psalm quoted here the reference is to the king of Israel. He therefore prefers the alternative translations, 'God is thy throne . . .' or 'This throne, like God . . .', suggesting that 'the meaning is rather that the king rules by divine right and is endued with the fulness of God's power'.[8]

Such writers cannot accept that, acting under the inspiration of God's Spirit, the author of Hebrews is using great Old Testament words to make a rich New Testament affirmation. Without denying their initial Old Testament reference (either to the actual or Messianic king), our writer transcends their original meaning and makes these words an appropriate vehicle for conveying a special truth about Christ's deity. He later insists that to forsake Christ and abandon the gospel is to 'crucify the Son of God on their own account and hold him up to contempt' (6:6). It is to spurn the Son of God and profane the blood of the covenant (10:29). But, before issuing these wavering and hesitant Christians with this warning, he presents a word picture of Christ as the true, eternal and only king of men, and all his regal symbolism is used to heighten their understanding of this majestic Christ. He has an eternal throne, a righteous sceptre, and a universal kingdom. The coronation anointing oil is a token of God's surpassing delight at the beauty of his Son's person, or his exultant joy at the completion and efficacy of his Son's work. In all this Christ

[8] Ps. 45:6–7; D. Cupitt, *Jesus and the Gospel of God*, p. 19.

is certainly beyond his *comrades*. As we have seen, the angels assisted him as he prepared for the cross, but he alone could bear our sins. By that saving death and victorious resurrection he has established his kingdom and invites our total allegiance as well as our sincere adoration.

5. His superior example (1:8b–9)

Possibly something else is indicated here by the deliberate introduction of moral and ethical qualities into this exposition of Christ's superiority over the angels. Remember that in the teaching of Scripture not all angels were good.[9] If these Jewish Christians chose to relegate Christ to the status of an angel, could they be sure that they would always regard him as 'good'? Many of their Jewish contemporaries did not believe him to be so. They regarded him as an impostor and blasphemer. But, whatever the precise moral quality of the angels, good or bad, Jesus far transcends them all. The good angels were not exposed to the grim hazards of human temptation. They knew nothing of the sinister voice of the evil one expressed not only directly in the lonely solitude of the wilderness, but also in the warm companionship of a well-meaning friend.[10] Christ lived valiantly among people and for people and exemplified in his spotless life the qualities of *righteousness*, for he loved it; and obedience, for he hated lawlessness (1:9); and joy, for he determined to honour the Father (5:8); and found true gladness (1:9) in humble submission, even to death on a cross (12:2). Therefore, says our author, the fact that he lived among us as a man, not as an angel, should encourage us to look again at the qualities of his rich exemplary life, as well as at the virtues of his sacrificial death.

6. His superior work (1:10–12)

The argument about the superiority of Christ over the angels is now presented in another form. The angels are but creatures, they are made for God's purposes (1:7); but Christ is not a creature. He is God's appointed agent in the work of

[9] Gn. 6:1–6; Mt. 25:41; 2 Pet.2:4; Rev.12: 7–9.
[10] Mt. 4:1–11; 16:23.

creation;[11] through him God 'created the world' (1:2). As part of the created order, the angels belong inevitably to that which is transient, temporary and perishable. Even the beautiful earth and the resplendent heavens will perish, but he remains the unchanging Christ. It is interesting to note that the first readers of this letter were reminded that, in a world characterized by change, they could be assured of the companionship of the changeless Lord Jesus Christ. The word must surely have come to them with encouraging assurance: *Thou remainest.* He is the same and his *years will never end.* This inspiring conviction not only comes at the beginning of the letter but is also asserted at its close. He is 'the same yesterday and today and for ever' (13:8).

7. His superior achievement (1:13a)

The letter began with a reference to his work as redeemer as well as creator. He 'sat down at the right hand of the Majesty on high' (1:3). As the author draws to the close of his exposition of Christ's superiority over the angels, he refers again to Christ as the One seated in the eternal realm. No angel was ever invited to sit at the right hand of God. They gladly hurried on God's errands, but their work lacked the finality of Christ's perfect work. *To what angel has he ever said, 'Sit at my right hand'*? None indeed, because no angel could feel for people, or atone for mankind as Christ did, or plead for them as he now does. Angels can serve us (1:14), but they cannot save us. His name is more excellent because he is not only a Son but a Saviour.

8. His superior destiny (1:13b)

'Sit at my right hand, till I make thy enemies a stool for thy feet.'[12] No angel has ever been addressed like that, because no angel has ever deserved such acclamation and exaltation. The angels are among the exultant multitude who recognize Christ's superlative revelation, his unique person, his finished work, his eternal deity and his matchless achievement. In the first century, God's servant John, exiled on Patmos, a pris-

[11] Ps. 102:25–27. [12] Ps. 110:1.

oner for his faith, heard the rapturous cry of heaven's worshipping throng and it included 'the voice of many angels'. They adored Christ as they praised him, saying with a loud voice, 'Worthy is the Lamb.'[13] In that great day which is to come, every tongue will acknowledge his supremacy, including those who dwell in heaven.[14] That is Christ's appointed destiny. No angel is worthy of honour such as that. The entire host of heaven will be subject to him.[15]

Yet, in addition to their exultant ministry in heaven, the angels have a supportive ministry on earth. They are *ministering spirits sent forth to serve* the heirs of salvation. What is late-twentieth-century man to make of an assertion of this kind? Is the problem, even for the Christian, that of doubting the supernatural? In his exposition of these verses, Jean Héring says that speculations about angels 'seem to be void of interest for many contemporary Christians, who have ceased to believe in their existence. But Christian theology would be wrong to conform to the demands of our obscurantist age which denies everything that does not fall under sense-perception'. Belief in the supernatural seems to attract increasing numbers to the occult with its allegiance to unseen powers. Héring makes a prediction: 'The day is not far distant when only the New Testament doctrine of angels will form a barrier against certain gnostic or "religious" movements which, intentionally or otherwise, run the risk of making many believers fall back into the cult of angels, dominions, and "elements".'

It would seem that some Christians, who say little or nothing about angels, entertain no doubts whatever about the existence of demons. Exorcism is fashionable whilst the doctrine of angels is neglected. Yet is it sensible for a believer to accept the biblical evidence about evil influences and ignore its testimony to the good powers? Is it not possible that this letter's assurance about the ministry of angels is intended as an encouragement to all believers, especially those in danger or serious adversity? First-century believers under the sinister threat of renewed persecution found comfort in the assurance that God's unseen messengers would help them in trouble. In our own century, Marie Monsen, a Norwegian missionary

[13] Rev. 5:11–12. [14] Phil. 2:10 [15] 1 Pet. 3:22.

serving in North China, testified to the intervention of angels at times when Christians were in danger. On one occasion, when looting soldiers surrounded her mission compound, those who had taken refuge within its flimsy walls were astonished to find that they were left in peace. A few days later the mirauders explained that they were ready to enter when they noticed tall soldiers with shining faces on a high roof in the compound. An unbeliever asked: 'Who were standing out on the east verandah all last night . . . there were many people there each time I opened the door to see if there was a fire anywhere near us.' Marie Monsen said, 'The heathen saw them, it was a testimony to them, but they were invisible to us. It came powerfully to me and showed me how little we reckon with "The Lord, the God of Hosts", who sends forth his angels, mighty in strength "to do service for the sake of them that shall inherit salvation" (Heb. 1:14 RV).'[16]

[16] M. Monsen, *A Present Help* (Lutterworth, 1960), pp. 37–38.

2:1–4

3. The danger of drifting

Therefore we must pay the closer attention to what we have heard, lest we drift away from it. [2]For if the message declared by angels was valid and every transgression or disobedience received a just retribution, [3]how shall we escape if we neglect such a great salvation? It was declared at first by the Lord, and it was attested to us by those who heard him, [4]while God also bore witness by signs and wonders and various miracles and by gifts of the Holy Spirit distributed according to his own will.

We come now to an important development in the author's teaching. The word 'Therefore', frequently used in the letter, introduces a fresh stage in the argument and clearly reflects on the teaching which has gone before. This parenthesis deals with the gospel of God. It is the logical outcome of the author's insistence on the superiority of Christ. If Christ is all that this letter so clearly asserts, then it is essential for us to hold to his gospel. In the passage before us he emphasizes the transcendent superiority of the gospel and insists that the good news of this revelation of God must make a practical difference in our everyday lives. Christ is the prophet, but his message must be obeyed just as the priest's sacrifice must be appropriated, and the Son's pre-eminence recognized. In this parenthesis the writer reminds us of the Christian revelation in the gospel and emphasizes its importance, authority, exposition, reception, and effect.

1. Its importance (2:1)

Despite its attractively multiform character and vivid presentation in Scripture (1:1), this eternally significant message of Christ and his salvation can still be ignored, dismissed or forgotten. The author pleads for *closer attention* to its teaching and in doing so compresses within one Greek word a vivid picture. Our failure carefully to attend to what God is saying to us in the gospel of Christ is arrestingly explained with the use of a word (*pararuōmen*) which is used in other contexts to describe a boat which is allowed to *drift away* aimlessly, so missing the landing point. It is also used of a ring which slips off a finger, or of water which leaks away from a faulty jar. Similarly, he says, we can allow these great truths to be lost, however majestic their presentation in Scripture or perfect their revelation in Christ. Unless we give ourselves to them, we too can drift along, carried by alien currents into dangerous waters, or lose something infinitely precious. Whilst retaining their loyalty to God's word in Old Testament Scripture, some of these first-century Jewish Christians were in serious danger of dismissing God's finest word to man, the good news of Christ. Remember that it is the devil's ambition to rob us of God's truth. It is the Holy Spirit's work to guide us into truth and bring this saving message constantly to our remembrance.[1]

2. Its authority (2:2–3a)

The important revelation of God's mind in the Old Testament was *declared by angels.* The reference follows naturally after the series of Old Testament quotations demonstrating the superiority of Christ over the angelic host. The part played by the angels in the communication of the law was often discussed by Jewish teachers in the pre-Christian era. It appears in the Greek version of the Old Testament (the Septuagint) at Deuteronomy 33:2 where the text says that when the Lord came from Sinai 'at his right hand were angels with him', and the theme is also mentioned in two different New Testament contexts. When Paul wrote to the Galatians he

[1] Jn. 14:26.

explained that the law 'was ordained by angels' and in what proved to be his last sermon Stephen describes his hostile congregation as those 'who received the law as delivered by angels and did not keep it'.[2] If the angels' message had to be obeyed, how much more the Son's word with its good news of *such a great salvation*. Hughes expresses the warning in these terms: 'If the breakers of the law did not go unpunished, certainly despisers of the gospel cannot expect to do so.'

3. Its exposition (2:3b)

This gospel message of such eternal significance was *declared at first by the Lord*. At this point our author refers to the teaching ministry of Jesus and so introduces us to a theme which is of the greatest possible importance to him, the earthly life of Jesus. There is more about Christ's ministry on earth in this letter than in any other New Testament book outside the gospels. Although he has so much to say about Christ's present work in heaven, he is equally attracted to Christ's former work on earth. Christ taught his disciples and instructed the hundreds of people who came eagerly and expectantly to attend to the word he shared with them. Jesus declared his word to those who were easily robbed of its message, easily deflected by adversity, or easily preoccupied by either anxiety or avarice.[3] He also declared it to people who were delighted to accept it, ready to obey it, and eager to believe it.[4] We must have a similar response if we are not to drift along in life without aim and purpose.

4. Its reception (2:3b)

Like ourselves, the author of the letter cannot claim actually to have heard Christ preach, but confesses that *it was attested to us by those who heard him*. He rejoices in the testimony of eye-witnesses who remember the words and sayings of Christ during his ministry on earth. It is just possible that the author is hinting at the easy defection of some of his readers from the truth of the gospel. Will they follow erroneous

[2] Gal. 3:19; Acts 7:53. [3] Mk. 4:15–19.
[4] Mk. 4:20; Lk. 6:46–48; Jn. 4:50–53.

doctrine in preference to the good news so perfectly revealed in Jesus and so gladly received by his believing contemporaries? Will they casually ignore or wilfully abandon the gospel as welcomed and practised by so many of their fellow Christians earlier in the first century? Were such holy and valiant people all wrong in committing themselves completely to this changeless word of God, this message of the eternal Son, Jesus Christ?

5. Its effect (2:4)

The word did not rely solely on human testimony for its reality. God himself confirmed its veracity by demonstrating its power. Signs, wonders, miracles and gifts were in abundant evidence; not only to confirm God's truth but to demonstrate God's sovereignty. The miraculous evidences of God's power and the generous gifts of God's grace were intended not merely to arouse human astonishment but to manifest God's kingly rule. He works by miraculous deeds *according to his own will.* He acts in mercy; people need the signs to help them. He acts in power; people need the miracles to encourage them. He acts in grace; people need the gifts to serve and glorify him. This gospel is still 'the power of God for salvation to every one who has faith'[5]

We must pay the closer attention ... lest we drift away from it (2:1). These words, with their intentionally startling warning, compel us to examine afresh our own response to the gospel of Christ. Three issues are of contemporary importance: the historicity, distinctiveness, and eternal significance of Christ's gospel.

a. The words of Christ

It was declared at first by the Lord (2:3). The clear conviction of our author stands in striking contrast to the scepticism and uncertainty propounded by some New Testament critics who doubt the authenticity of the words of Christ in the four gospels. Don Cupitt asserts that the 'false cult of Jesus as a

[5] Rom. 1:16.

human god must go, so that the words of the real Jesus can be heard again'. But 'which words?', we may ask, for Cupitt denies the reliability and trustworthiness of most of the sayings in the gospels. 'Just how much of this material can be confidently ascribed to Jesus himself we shall never know with certainty.'[6] Inevitably, this kind of rejection or doubt about the New Testament evidence concerning the person of Christ has unhelpful implications for our Christian lives: 'Nothing could be more false to him than to make of him the principle object of worship . . .'[7] The message of the New Testament about Jesus is thus rejected.

We ought to be grateful that reputable conservative scholars continue to apply their best minds to important critical questions of this kind.[8] The question at present under discussion in New Testament studies is not whether the sayings of Jesus in the gospels are authoritative, nor whether they are Christlike in content, but whether Jesus really said them. Obviously, this is not the place to debate such matters, but it is the right context in which to affirm our confidence in the genuine and reliable nature of this New Testament evidence and applaud the strenuous work of those scholars who dedicate their energies to such central issues in biblical studies. It is also an appropriate place to be reminded of the necessity of a well-informed understanding of such subjects, so that we can confidently present the message of Christ's gospel to those whose faith has been undermined by the doubts and scepticism of radical and destructive gospel criticism.

b. The gospel of Christ

But there is something else here. The gospel is not only genuine and reliable, but also distinctive. In almost every period of Christian history there have been those who have offered a substitute message. These persuasive but dangerous innovators have expounded a gospel of salvation by religious observance, or by moral effort, or by humanitarian benevol-

[6] D. Cupitt, *Jesus and the Gospel of God*, p. 58.

[7] *Ibid.*, p. 67.

[8] See, for example, R. T. France, 'The Authenticity of the Sayings of Jesus' in C. Brown (editor), *History, Criticism and Faith* (IVP, 1976); and I. H. Marshall (editor), *New Testament Interpretation* (Paternoster, 1977).

ence, or by political involvement, or by social action. Nobody denies some place for all these things, but not as substitutes for the gospel of God's undeserved grace and Christ's redemptive work. The deliverance which man can experience through this once-for-all event is *such a great salvation.* Its message must not be perverted and it should not be neglected (2:3).

c. The judgment of Christ

One of the ways in which the message of the gospel has become distorted, in recent decades particularly, has been by the presentation of 'universalism'. J. A. T. Robinson asks, 'May we not imagine a love so strong that ultimately no one will be able to restrain himself from free and grateful surrender?'[9] He is persuaded that 'hell is an ultimate impossibility, because *already* there *is* no one outside Christ'[10] . . . 'The world *has been* redeemed. Hell has been harrowed, and none can finally make it their home.'[11]

This teaching ignores or explains away the serious, warning passages of Scripture about man's accountability to God and suggests that, because God is love, ultimately and inevitably all people will be saved. Such a message can only be described as a most serious misrepresentation of New Testament teaching. It springs from a totally unbalanced doctrine of God, Christ, man, sin and its eternal consequences. This passage in Hebrews talks plainly about the *just retribution* of those who disobeyed God's word and goes on to ask how we can possibly escape even more serious punishment if we deliberately choose to reject Christ and his *great salvation.* Emphasizing Christ's mercy and generous pardon, a great deal of universalist teaching ignores the fact that the judgment-theme figures prominently in the preaching of Jesus himself.[12] It was because of his perfect love for lost mankind that Christ spoke so directly and unmistakably about our accountability to God. He talked about hell as well as heaven. Men and women cannot hope to *escape* from a *just retribution* if they disregard the Christ who made their salvation possible and

[9] J. A. T. Robinson, *In The End God* (Fontana, 1968), p. 122.
[10] *Ibid.*, p. 130. [11] *Ibid.*, pp. 132–133.
[12] Mt. 5:29–30; 8:11–12; Jn. 3:16–18, 36.

who ultimately will be their judge.[13] Leon Morris has reminded us that man's response to these great truths determines our destiny: 'This Epistle leaves us in no doubt but that those who are saved are saved from a sore and genuine peril. Christ's saving work is not a piece of emotional pageantry rescuing men from nothing in particular.'[14]

[13] Jn. 5:22–23, 25–27; Acts 10:42; 17:31.
[14] L. Morris, *The Cross in the New Testament* (Paternoster, 1965), p. 274.

2:5–13

4. Christ our pioneer

We have already noticed that 2:1–4 is a parenthesis. So, in order to understand the flow of the author's argument, we ought to read directly from 1:14 to 2:5, omitting the parenthetical section. Before his brief digression about the importance of God's word in the gospel, he was writing about angels, the 'ministering spirits' sent by God as his servants to Christians. But the writer of this letter has introduced the theme of the angels and their work only in order to emphasize the superiority of God's Son, the perfect and unique intermediary, the 'one mediator between God and men, the man Christ Jesus'.[1] He transcends the angelic order and far surpasses the brightest of angels in his person, dignity, work and office. Following the brief parenthesis the author presents his readers with a further series of word-pictures of Christ. He is not only their prophet, priest and king, the Son of God; he is also their pioneer, liberator, and apostle.

5For it was not to angels that God subjected the world to come, of which we are speaking.

It has already become clear that angels are extremely important to the writer of this letter. The Jewish people believed that in past times the angels shared in the mediation of God's word (2:2) and that in the present age they participate in the administration of God's world. We have noted earlier that some scholars maintain that the first recipients of this letter

[1] 1 Tim. 2:5.

may well have been a company of believers originally committed to or influenced by the teaching of the Qumran community with its treasured Dead Sea Scrolls. The scrolls had a good deal to say about the role of angels. This sect awaited the appearance of two Messianic figures, one kingly, the other priestly (the priest being the greater), both of whom would become subordinate to Michael, the archangel. In their thinking, the *world to come* would eventually be subjected to the authority of angels. But our author insists that this world to come is certainly not included within the range of angelic responsibility. In the new world-order 'the place of honor and authority belongs to the glorified Son, not, as . . . the Dead Sea sect imagined, to angels or archangels' (Hughes).

But what does our writer mean when he mentions the world to come? It is surely the same as the 'last days' referred to in 1:2. A similar phrase, 'the age to come' is used later in the epistle (6:5). The author says it is the world of which he has been speaking, and he has certainly been expounding the message of salvation (2:3). The world to come is the totally new world-order which has already begun in Christ. In other words, it is the new age, the era of salvation. It is not, therefore, something reserved entirely for the future, even though it has a future dimension of rich and exciting significance. In Christ we have already entered God's stupendous future.

The Son's responsibility for inaugurating this new age is given vivid expression in a new title given to Christ and first introduced in this section of the letter. Jesus is described as the 'pioneer' of our salvation (2:10). He led the way and opened up the road for those who followed him. The word used here (*archēgos*) is quite common in the Greek version of the Old Testament, so well-known to the writer. It is sometimes used in secular Greek literature to describe the head of a clan, a hero, a founder of a school of thought, or the originator of a particular course of action. Christ has opened the way to glory for God's 'many sons'. Three important aspects of the theme are developed here, the pioneer's humanity, mission and achievement.

1. The pioneer's humanity (2:6–9)

6 *It has been testified somewhere,*
'What is man that thou art mindful of him,
or the son of man, that thou carest for him?
7 *Thou didst make him for a little while lower than the angels,*
thou hast crowned him with glory and honour,
8 *putting everything in subjection under his feet.'*
Now in putting everything in subjection to him, he left nothing
outside his control. As it is, we do not yet see everything in
subjection to him. 9 *But we see Jesus, who for a little while was*
made lower than the angels, crowned with glory and honour
because of the suffering of death, so that by the grace of God
he might taste death for everyone.

He opened this exclusive way, this only route to glory, because he knows every step of the road from personal first-hand experience. This saving work could not possibly have been entrusted to angels. Only Christ could achieve our salvation and in order to do so became man, not taking upon himself the nature of angels but being made 'like his brethren in every respect' (2:16–17). At this point in the argument the writer makes striking use of some verses from Psalm 8. He has used Old Testament Scripture in chapter 1 to portray Christ's superiority over the angels as the Son of God. Here he presents Christ as for a time lower than the angels, the Son of man. When Jesus assumed our human nature he willingly took upon himself our frustrated, suffering and threatened humanity.

a. Our frustrated humanity

Christ knew that it was a humanity marked by frustration. Man is not what he was intended to be. Psalm 8 expounds the dignity and destiny of man in God's original purpose. First, he was intended to be a creature of *supreme favour.* God was 'mindful of him' and cared for him (2:6). Next, he was intended to be a creature of *special privilege*, only 'for a little while lower than the angels' (2:7). Moreover, he was meant to be a creature of *unique dignity*, the treasured aspect of God's creation, 'crowned . . . with glory and honour'

(2:7), the recipient of God's special favour. He was, furthermore, marked out initially as a creature of *unrivalled dominion*, with all the created order under his control, 'everything in subjection under his feet' (2:8). It is all a direct echo of Genesis 1:26. But this is not man as we now see him. From our observations we see him despising God's favour, abusing his privileges, ignoring his dignity and, through sin, limited in his dominion. Man is certainly not as he should be. But, says our author, in Christ's person we see him as he can be and through Christ's work we see him as he will be: *we see Jesus* and acknowledge afresh that he came to be our pioneer. He had to take our nature and become like us, but without those sinful and rebellious characteristics which mar our nature.

b. Our suffering humanity

Moreover, it is obvious from these verses that Christ took upon himself our humanity in all its suffering. Becoming man, he entered directly and personally into the arena of our anguish. 'Suffering' is an important idea in this letter and is specially significant in view of the readers' earlier troubles and future prospects. The word is used here for the first time in the letter (2:9), but it is to recur later both in its description of Christ's anguish throughout life and in death, and of the tribulations of God's people.[2] When Christ assumed our humanity he became like us, exposed to all the hazardous perils of our life and death. He was not protected from trouble and adversity. When we find ourselves immersed in the harsh realities of human experience, he knows exactly how we feel.

c. Our threatened humanity

At the incarnation Christ also took upon himself a human nature exposed to the anguish of death. Throughout his days man lives under the threat of death. Jesus himself tasted death, went through the physical sensation of dying and did so under the worst possible conditions *for every one* (2:9). Death was the terrifying problem of the ancient world and if Jesus was

[2] Heb. 2:18; 5:8; 10:32; 11:26, 36; 13:12.

to be really and truly 'like his brethren' (2:17), he had to go through its grim experience. The angels could not feel these pangs of human desolation. Death was unknown to them. In the later verses of this chapter the author is to exult in the fact that Christ did not merely experience death; he conquered it (2:14–15). As our pioneer, he has gone through all this in advance of us. His feet have moved through that lonely territory of death and he has triumphed over its power for us. The forerunner (6:20) has gone on before us and those who know him have nothing to fear about the future.

With the aid of Psalm 8, the writer wants to emphasize not only that Jesus has entered fully into our humanity, but more especially that he is the ideal man, man as God really intended him to be. The phrase *But we see Jesus* (2:9) brings the quotation from the Psalm to a dramatic climax. Man is certainly not remotely like the ideal humanity portrayed by the psalmist, but Jesus has come into the world to show us what man is like in God's original purpose and what man can be through Christ's effective work.

Before we leave these verses one further point needs to be made. Our writer has repeated the psalmist's words that when God made man he *left nothing outside his control.* Although sin has restricted man's dominion in creation, it has not entirely obliterated it. Man's qualified mastery over created things indicates that in God's purpose we have a divinely given responsibility towards creation. Many of our contemporaries are rightly concerned that, far from acting responsibly, man is plundering the limited resources of our beautiful world. Although some writers on pollution and related subjects may occasionally sound alarmist, few informed people would deny that the problem is fast approaching crisis proportions. Sinful man ignores the fact that 'the earth is the Lord's',[3] not ours. These rich resources belong to our creator and we are meant to serve God in the created order as his responsible stewards.

What can the Christian do to give practical expression to this responsible stewardship? Like the psalmist, we ought to begin simply by admiring the created world. Some Christians

[3] Ps. 24:1.

are far too busy rushing here and there to look at the beautiful things around us that God has made for our enjoyment.[4] Next, we ought to recognize that creation can become the instrument of God's revelation to us,[5] a vivid colourful exposition of his power, majesty, beauty, providence, infinite love and care for detail, as well as his sovereignty. For these reasons we ought to value it and stand alongside all those with whom we can conscientiously identify in the campaign for a responsible attitude to our environment. It is both sinful and selfish greedily to squander for ourselves the resources which our children and grandchildren also have the right to enjoy.[6]

2. The pioneer's mission (2:10)

For it was fitting that he, for whom and by whom all things exist, in bringing many sons to glory, should make the pioneer of their salvation perfect through suffering.

Christ came not only to share our humanity, but to transform it. On account of sin man is not crowned; he is degraded. Creation is not subject to him; he is in subjection to it, dominated by its immense power and under its sovereign control. But God has a brighter prospect for his people. Things can be different. Within the compass of this brief verse, three biblical themes are given prominence – God's wisdom, man's destiny and Christ's perfection.

a. God's wisdom

Man's salvation begins in the heart and mind of God. If fallen humanity is to be brought ultimately into the presence of God as a redeemed and changed personality, it can only be because God has chosen to effect this miracle by his saving intervention in human history. Notice the initiative and action of God in all this. It is 'by the grace of God' (2:9) that Christ

[4] Ps. 8:13; 1 Tim. 6:17. [5] Ps. 19:1–6; Rom. 1:20.

[6] See R. J. Sider, *Rich Christians in an Age of Hunger* (Hodder & Stoughton, 1977); E. Rogers, *Plundered Planet* (Denholm House Press, 1973); R. J. Berry, *Ecology and Ethics* (IVP, 1972); R. Elsdon, *Bent World* (IVP, 1981); R. Moss, *The Earth in Our Hands* (IVP, 1982).

experienced death for us and it is through the wisdom of God (2:10) that such a death is savingly effective for mankind. God made it possible because God knew it to be right. This sacrifice was *fitting*, 'clearly fitting' (NEB), and part of God's compassionate plan for the redemption of mankind. The creator, *for whom and by whom all things consist*, is in charge of the universe he has made and it is he who determines this way of salvation by which the Son made purification for sins.

It is important to pause for a moment here. Some contemporary expositions of the idea of salvation choose to begin not with what is 'fitting' in the mind of God, but with what is congenial to the desires of men. There are those who earnestly seek to be saved from oppressive political powers, and we sympathize with their desire for such liberation. But some contemporary theologians have chosen to identify and confuse human efforts for individual or corporate liberation with the divine purpose for man's personal salvation. In no sense do we condone human oppression when, with the teaching of this letter, we assert the prior necessity of divine salvation. As P. E. Hughes observes: 'The purpose of this verse and the following verses is to show how *fitting* this method of salvation is and, by implication, how totally inappropriate any other notion must be.'

This verse is appropriate not only for the political liberationist, but for the religious pluralist. In a society where most of the world's main religions now have dedicated representatives, if not active propagandists, in all parts of our country, Christian believers need to be reminded that all ways do not lead to God. John Hick expresses a different view, fundamentally at variance with the apostolic insistence that 'there is no other name under heaven given among men by which we must be saved'[7] and Christ's own assertion that he alone is the way:

> We must thus be willing to see God at work within the total religious life of mankind, challenging men in their state of 'natural religion', with all its crudities and cruelties, by the tremendous revelatory moments which lie at the basis of the great world faiths . . . All salvation – that is,

[7] Acts 4:12.

> all creating of human animals into children of God – is the work of God . . . But what we cannot say is that all who are saved are saved by Jesus of Nazareth . . . On the contrary, we would gladly acknowledge that Ultimate Reality has affected human consciousness for its liberation or 'salvation' in various ways within the Indian, the semitic, the Chinese, the African . . . forms of life.[8]

Convictions of this kind are hardly supported by the message of Hebrews with its repeated affirmation that Christ's sacrifice is the only *fitting* means for the salvation of all mankind. In our own day there is a commendable desire to study, understand and respect the religious convictions of others, but the believer who takes this letter seriously realizes that there is only one way by which man can be redeemed, one and one only. All other ways have been just as certainly abolished by Christ as was the way of Jewish ritualism described as obsolete in our epistle.

b. Man's destiny

God's purpose for mankind is to bring *many sons to glory.* The file-leader, the pioneer of our salvation, endures the bitter experience of death for us in order to lead us up to the throne of God. He goes in front of us and clearly marks out the way that leads to salvation. In this context salvation is presented as a future prospect, although elsewhere in the letter it is portrayed as a present possession. Both aspects of truth are expounded in the New Testament. The believer finds encouragement and strength in both. He will be brought to glory by the Christ who suffered for him. As the teaching of the letter proceeds, we shall be encouraged more than once by our future hope. Believers march toward the 'city which has foundations', their 'homeland', 'the heavenly Jerusalem'. They belong to the 'kingdom which cannot be shaken', and pursue their journey to 'the city which is to come'.[9] We are called to pilgrimage and need to press on to our promised rest. There is something that remains yet to be possessed.

[8] J. Hick (editor), *The Myth of God Incarnate*, pp. 180–181.
[9] Heb. 11:10, 14, 16; 12:22, 28; 13:14.

Our race has yet to be run to its rewarding conclusion.[10]

Yet this is only part of the story. Salvation is also a present possession. Already Christ has made 'expiation for the sins of the people'. He is 'able for all time to save those who draw near to God through him'. He *has* secured 'an eternal redemption' for us, and our sins have been 'put away'.[11] We do not wait, tentatively and without certainty, hoping that we might be saved. This letter, more than anywhere else in the New Testament, asserts that Christ's work is finished and complete. We can enjoy its benefits and experience its blessings.

This verse's teaching about the Christian life announces that believers have both certainty (they are *sons*) and destiny (they will be brought to *glory*). It is also a necessary corrective to some forms of contemporary theology which suggest that salvation is now to be interpreted primarily as a 'this-world' ideal for which man must struggle and strive during this life. Man is a sinner and, even when he tries to change society for the better, his motives are not always pure and his methods may bring pain instead of peace. His destiny is determined not by man's fleeting success, but by God's eternal intervention.

c. *Christ's perfection*

The third great theme announced in this important verse concerns the person and work of Christ. In these initially bewildering words Jesus is described as one made *perfect through suffering*. What does that mean? In this letter (7:26), as elsewhere in New Testament teaching,[12] Christ always has been perfect in a moral sense. He *is* sinless. The word translated *perfect* here frequently recurs throughout this letter. It signifies the completion of a process. F. D. V. Narborough says that 'its use here means that Jesus became *fully qualified* as pioneer of man's salvation by undergoing experience of human sufferings, inasmuch as through suffering is the way to salvation'. Although Christ was morally perfect and sinless, his life and work were brought by suffering to a form of

[10] Heb. 3:14; 4:1, 9, 11; 12:1. [11] Heb. 2:17; 7:25; 9:12, 26.
[12] 2 Cor. 5:21; 1 Pet. 2:22; 1 Jn. 3:5.

perfection or completion which cannot have been possible without them. First, he became perfect in his vocation. He determined to do God's will in every part of his life (10:7, 9). Secondly, he became perfect in obedience. Christ was in perfect union with his Father in eternity, but by fulfilling the divine purposes in the incarnation he did what God desired of him and his obedience was brought to perfection. Thirdly, he became perfect in his identification. Although Christ certainly loved us in his pre-existence, this letter is about to emphasize that he had to become like us in our humanity in order to achieve our eternal redemption. Finally, he became perfect in his conquest. Supremely, it was through his sufferings that Christ became fully qualified to be known eternally as man's Saviour.

Leon Morris makes use of a helpful illustration in an exposition of this verse. He believes that the meaning here is 'that sufferings introduce a new perfection, a perfection of testedness. There is one perfection of the bud and another of the flower . . . In the same way there is a perfection involved in actually having suffered, and which is not implied in any previous perfection. It casts no doubt on the previous perfection, but it adds something to it.' Helpfully, Morris goes on to reflect that 'for Christians, as for their Master, there is a perfection in suffering. Little as we may like them, the fires of affliction are the place in which qualities of Christian character are forged. No one wants to suffer. No one looks forward to suffering. But the Christian cannot regard suffering as an unmitigated evil. He can agree that it is an evil, but he knows also that, borne in the right spirit, it is the means of an increasing Christlikeness.'[13]

3. The pioneer's achievement (2:11–13)

[11]*For he who sanctifies and those who are sanctified have all one origin. That is why he is not ashamed to call them brethren,* [12]*saying,*

'I will proclaim thy name to my brethren,
in the midst of the congregation I will praise thee.'

[13]*And again,*

[13] L. Morris, *The Cross in the New Testament*, p. 281.

'I will put my trust in him.'
And again,
'Here am I, and the children God has given me.'

Although believers are moving, day by day, towards their future destiny as sons of glory, something is also happening to us in the present. We are being changed, here and now. In Christ we are sanctified, set apart for God's use and made 'holy'. Sanctification is another dominant theme in this letter (10:14, 29; 13:12). It is the imagery of the temple. In Old Testament times, certain people, selected vessels and appointed days were 'set apart' for God's use. By his death our pioneer has not only prepared our way to glory, but has made us fit to tread that holy way. He sanctified us by becoming one of us in his humanity and by making us one with him (2:11). He who sanctifies and those who are sanctified 'are all of one stock' (NEB). They 'are of the same family' (NIV). The opening verses of this epistle have made it clear that Christ came to obtain our purification (1:3), but in one sense simple 'cleansing' is not enough. In that act of purification we are also 'set apart' for the use of God. We are cleansed in order that we might 'serve the living God' (9:14). In this service we are one with Christ and he is pleased to call us 'brothers'.

The writer uses the words of both psalmist and prophet to impress upon his readers their oneness with Christ. Isaiah 8 reflects the context of hope in time of despair. The Lord is hiding his face from Jacob, but God's servant says, 'I will hope in him.' Similarly, Jesus puts his complete trust in his Father in the most desolate moment of his life and in the darkest hour of world history when he bore our sins in his own body on the cross. Through that saving and transforming anguish and death we become his sons (2:10), brothers (2:11–12; 11:16) and children (2:13). Christ rejoices in the companionship of the household of God (3:6);[14] they are the children God has given him,[15] and they will be his for ever.

If we are sanctified, then we must be what we are. It is possible only by his grace and in his strength,[16] but it is

[14] Eph. 2:19. [15] Jn. 17:6, 9.
[16] 2 Cor. 12:9–10; Eph. 3:16; Phil. 4:19.

certainly possible. All too often sin, ignorance or apathy keeps us from what we ought to be and can be with his help. We live well below our spiritual potential. If, through his work for us, we are sanctified, then let us see that our daily lives are 'set apart' so that what he achieved may be not only an item of theology, but a fact of experience.

What does this mean in practical terms? It means that those who are 'set apart' for him recognize that he has the first claim on their lives. They recognize that such gifts that they have are set apart for God's use in the world. Their possessions are set apart, clearly acknowledging that they too belong to God. The sanctified man or woman does not spend enormous sums of money on items for self-satisfaction and then casually give a mere pittance to Christ's work. Moreover, time is set apart for the service of Christ. The Christian who has hours of time for leisure but no time for some practical work for Christ in church, college or community, is hardly sanctified in any practical sense. What is potentially there needs to be practically implemented.

2:14–18
5. Christ our liberator

[14]Since therefore the children share in flesh and blood, he himself likewise partook of the same nature, that through death he might destroy him who has the power of death, that is, the devil, [15]and deliver all those who through fear of death were subject to lifelong bondage. [16]For surely it is not with angels that he is concerned but with the descendants of Abraham. [17]Therefore he had to be made like his brethren in every respect, so that he might become a merciful and faithful high priest in the service of God, to make expiation for the sins of the people. [18]For because he himself has suffered and been tempted, he is able to help those who are tempted.

The writer now develops his theme of Christ's identification with our humanity by describing his liberating work for all mankind. During the past decade 'liberation' has become a highly fashionable theological idea. This passage expounds the theme of man's greatest deliverance, but it does not figure prominently in the teaching of so-called 'liberation theology'. It is important for us to discern what our author believes to be man's most serious form of bondage and how Christ effected his release from such a grim prison. Christ's liberating mission is here presented as an urgent necessity, an accomplished fact and a continuing process.

1. Liberation as an urgent necessity

The liberation theologians of South America and elsewhere focus attention on man's need for political and social deliverance. Genuine Christians are portrayed as those willing to take up the cause of the powerless masses. Liberty and freedom are presented in terms of human salvation from inhuman regimes and oppressive structures. It is important here to emphasize again that Christians have cause to be deeply troubled about any form of human deprivation. It is certainly no part of the Christian gospel to ignore the crying needs of the oppressed. Jesus cared for people deeply, fed the hungry and helped the outcast members of his contemporary society. But this letter makes it abundantly clear that even if, rightly, all forms of oppression are removed from man's experience, he will still be crushed and broken by a far greater power than that exercised by loveless megalomaniacs, selfish employers, or indifferent politicians. In other words, the worst tyranny is within. These verses vividly portray helpless man, the terrified victim of a triple enemy, sin, death and the devil. Our writer asserts that, as our perfect pioneer, Christ had to meet these sinister powers and malevolent influences. It was necessary for him to partake *of the same nature* as ourselves in order to deal effectively with them.

The first enemy is *sin*. We have already seen that it is starkly portrayed in the opening verses of this letter as an ugly stain which must be purged away if we are to be purified (1:3). It is a hostile, destructive, inward power which will always prevent us from being the people we might genuinely want to be. To meet our need of purification, Christ came as a priest to offer the sacrifice of himself. He makes *expiation for the sins of the people* (2:17).

The second enemy is *death*. Death is the direct result and inevitable fruit of sin[1] and man is haunted by its constant threat. Throughout our lives we are *through fear of death ... subject to ... bondage* (2:15). Enslaved convicts, we are in powerless 'servitude' (NEB) and need to be released. By taking our nature and experiencing death (2:14), Jesus deals effectively and eternally with this immense tyrant.

Perhaps even the early Christians who received this letter were a little fearful when they thought of death. Persecution was imminent and, understandably, one might have been a little afraid of the actual experience of dying, especially as it

[1] Gn. 2:17; 3:3–4; Rom. 5:12; 6:23; 1 Cor. 15:21, 56.

might well involve intense physical suffering. Such believers stood in need of a reminder that death has no fears for the Christian. But if Christians might occasionally be afraid when they contemplated death, unbelievers in the first century were terror-stricken when they considered its shattering prospect. The pagan had no hope for the future. He could only live for the present. Some lines from Euripides indicate something of the crippling despair in the mind of the ancient pagan when he considered the fact of death. The Greeks thought about it this way:

> But if any far-off state there be,
> Dearer than life to mortality;
> The hand of the Dark hath hold thereof,
> And mist is under and mist above.
> And so we are sick for life, and cling
> On earth to this nameless and shining thing.
> For other life is a fountain sealed,
> And the deeps below us are unrevealed
> And we drift on legends for ever![2]

The most that the Romans could believe about the life to come is that a good man might hope to 'live on' in the minds of those who cherished his memory, but there was little thought of personal survival. With what excitement the early Christian preachers must have proclaimed the authoritative words of Jesus to men and women in despair about death: 'I am the resurrection and the life; he who believes in me, though he die, yet shall he live, and whoever lives and believes in me shall never die.'[3] The unbelieving world has no such assurance. It is absent, for example, from both Communism and humanism. During the second world war Sir John Lawrence attended what he describes as 'a sort of Communist memorial service' to Stanislavsky in the Moscow Arts Theatre. He says,

> There was a closed coffin on the stage, draped in a red flag, and the dead man's colleagues came and said goodbye to

[2] The words of Phaedra's nurse in *Hippolytus*, Gilbert Murray's translation (London, 1915), p. 12.
[3] Jn. 11:25–26.

> him in set speeches. One heard some of the world's greatest actors and actresses speaking of their teacher and leader on what should have been a moving occasion, but the experience was empty. I was not at that time a Christian believer, but even so it struck me that Communism has nothing to say about death. There was no development of a theme such as one gets in the prayer book service for the Burial of the Dead. In the same way, to visit the Mausoleum where Lenin lies, and where Stalin lay for a few years beside him, is for me a disturbing experience precisely because it has no content.[4]

Or take the humanist attitude to life with its sad stark pessimism and restricted horizons. Bertrand Russell says:

> Brief and powerless is man's life; on him and all his race the slow, sure doom falls pitiless and dark. Blind to good and evil, reckless of destruction, omnipotent matter rolls on its relentless way; for man, condemned today to lose his dearest, tomorrow himself to pass through the gates of darkness, it remains only to cherish, ere yet the blow fall, the lofty thoughts that enoble his little day; . . . to worship at the shrine his own hands have built.[5]

The third enemy is the *devil.* Jesus has robbed death of its anguish by defeating the one who constantly makes use of it. The devil is a reality to the biblical writers. Some modern scholars, embarrassed by the references to his work in Scripture, have endeavoured to dismiss the force of such sayings by suggesting that the idea of the devil is a Persian religious notion which came into Old Testament thought rather late in the day. The argument then proceeds that the New Testament writers inherited this conception and utilized it, but in our more enlightened times we can dispense with it. Those who are committed to the authority and reliability of Scripture believe that the entire book is given for our instruction[6] and choose to be neither dismissive nor derisive concerning the

[4] J. Lawrence, *Russians Observed* (Hodder & Stoughton, 1969), p. 118.
[5] B. Russell, *A Free Man's Worship and other essays* (Unwin Paperbacks, 1976), pp. 18–19.
[6] 2 Tim. 3:16.

biblical teaching about the devil.[7] Jesus did not appear to minimize his power or rationalize his sinister influence,[8] and in his teaching openly identified him for what he is, murderer, liar, thief.

2. Liberation as an accomplished fact

The New Testament makes it clear that the coming of Jesus was the beginning of the end for the devil. Hebrews adds to this incontrovertible testimony that Christ has overcome the devil's power, and our writer makes his point in three ways. He is convinced that his victory for us began with the incarnation, was revealed in his sinlessness, and achieved by the atonement.

It was necessary, first of all, for the liberator to partake of the same nature as ourselves. In this way he experienced the full force and relentless power of temptation but resolutely refused to be influenced by its onslaughts. He was tempted not less than we are, but more. All too often we succumb to temptation, we yield to its power when the pressure is on. We give in long before its full force has been really felt. As Hughes puts it, Christ 'knows the full force of temptation in a manner that we who have not withstood it to the end cannot know it.'

But our victory over the triple-enemy of sin, death and the devil, needed something more than his incarnate life and his moral perfection. To become man's perfect liberator, God's Son had to experience the process common to all *flesh and blood*, the experience of death. It was also necessary for this spotless, pure, undefiled (7:26) conqueror to take upon himself in death the weight and burden of our sin, doing for us at the cross, as our substitute, that which we could not possibly do for ourselves. By that death he obtained for sinful mankind the pardon of our sin and the removal of our guilt. This is how the devil was 'rendered impotent', which is the true meaning of the word *destroy* here (2:14).

But, understandably, the question may be asked: If, at the cross of Christ, the devil was rendered impotent, why is he still so very much alive in the world, and in what sense are

[7] Gn. 3:1; Rev. 12:9; 20:2. [8] Mt. 4:1–11; 13:19; 16:23.

we free from his aggressive power? Surely he is still far from being 'destroyed' in any final sense? Does he not still, as in Peter's day, stalk around the entire world like a roaring lion, constantly looking out for someone to terrorize, molest and destroy? Christ's victorious death robbed the devil of his earlier power and stranglehold over men. Ultimately, the devil will be destroyed completely,[9] but until then believers need to recognize that his power is a limited power.

In my early twenties I used to be a postman. One day I had to deliver a letter to a house I had never visited before. I opened the garden gate only to find myself confronted by the largest and most vicious dog I had ever seen! It barked furiously and then leapt towards me. I stood there helpless and terrified until, to my immense relief, I saw that this massive, angry dog was chained to a huge stake set in concrete. The chain was a long one and the dog had considerable freedom, but not enough to reach me. I saw I could easily deliver the letter and did so. The incident became like a parable to me. As a matter of fact, whenever I had to visit that house in the course of my work, I took little notice of the aggressive dog. I always kept my eye on the strong stake! At the cross the enemy of souls, the devil, was made impotent, limited and chained down. When he has 'bitten' us it is usually because we have been far too near.

3. Liberation as a continuing process

The author of this epistle is deeply persuaded that this eternally significant, divinely planned, conquest of sin, death and the devil by Christ took place once for all in history. He knows, however, that this victory is likely to prove effective in the lives of individual believers only if they recognize that its achievements must be appropriated and its blessings applied in daily living. He is assured not only about what Jesus has done but about what he continues to do for his people. Whatever the hazards of daily living, *he is able to help those who are tempted* (2:18). There are numerous ways in which this promised help comes to the children of God.

First, he helps us by removing our fears. There is little that

[9] Rev. 20:10.

paralyses us and inhibits us more than being afraid. Here the writer has asserted that, before Christ comes into our lives, our greatest fear is that of death. A truly committed Christian has no need to fear death. In his exposition of these verses, Martin Luther wrote: 'He who fears death or is unwilling to die is not a Christian to a sufficient degree; for those who fear death still lack faith in the resurrection, since they love this life more than they love the life to come . . . He who does not die willingly should not be called a Christian.'

Secondly, he helps us by manifesting his mercy. He became like us in order that he might adequately minister to our needs as a *merciful . . . high priest*. Death is the fear of the future. Guilt is the fear of the past. Through his 'great salvation' he has made expiation or propitiation for the sins of the people. The word used here (*hilaskesthai*) is translated 'to make expiation for' (or 'to expiate', NEB). It is grammatically permissible to translate this verse (2:17) as a reference to Christ's work in making 'expiation', but as Bruce has made clear, 'if sins require to be expiated, it is because they are sins committed against someone who ought to be propitiated.' An Old Testament priest committed himself to 'the service of God' and part of his essential ministry on behalf of the congregation was to make propitiation for the sins of the people. As Leon Morris puts it: 'The just wrath of God was exercised toward men on account of their sin. But Christ dealt with that situation. He made the propitiation that was necessary, and so sin is no longer operative.' Morris has shown that elsewhere in Scripture *hilaskomai* has to do with the averting of the divine wrath.[10] This does not in any sense imply that a merciful Christ has to die in order to placate the anger of a God initially unwilling to do anything about man's sin other than destroy the sinner. Far from it. Hughes reminds us that this is a perilous caricature of biblical truth in that it 'introduces an intolerable dichotomy between the Father and the Son, as though the Son by acting independently could somehow induce a change in the Father's attitude'. Such a view is certainly not supported by the teaching of this letter. We have already seen that God acted in this way for man's redemption

[10] L. Morris, *The Cross in the New Testament*, p. 299; see his *Apostolic Preaching of the Cross* (IVP 1955), chapters 4 and 5, for a full discussion of this important term.

because it was fitting for him so to do (2:10). A later passage makes it even more clear that his incarnation and death were an expression of Christ's obedience to and harmony with the saving purpose of God for mankind (10:7–10).

Nothing is quite so debilitating and demoralizing as an acute sense of failure. It severs the nerve of moral action, floods our disturbed minds with a sense of remorse, and cripples us at the very point where we need power not to fail again. Jesus is able to help us when we are tempted because he declares to us, clearly and unmistakably, by his word and his work, that our sin is forgiven, our guilt taken away, our pardon assured. We are thus given a clean start; the failures of the past need not in any sense keep us back from the potential victories of the future.

Thirdly, he helps us by proving his faithfulness. He is a *faithful* as well as merciful high priest in God's service. It is possible, of course, to suggest here that in his high-priestly service Christ is merciful to man and faithful to God, the twin-title reflecting the manward and Godward aspects of his priestly ministry. But it is equally true that he is faithful to us. The trustworthy and reliable Christ is the one who comes to our help when we are tempted, not a vascillating, capricious, occasionally unavailable helper, but one who has proved himself fully dependable and completely adequate in every experience of life.

Fourthly, he helps us by sharing our sufferings. Jesus did not live a detached life, free from adversity and trouble. He experienced first-hand its hazards and hardships, and went through anguish we shall never have to contemplate, and he did it all for us. The first readers of this letter were also up against persecution, rejection, physical assault and social deprivation. It is essential for them to know that the Christ their contemporaries reject is that Lord who understands their constantly changing needs. This means surely that whenever we are up against it, prayer is our immediate aid. We turn instinctively to the one who has suffered, knowing that he feels for us. The help is not simply emotional, however, though in any kind of trouble we know the immense value of sympathetic understanding from someone who has been through the same grim experiences. He not only feels; he instructs. Having been through all the testings of life, he can reveal to us, especially by his radiant example and his matchless words, how we should react to sufferings or temptations. Moreover, he does not simply teach, he supports.

Finally then, he helps us by supplying our strength. Jesus pledges his strong and sure support, his own invincible and available power. He serves effectively as our priest 'by the power of an indestructible life' (7:16). All the forces of evil were hurled against him as he hung upon the cross, but he was 'brought again from the dead' (13:20) by the eternal, almighty God. When we are humanly at the end of our tether, with seemingly no resources left, moral or physical, Christ comes to his 'sons' with the promise that he is fully qualified to bring them to his ultimate glory. For that journey they will need all the power they can get. Many Christians today work, study, live and serve in surroundings far from congenial for a believer. Christ's name is used only blasphemously, moral standards are a thing of the past, materialistic concerns are dominant, secular interests and preoccupations form the very air we breathe. Many of our contemporaries cannot cope with the pressures. Disillusionment, loneliness, moral frustration and emotional despair lead some seriously to contemplate the possibility of putting an end to it all. But the one who endured the world's greatest suffering, the bearing of human sin and separation from God, and yet triumphed, is certainly able to help anyone who turns to him. He is able to help us in our moment of fierce temptation. He is able for all time to save those who seek (7:25). He is able to do far more for us than we would ever dare to pray about or even think about. He is able to keep us from spiritual collapse and present us to the eternal God as his redeemed children. However great the pressures, the New Testament assurance that he is 'able' should encourage us to deeper trust and renewed confidence in his unfailing ability not only to see us through the troubles, but make us conquerors[11] over them.

[11] Eph. 3:20; Jude 24–25; Rom. 8:37.

3:1–6

6. Christ our apostle

Therefore, holy brethren, who share in a heavenly call, consider Jesus, the apostle and high priest of our confession. [2]*He was faithful to him who appointed him, just as Moses also was faithful in God's house.* [3]*Yet Jesus has been counted worthy of as much more glory than Moses as the builder of a house has more honour than the house.* [4]*(For every house is built by some one, but the builder of all things is God.)* [5]*Now Moses was faithful in all God's house as a servant, to testify to the things that were to be spoken later,* [6]*but Christ was faithful over God's house as a son. And we are his house if we hold fast our confidence and pride in our hope.*

At this point in the letter the author makes another pastoral exhortation, similar to the one we have already noticed at 2:1–4. At the beginning of chapter 2 he urged them to give their careful obedience to the gospel of God; now he pleads with them to give their submissive attention to Jesus, the *apostle and high priest* of their confession. The writer urges these Jewish Christians to reflect on all that Christ has done for them, and describes these believers in terms equally reminiscent of his earlier teaching. First-century Christians are here portrayed in terms of their relationship, nature and privilege.

First, he mentions their *relationship*. They are brothers (3:1). Christ is not ashamed to acknowledge them as such (2:11) and rejoices in their fellowship. He was made like them in every respect (2:17) in order to meet their spiritual and moral needs. They are also described in terms of their *nature*.

They are holy brothers. If 'brothers' describes their union with Christ, 'holy' defines their most important characteristic. They have been made 'holy' or sanctified by Christ's atoning work (2:11). These Christians are then described in terms of their *privilege*. They are not only holy brothers, but heavenly partners; they have rich privileges, having become partakers or sharers in a heavenly call. This word 'partakers' (*metachoi*) recurs at various points in this letter. It 'describes participation in some common blessing or privilege . . . The bond of union lies in that which is shared and not in the persons themselves' (Westcott). The same word 'sharers' is used later in the letter when Christians are described as sharers in Christ (3:14), partakers of the Holy Spirit (6:4) and participators in discipline (12:8).

It is of special interest that these terms are used in a section which is about to expound the work of Christ in relation to that of Moses, for Moses certainly received *a heavenly call* from God. Clearly and unmistakably the Lord God *called* to Moses out of the bush. Moreover, Moses was *sent* by God to the work which had been prepared for him[1] and this passage describes Jesus as the one who has been *sent* by the Lord God. He is the *apostle* of our confession. We too have been made 'partakers' in a heavenly call. We have been called *from* heaven. The Lord God has addressed us in Christ so clearly and perfectly. He has 'spoken to us by a Son' (1:2). But we are not only called *from* heaven; we are called *to* heaven. We are sharers with other believers in the call which Paul mentioned when he wrote to the Philippians, 'the upward call of God in Christ Jesus'.[2] He is calling us on to glory and to the great future he has prepared for us.

These sanctified brothers are urged to *consider Jesus* or fix their attention continuously on the Lord Jesus. In more than one place in this letter believers are given similar advice. They are to 'consider' Jesus and 'scan closely' the one who has done so much for them (12:2–3). A threefold theme is presented here, Christ's apostolic and priestly work in relation to man, Moses and God.

[1] Ex. 3:4, 10, 14. [2] Phil. 3:14.

1. Christ's work and ourselves

The first readers of this letter are expected to look to Christ, and the terms used to describe the Lord are rich in spiritual significance. They are to consider the human Jesus, the divine apostle and the gracious priest.

a. The human Jesus

These believers were urged to turn away for a moment from their persecuting contemporaries to the Lord Jesus himself. In looking to him they are giving their best thoughts and highest love to the one who has himself been through testing, adversity and bitter opposition. Only then can they hope to cope with their own trials and be brought to the place of abiding peace and ultimate conquest. They are urged to look earnestly to *Jesus* and, as in other contexts in the letter, the author quite deliberately uses the human name of Christ to heighten the appeal of his words: 'But we see *Jesus*', 'consider *Jesus*', 'we have a great high priest . . . *Jesus*', 'In the days of his flesh, *Jesus* offered up prayers', 'the inner shrine . . . where *Jesus* has gone as a forerunner'.[3] He lived amongst us, suffered alongside us, died for us, prays for us, as one who fully and completely understands our needs. Consider Jesus for he constantly considers you and enters deeply and sympathetically into your needs. This is one of the author's most compelling and attractive themes.

b. The divine apostle

They are to consider Christ as *apostle*. He is God's envoy, messenger, or ambassador, sent by the Father.[4] In first-century thought and practice the specially appointed envoy possessed the full powers and was regarded as the personal representative of the one sending him. Jesus has been sent to fulfil a definite mission for God. He was sent not only to proclaim the truth but also to manifest it (1:2–3). Moreover, in this passage we may also discern a further aspect of his work as God's apostle. He is also sent to form or establish

[3] Heb. 2:9; 3:1; 4:14; 5:7; 6:19–20.

[4] Jn. 17:3, 8, 18; 20:21.

a *house*, or household, a redeemed community (3:6).[5] The preceding chapters of the letter have already hinted at the writer's doctrine of the church; in Christ we are sons, brothers, children and partners.[6] But here we begin to realize the importance of the Christian family in the thinking of the author. Christ came not only to save fallen individuals but to gather a vast company of his followers, the redeemed people of God. This epistle has little time for the spiritual individualist. Believers are to recognize the immensely important ministry that they can exercise towards other Christians and to take such responsibility seriously: 'Let us consider how to stir up one another to love and good works.' The regular meeting for worship and fellowship must not be neglected and Christian people must give all the encouragement they can to other believers. Christians are here described as those who belong to God's house, and Christ was sent into the world to save them and bring them into this enriching, secure and eternal company.[7]

c. The gracious priest

Earlier in the letter, Christ is expounded as the effective, merciful and faithful priest. Here he is the high priest *of our confession*. Some first-century Jewish Christians had abandoned their faith. He was no longer the priest of their confession, but others rejoiced that Christ was true to them and they in turn longed to make public confession of him as their apostle (the one sent from God to us) and priest (the one sent from the presence of needy people into the presence of God), whatever the cost of such a bold confession.

If these tempted and tested believers are to maintain their spiritual *confidence* and commitment to Christ in a hostile environment, then they must *consider* or 'fix their gaze' on Christ. The word means 'to apply one's mind diligently to something' (Hughes). It 'expresses attention and continuous observation' (Westcott). It is used in the gospels when Jesus invites his hearers to think about the ravens and the lilies[8] and

[5] Eph. 2:19–22; 1 Tim. 3:15; 1 Pet. 4:17. [6] Heb. 2:10–13, 17; 3:1.
[7] Heb. 3:6, 13; 4:9; 6:10; 10:24–25. [8] Lk. 12:24, 27.

appears again later in this epistle when its author urges his readers to give serious attention to the means by which they can help their fellow Christians (10:24). If we are to progress to maturity in the Christian life, some time in each day must be devoted to a careful consideration of the person, teaching and work of Christ. In other words, believers must meditate or fix their thoughts on Jesus. Meditation is a lost art. Time for quiet reflection is at a premium. In the contemporary world life is so busy, hurried and rushed, yet to neglect meditation is to run the risk of having a shallow understanding of spiritual truth.

Christian meditation is all the more important surely at a time, when, convinced of the value of meditation, so many people in western society are feeling the attraction of some eastern religions with their emphasis on forms of meditative prayer. Frustrated by the disappointments of secularism, materialism and rationalism, thousands of our contemporaries – especially, but not exclusively, thinking young people – respond eagerly to the advice of eastern mystics. Pictures of gurus smile down on us from hoardings; their followers are in all our cities. It is surely all the more important for committed Christians not only to recognize the pagan nature of such teaching, but also to give themselves to meditation of a biblical, instructive, positive and helpful kind. In Transcendental Meditation the mind is not required to make judgments. Adherents of the cult confess to a general feeling of well-being. That is the goal. Resignation is the outcome. But Christian meditation does not involve the believer in selfish disregard of others, pious detachment, or moral indifference. It involves the use of a dedicated mind. The Bible teaches that our meditation must be acceptable to God. We should meditate on God's word, not repetitive, empty Hindu mantras, and on God's Son, not the eastern gurus.[9] This letter to the Hebrews invites us to apply our minds and offer our adoration to Jesus, the apostle sent from God to meet our need, and the priest who has entered into God's presence as our eternal saviour, present intercessor and constant friend.

[9] Ps. 1:2; 19:14; 104:34; 119:15. For helpful introductions to Christian meditation, see M. V. Dunlop, *Stillness and Strength* (Fellowship of Meditation, Guildford, 1976) and E. P. Clowney, *Christian Meditation* (IVP, 1980).

2. Christ's work and Moses

Obviously Moses was a most significant figure in Jewish faith and thought. He was used to communicate God's word to his people. It is important for the writer to make it absolutely clear that in exalting Christ, believers are not thereby depreciating Moses. The eternally valid moral law was 'declared by angels' and Moses, the giver of the law, was *faithful* (3:2, 5).[10] But Jesus is worthy of *much more glory* than Moses. Moses was a temporary *servant*, whereas Christ is the eternal *son*. Moses was a witness, testifying to the things which are to appear later, the better and fuller revelation that was to come, whereas Christ is the revelation itself (1:1–3). Moses was a faithful steward in the house, but Christ is its owner. Moses could be only a part or a portion of the house, whereas Christ is the *builder*. He is over it and he is its founder (3:6). Moses loved God, but Jesus is God. The implication is plain. To forsake the way of Christ for the way of Moses is to go from the greater to the lesser. It is to abandon the permanent in favour of the temporary.

It is quite possible, of course, that this section of teaching is not only occasioned by the theological problem of the relationship of Christ and Moses, gospel and law, but also by a practical and pastoral issue. Formally 'cut off' from Judaism because of their new-found Christian faith, isolated from family and friends, some of these Jewish Christians felt bereft and alone. It was necessary to remind them that in Christ they most certainly belong to the house of God and as such are eternally safe and secure. They may have been cast out of the local synagogue, but they have not been cast out by God. *We are his house* (3:6). The words ring out with sustaining assurance. *If we hold fast*; the privilege is retained by those who, through his strength alone, maintain their loyalty and hold on to their boldness, whatever the opposition, and to their hope, however attractive the alternatives.

[10] Nu. 12:7.

3. Christ's work and God

The most majestic theme in this section, however, is the supremacy of Christ, expounded in such inspiring detail in the letter's opening chapters. The writer appeals to these early Christians to fix their thoughts on Jesus, so that they may consider his relationship to God as well as to themselves in the present and Moses in the past.

Moses responded to God's will recognizing that he had been appointed by God to a particularly exacting assignment. Christ was appointed by God to a far more responsible and eternally significant mission. He came to it not unwillingly (as Moses did at first), but gladly, even though it involved death on a cross. The epistle began by mentioning Christ's appointment and his future destiny. Christ is 'appointed the heir of all things' (1:2). Here we read of Christ's appointment in the past. He *was* appointed by God as a faithful apostle. A later passage in this letter tells of Christ's appointment and its present significance. He *is* appointed as our high priest (5:1, 5). Although the Lord Jesus is portrayed in this letter in exalted terms of absolute deity, he did not take these honours and glories upon himself. He 'did not exalt himself to be made a high priest' (5:5). Although he was a Son, he waited in the eternal presence until he was appointed by God as the apostle and ambassador of our salvation.

Moses was faithful. He did everything God required of him,[11] but his obedience and zeal were far surpassed by the faithfulness of Jesus. The Lord God knew that he would fulfil the eternal responsibilities which had been assigned to him.

It is appropriate for us to note, in conclusion, the perfect balance in this passage, and throughout this letter, between the believer's promised security and his necessary perseverance.

First, the believer's security is assured. Christians will not fail if they look dependently to their merciful and faithful high priest. So many temptations and pressures, insidious as well as blatant, can lure us away from Christ and the faith we profess. This epistle seems to demand so much from us in

[11] Ex. 40:16.

relentless pilgrimage, strenuous running and persistent continuance, but that is only part of its message. Time and again its firm truths sound out with ringing certainty: 'He is able to help.' 'We are his house.' 'We share in Christ.' 'We have a great high priest.'[12] This is the ground of our confidence. We do not place our hope in what *we do*, but what *he has done*. Believers do not rely on what *they* are; that would be a religion of merit. They base their entire spiritual confidence on what *he* is.

Secondly, the believer's continuance is essential. It is important to recognize the seriousness of this letter when it rightly insists on perseverance. F. F. Bruce describes this persistent endurance as 'the test of reality'. There is no casual easy-going presentation of Christianity in these chapters. William Manson is perfectly right when he insists that to the author of this epistle, Christianity is 'not a matter only of repenting and obtaining forgiveness, but of irrevocable commitment of life to a supernatural end.'[13] We are certainly in God's house by faith in Christ but, to be real, that belief must be something more than the occasionally faltering faith which initially takes hold of Christ, or that excited faith which, with adoring gratitude, first renounces sin and comes to Christ for liberating pardon. It is hardly that vascillating faith which calls out in moments of bewildered dejection: 'I believe; help my unbelief!'[14] It is a persistent faith which holds fast to its boldness and rejoices in the certain hope of better things. True Christian confidence is unwavering faith in a trustworthy God. He who has promised to keep us is eternally faithful and will not disappoint his people,[15] but that truth is not meant to encourage careless complacency. Committed Calvinist that he was, Bunyan agreed with the author of our letter that the Christian life is a rewarding yet strenuous race. His aim was not 'to run a little now and then, by fits and starts, or half way, or almost thither; but to run for my life, to run through all the difficulties, and to continue therein to the end of the race, which must be to the end of my life'.[16]

[12] Heb. 2:18; 3:6, 14; 4:14. [13] Manson, p. 85.

[14] Mk. 9:24. [15] Heb. 10:23; 11:11; 13:5–6.

[16] J. Bunyan, 'The Heavenly Footman', in G. Offor (editor), *The Works of John Bunyan*, 3 (London, 1885), p. 381.

3:7 – 4:13

7. Firm to the end

We are about to consider an extended passage which is not one of the easiest sections in the book to understand and interpret. We have to realize at the start that it is a highly compressed argument in the course of which our author makes occasionally abrupt use of Old Testament passages. But the main idea is clear enough. He has been expounding the superiority of Christ over Moses, but he has made it abundantly evident to these Jewish Christians that in exalting Jesus he has not the slightest desire to denigrate Moses. Moses was faithful (3:2, 5), but unfortunately Moses' faithfulness was not typical of the Israelites. They were faithless and did not enter into the rest of the promised land. Writing to Jewish Christians, deeply convinced that God has addressed his people 'in many and various ways' and with his own intense love for Scripture, it is natural for him to use the sad historical event of the wilderness wanderings as a parable or type of Christian pilgrimage and its attendant perils.

It is not at all unusual for New Testament writers to regard the Christian life as a new exodus. Luke describes Christ's death in those terms (*exodos*).[1] Paul declares that the Lord Jesus is the Passover Lamb[2] who has been sacrificed for us. Peter says that Jesus is 'a lamb without blemish or spot'.[3] 1 Corinthians 10:1–10 has many such 'exodus' allusions and Paul asserts that such events 'were written down for our instruction.[4] The author of Hebrews has a similar approach

[1] Lk. 9:31. [2] 1 Cor. 5:7. [3] 1 Pet. 1:19.
[4] 1 Cor. 10:11; Rom. 15:4.

to these Old Testament narratives. We too are pilgrims, he says. Those Israelites made a splendid beginning, but they did not continue in faith and so failed to reach their promised rest. It is not enough for us to make a decisive start. That undoubtedly memorable beginning must be followed by continuing faith and loyal obedience.

The author's choice of the 'Israel in the wilderness' theme has even greater significance for the first readers of this letter if, as many scholars believe, they were Christian believers influenced by the teaching of the Dead Sea Scrolls. That sect consisted of people who had deliberately withdrawn themselves from everyday Judean life in order to re-enact the exodus events. This Qumran community used the 'forty years in the wilderness' as a model or pattern of life to prepare themselves for eventual re-entry into a Jerusalem purged of a corrupt temple and its false leadership.

This passage presents its readers with a warning, an appeal and a promise.

1. God's word from the past: a serious warning (3:7–11)

7*Therefore, as the Holy Spirit says,*
'Today, when you hear his voice,
8*do not harden your hearts as in the rebellion,*
on the day of testing in the wilderness,
9*where your fathers put me to the test*
and saw my works for forty years.
10*Therefore I was provoked with that generation,*
and said, "They always go astray in their hearts;
they have not known my ways."
11*As I swore in my wrath,*
"They shall never enter my rest."'

We have already noticed that this letter addresses itself to the problem of apostasy. Some members of the church were in danger of turning back and giving up. These believers are reminded of Israel's fatal mistake in the wilderness. God requires his people to exercise *persistent* faith. He is asking them to rely on his power not only to change them, but also to keep them. They must 'go on' (6:1). Christians are the privileged members of God's house, but it is not unconditional membership. We certainly share its security and favours, but only if 'we hold fast our confidence firm to the end' (3:14).

In this passage, as earlier, the emphasis is on God's word, its seriousness and relevance. The author reflects on the message of Psalm 95, a highly appropriate passage to expound in this context. The psalm was regularly used each sabbath day in first-century synagogue worship and it would therefore provide a most fitting introduction to the idea of the eternal sabbath, the promised rest which God had provided for his faithful people. This psalm unites 'worship' and 'loyalty' as two inseparable ideas. What is the point of offering our praise to God, if the words we use are merely slick and religiously appropriate phrases which do not in fact reflect our hearts' love and obedience? Worship must be expressed in action as well as in language. Those who choose to 'come into his presence with thanksgiving'[5] must also come with attentiveness ('hearken to his voice') and obedience. They must not disregard God's ways as their ancestors did.[6]

It is important to note that, in the view of the author, God is still speaking to them through this Old Testament scripture. In his view the Psalms are something more than memorable hymns of rich poetic beauty. They are vehicles of God's *present* revelation to his people. 'Therefore as the Holy Spirit *says*'. The Spirit issues this eloquent appeal and, in order to press home its immediate, present significance, there is an important change in the quotation from Psalm 95. It strictly reads, 'I loathed *that* generation', but he makes it read, '*this* generation'. He knows only too well that even Christians can develop hard (3:8), then wayward (3:10) hearts. The psalmist is himself reflecting on the unhappy incidents recorded in Exodus 17:1–7 and Numbers 20 when the redeemed Israelites forgot the Lord's earlier deliverance and complained about their present circumstances. Passing through the Red Sea was fine, but once they came up against difficulties, they rebelled against God by opposing his servant. They doubted God's presence by saying, 'Is the Lord among us or not?' The names given to these places of revolt described in the Old Testament were 'Exasperation' and 'Contention'. God was deeply

[5] Ps. 95:2. [6] Ps. 95:7–11.

grieved by his people's doubt and disloyalty and swore they would not enter into the land of rest which had been promised to them and prepared for them. This warning from the past would certainly not be lost on these Jewish Christians in danger of defection and apostasy.

2. God's word in the present: an earnest appeal (3:12–19)

[12]*Take care, brethren, lest there be in any of you an evil,*
unbelieving heart, leading you to fall away from the living
God. [13]*But exhort one another every day, as long as it is called*
'today,' that none of you may be hardened by the deceitfulness
of sin. [14]*For we share in Christ, if only we hold our first*
confidence firm to the end, [15]*while it is said,*
'Today, when you hear his voice,
do not harden your hearts
as in the rebellion.'
[16]*Who were they that heard and yet were rebellious? Was it*
not all those who left Egypt under the leadership of Moses?
[17]*And with whom was he provoked forty years? Was it not*
with those who sinned, whose bodies fell in the wilderness?
[18]*And to whom did he swear that they should never enter his*
rest, but to those who were disobedient? [19]*So we see that they*
were unable to enter because of unbelief.

Our author is not only a gifted expositor; he is a devoted pastor. It is not enough for him to remind his readers of these Old Testament narratives and this warning from the Psalter. He presses his message home with compelling earnestness. He is saying in effect: 'Take care, brothers. That same evil, unbelieving heart which you despised in the ancient Israelites can be in you, in *any* of you.' There is no naively optimistic view of human nature in these verses. The situation is serious. Some of these believers might be kept from the eternal and promised homeland, their lasting city, because, like the stubborn, unbelieving Hebrews of earlier centuries, they rebel against the God who loves them. They must take care lest in the oppressive days of persecution, they also *fall away from the living God.* Notice the grim description in these verses of the human condition without God's transforming grace and continual help. Our hearts can become rebellious, wayward, ignorant and undiscerning, evil, faithless, hardened, deceived and disobedient.[7] This is a picture not of casual drifters, but deliberate deserters.[8] *Take care.*

How can these early Christian believers avoid a fate similar to that of the rebellious Hebrew pilgrims of bygone centuries? The author insists that, if we desire to bring our pilgrimage to that great rewarding conclusion which God has prepared for Christians, we must make our glad and obedient response to his word. We are required to hear, believe, obey and share the word of God.

a. Hear the word

His voice must be heard (3:7, 15; 4:7). On three separate occasions the eloquent appeal of Psalm 95 is repeated in this section, obviously for emphasis and in clear recognition of its immense importance. We must read the word of God privately and personally, meditating on its life-changing message. Each new day demands a fresh appointment with God, made real through systematic Bible reading and prayer. It must not be hurried; we need this daily meeting with God so that we do not neglect 'the hearing of the word' in our own hearts and minds. In our own day, some Christians, fearful of inhibiting legalism or mere conventionalism, have spoken or written disparagingly of the daily time with God. In a society where discipline is discouraged and authority despised, it does not require great perception to see how some unhelpful and destructive modern thought-forms have influenced contemporary Christian thinking. The Christian who does not make a special point of setting aside in each day a particular time for the cultivation of his spiritual life is not likely to make significant progress in spiritual maturity.

Moreover, this is not a merely private matter; we must hear the word publicly and study it corporately. The writer of this epistle knows the supreme value of edifying teaching, as well of compassionate service, corporate worship and encouraging fellowship. Regular attendance at public worship, Bible-study meetings and opportunities for Christian teaching is warmly encouraged by our writer (10:25).

[7] Heb. 3:8, 10, 12–13, 18.
[8] Heb. 3:12 NEB: 'wicked, faithless heart of a deserter'.

b. Believe the word

It is one thing to hear it; it is another to accept its message in responsive faith. The person with the unbelieving heart will certainly *fall away from the living God* (3:12). If we refuse to accept the living word (4:12), how can we hope to know the living God who is its almighty author? The rebellious Hebrews who failed to enter the land of promise fell in the wilderness *because of unbelief*. They rendered themselves morally and spiritually incapable of possessing their inheritance, and all because, in their lust for the immediate, they lost their hope in the ultimate. Stark and persistent unbelief, the stubborn refusal to take God at his word and to put their confidence in him alone, kept them out of the *rest* which God had prepared for his people. Because these rebellious Hebrews did not combine the given word with their own faith in it, the privileged revelation of God 'did not benefit them' (4:2). Faith in what God has said and in what Christ has done is of supreme importance in this letter.

c. Obey the word

The word must be not only heard and believed. We must act upon it immediately and unreservedly and express our faith in obedience to its commands. *Those who were disobedient* lost their reward. The point that is made here is repeated for emphasis in the next chapter; the disobedient Israelites 'failed to enter because of disobedience' (4:6), even though initially they received, presumably with enthusiasm, the good news of the glorious future God had prepared for them. But this is not only a disastrous past event; it is a frightening immediate possibility. These believers are later urged to make strenuous progress and stride forward in their Christian pilgrimage so 'that no one fall by the same sort of disobedience' (4:11). Obedience is a key idea in the letter. These first-century Christians are exhorted to costly obedience, knowing that even though the Lord Jesus enjoyed all the rich status of deity ('Although he was a Son'), yet 'he learned obedience through what he suffered'.

d. Share the word

We have already noticed that our author believes in the vital role of the Christian community. Here he makes it unmistakably clear that as sons, brothers and children, they stand in daily need of corporate encouragement and exhortation. Probably their attendance at worship was confined to a meeting in somebody's house early in the morning on the first day of the week. With such meetings the opportunities for mutual help were limited to weekly contacts, so he urges them here to repeat the warnings and promises of God's word on a daily basis when they meet one another (literally) 'day by day' (3:13), so that not one of them may be lured away by the deceptive attraction and subtle deceitfulness of sin. These believers had to be reminded not only of the superiority of Jesus and the importance of the word, but also the encouragement of the church. In frightened isolation they might fall, but in supportive companionship they would stand.

In the past some church members have placed far too much responsibility on the shoulders of their ministers, limiting themselves mainly to church attendance as relaxed and appreciative passengers. But one needs to encourage the exercise of *corporate* responsibility. Not all are destined for a preaching role (mercifully!), but in the local church all must accept a pastoral role. The word translated *exhort* (*parakleite*) is the word of strong encouragement. It is the word of the confident, heartening captain before battle. It is often used in secular Greek literature of the naval or military commander putting strength into his sailors or soldiers. Believers are expected to exercise a daily, cheering ministry to other Christians. It is never fitting for believers to adopt the depressing pessimistic outlook of a godless world. With God things can always be better, and Christians ought to be the first to *say* so. It is far from easy for many believers to live and witness effectively for Christ in contemporary society. Every Christian ought to be able to count on the cheering encouragement of his fellow believers. To make that possible, every member of the body of Christ should grasp opportunities in every day to speak the uplifting word and do the supportive thing for his Christian partners in Christ.

3. God's word for the future: a dependable promise (4:1–13)

Therefore, while the promise of entering his rest remains, let us fear lest any of you be judged to have failed to reach it.
2For good news came to us just as to them; but the message which they heard did not benefit them, because it did not meet with faith in the hearers. 3For we who have believed enter that rest, as he has said,

'As I swore in my wrath,
"They shall never enter my rest,"'

although his works were finished from the foundation of the world. 4For he has somewhere spoken of the seventh day in this way, 'And God rested on the seventh day from all his works.' 5And again in this place he said,

'They shall never enter my rest.'

6Since therefore it remains for some to enter it, and those who formerly received the good news failed to enter because of disobedience, 7again he sets a certain day, 'Today,' saying through David so long afterward, in the words already quoted,

'Today, when you hear his voice,
do not harden your hearts.'

8For if Joshua had given them rest, God would not speak later of another day. 9So then, there remains a sabbath rest for the people of God; 10for whoever enters God's rest also ceases from his labours as God did from his.

11Let us therefore strive to enter that rest, that no one fall by the same sort of disobedience.

Now that he has made special use of the idea of the promised rest for the people of God, our writer is at pains to emphasize that such a 'rest' was not limited to the historical circumstances attendant on the Canaan event. The true 'rest' promised by God has not yet been received; it belongs to the future. Actually, nobody could imagine, he says, that the 'rest' to which he and the psalmist refers is the land of Canaan, because later in Hebrew history David wrote about it in anticipation,[9] and naturally they were all well and truly settled in the land when such words were first recorded in that psalm.

[9] Ps. 95:11.

Once God had completed his work of creation he began his rest, and he longs that ultimately all his people should enter into that rest. God's gracious promise of rest has not been withdrawn. The invitation is still open, but we must realize that in the course of our pilgrimage the pursuit of this rest might well be costly. We must strive and apply ourselves diligently to the journey ahead. But we should not imagine that it can be attained by works.[10] It is God's rich *gift* to the faithful and obedient pilgrim at the end of his days when he *ceases from his labours as God did from his.*

The idea of the 'rest' promised here has sometimes been interpreted in terms of the *present* rest of the sanctified believer. These two chapters have figured quite prominently in the teaching of some holiness movements which have emphasized the necessity of a 'second blessing' for the Christian. The exodus imagery is used to support the idea that at conversion the believer gratefully emerges from a tyrannous Egypt, but he has yet to become sanctified by entering the promised Canaan of God's 'rest'. If by 'rest' such teaching is a figurative way of describing the present *peace* of the Christian, then few would want to quarrel with it. God certainly gives his people inward peace, but the imagery of 'rest' is not necessarily helpful when describing God's work of present sanctification in the life of a believer. It savours far too much of the 'let go and let God' concept with its suggestion that, in order to be a sanctified Christian, one has only to relax every nerve and abandon any thought of moral struggle. In this thinking, God undertakes to do it all; nothing is necessary but faith. It is true that no believer can hope to achieve his own sanctification no matter how hard he tries. It is God's work to make us holy. But neither can any Christian hope to be conformed to the likeness of Christ in his everyday life simply by making sure that he does nothing about it. It is a strenuous, costly business to be a Christian. Believers must *strive* to enter the rest of the people of God (4:11). The word that is used describes the intense concentration of energy necessary to reach a desired goal. It demands everything we have got, but always with the clear recognition that

[10] Eph. 2:8–9.

Every virtue we possess,
  And every victory won,
And every thought of holiness,
  Are his alone.[11]

The very desire to live at our best for Christ is an ambition he has planted into our minds; unbelievers care nothing for such things. The dependence we have on him day by day is something God has taught us clearly in his word. The strength which enables us to conquer temptation is a power which he has supplied by the indwelling life of his Holy Spirit. In that sense, it is all of him. But, without careful qualification, it is unwise to describe our present Christian life mainly in terms of 'rest'. After all, there were giants in the land! Joshua and his contemporaries soon discovered that life in Canaan demanded courageous heroes, not relaxed spectators.

Christian pilgrims in the contemporary world must realize that, in the light of a passage such as this, it will not do to confess a merely nominal allegiance to Christian truth or pay occasional lip service in meetings and services to faith in Christ. Our commitment must be sincere and genuine, and it can be so for two reasons given at the close of this passage: what God says and what God sees.

[12]*For the word of God is living and active, sharper than any two-edged sword, piercing to the division of soul and spirit, of joints and marrow, and discerning the thoughts and intentions of the heart.* [13]*And before him no creature is hidden, but all are open and laid bare to the eyes of him with whom we have to do.*

a. The word of God (4:12)

If God has spoken so clearly to his people, then it is a mistake to suppose that man can trifle with such a word. It is alive. It does not simply record the great events of the past. The 'yesterday' element is certainly not missing, especially in this letter, but God's word is something more than a mere historical record. 'Today' is a key term here. God is speaking to

[11] H. Auber, 'Our blest Redeemer, ere he breathed'.

us through his living word in this very day (3:7, 15). God 'sets a certain day, "Today"' (4:7) as he renews his appeal, and extends his promises, and repeats his warnings. The word not only lives; it works. It is an effective as well as a perpetually relevant word. Its activity is such that it cannot return void; it must accomplish his sovereign purposes.[12] The word is energetic. It is like a sharp sword cutting its way through this substance or that without any kind of difficulty. This sword of the word[13] can penetrate deeply into the human heart and mind. It can scrutinize the unspoken thoughts and hidden conceptions of the heart of man. It can reach deep down where, because of earth's bewildering and preoccupying noises, no other voice can easily be heard. This word probes more deeply than the mere voice of man however interesting or eloquent. It goes to 'the inmost recesses of our spiritual being and brings the subconscious motives to light' (Bruce).

b. The nature of God (4:13)

This flows naturally from what has gone before. God uses his word to penetrate man's stubborn and rebellious heart, for he knows how much we need it; he sees what is really there. He looks right below the extremely thin veneer of merely outward piety to the true thoughts of man. He can test man's sincerity. Nothing whatever is hidden from his searching gaze. Everything is exposed to his sight. In view of this, how ridiculous is our pretence and how nauseating our hypocrisy. The words *with whom we have to do* can be translated 'before whom we must render account'. Whether he likes it or not, man is moving to his destiny. The message of one who has gone before as pioneer and priest is a word of immediate relevance. Christ's essential work for man has been effectively accomplished. Our part is to hear, believe, obey and share this word of abundant life.

[12] Is. 55:11. [13] Is. 49:2; Eph. 6:17; Rev. 1:16; 2:12.

4:14 – 5:10

8. A great high priest

God's word exposes man, and God's nature is such that, in his omniscient wisdom, everything is laid open to the searchlight of his scrutiny. Bereft of his sham securities and useless defences, man stands before God as he has always been and as he really is. The person so revealed is exposed in his sin and in his weakness. What can he do about his guilt? Even when he is purified and his pilgrimage begins, how can he hope to find the strength to continue? Such a person needs help, and at this point in his exposition our writer returns to a theme of majestic importance, the present, intercessory ministry of the Lord Jesus. He is eager to make four supreme assertions about our *great high priest*: he passed through the heavens; he is able to sympathize; he learned obedience, and became the source of our eternal salvation. In this way we are introduced to some of the most essential aspects of the priesthood of Christ.

1. A victorious priesthood (4:14)

Since then we have a great high priest who has passed through the heavens, Jesus, the Son of God, let us hold fast our confession.

The work of Christ has already been portrayed in this letter as a triumphantly victorious achievement (2:9, 14–18). These ideas are now compressed into a rich Christian confession: *We have a great high priest who has passed through the heavens, Jesus, the Son of God.* Our writer repeats his conviction that the mission of the priest is finished by Christ, accepted by God and effective among men. Jesus has passed through the heavens. The dominant idea in this writer's exposition of the work of Christ is that he is triumphantly ascended and eternally glorified. His major theme is the exaltation of Jesus. In asserting this great confession of faith, our author underlines the fact that to be a victorious priest with this transforming work for men finished, complete, adequate and efficacious, it was necessary for Jesus to be a great, human, and unique priest.

First, Christ is described as a *great* priest. He far surpasses all of his priestly predecessors. Their priestly work cannot possibly be compared with his in its range, nature, cost and efficacy. He alone is truly 'great'.

Secondly, Christ is here portrayed as a *human* priest. The one who has passed through the heavens is 'Jesus'. The human name of Christ, so often used in this letter by way of striking emphasis, is mentioned here in the context of his victorious ascension. There is a man in heaven; he understands us and knows our trials.

Thirdly, he is without doubt a *unique* priest. He is *the Son of God*. His deity, as well as his real humanity, is a central theme in this epistle. The letter began by asserting it, continues by proving it and goes on to expound it. It warns of the danger of denying it and rejoices throughout in the inspiring assurance which comes through affirming it.

These three elements of supremacy, humanity and deity were essential aspects of his victorious work. No other priest could have achieved such a victory over the power of sin, death and the devil. The fact that he has passed through the heavens and 'sat down at the right hand of God' means that his saving work is finished. It happened 'once for all' (9:26), a favourite phrase in this letter. The ascension of Christ was not just a dramatic end to the earthly ministry of Jesus. It was God's visible act of vindication, exaltation and glorification. The fight is over. The victory has been won. The work is complete. In the course of their duty, the various high priests of Jewish history passed through the veil in the material tabernacle or temple, but Jesus has passed into the presence of God himself.

The writer goes on to assert that, in the light of this victory, this is no time for cowardice. The *confession* of the faith we possess is a treasure beyond price. It cannot be lightly dismissed or thoughtlessly abandoned. It makes life worth living, and throughout the centuries hundreds of men and women have been prepared to die for it. These first-century believers were urged to *hold fast* to such a faith. This is not merely an appeal for endurance but an exhortation to fearless witness. Don't be robbed of your faith; advertise it. Hold it fast and hold it forth. In order to become our effective and adequate priest, Jesus suffered 'outside the gate' and we must be prepared to go out into the alien or apathetic, Christ-rejecting or Christ-ignoring, world, 'bearing abuse for him' (13:12–13).

2. A compassionate priesthood (4:15 – 5:3)

15*For we have not a high priest who is unable to sympathize with our weaknesses, but one who in every respect has been tempted as we are, yet without sinning.* 16*Let us then with confidence draw near to the throne of grace, that we may receive mercy and find grace to help in time of need.*

5:1 *For every high priest chosen from among men is appointed to act on behalf of men in relation to God, to offer gifts and sacrifices for sins.* 2*He can deal gently with the ignorant and wayward, since he himself is beset with weakness.* 3*Because of this he is bound to offer sacrifice for his own sins as well as those of the people.*

We have already noticed that this letter rejoices in the essential humanity of Christ. He had been tempted in every respect as these first-century Christians were now being tested. Naturally when this letter says that Jesus was tempted *in every respect* as we are our writer is not thereby implying that within his lifetime Christ encountered every possible different temptation. He could hardly have experienced personally the specific temptations peculiar, for example, to women, to married people, to the elderly, to those made redundant in a time of economic recession or to those who live in a modern technological society. Yet at the root of the different temptations encountered by men and women throughout the wide range of human experience there are a number of basic trials or tests, and Jesus certainly knew what it was to meet these and emerge victoriously from the struggle. He knew those temptations which, if unconquered, lead on to doubt, despair, disobedience towards God, lovelessness towards others and a selfish preoccupation with our own desires. It can be argued, surely, that far from being less than ours, Christ's temptations were even greater. As T. H. Robinson puts it in his exposition of this letter: 'His whole life was one of temptation, and the very fact that he had powers and abilities which we do not possess only added to the stress. He was the fullest and most vivid personality that this world has ever known, and the very richness of His human nature exposed Him all the more fully to the assaults of temptation.' No-one on earth, before or since, has ever been through such spiritual desolation and human anguish. For this reason he can help us in our moments of temptation. He is aware of our needs because he has experienced to the full the pressures and testings of life in this godless world.

If verse 14 tells us that, in a hostile world, we must not be ashamed of Christ, verse 15 assures us that we need not be lonely. The strength to make our confession comes from one who made his confession before Pilate.[1] He knows exactly how we feel. Such assurance of his sympathy (2:18) ought to encourage us and sustain us when things go wrong. It confronts us with one of the New Testament's most important invitations: *Let us then with confidence draw near to the throne of grace*. We dare not be prayerless. In the trials and temptations of life we find comfort in the deep assurance that 'Jesus knows', but our author's exposition of the high-priestly ministry of Christ includes an invitation to follow him with boldness into the holy place. It is here that we *receive mercy* to cover the sins of yesterday, and it is also here that we *find grace* to meet the needs of today.

P. T. Forsyth used to insist that prayerlessness is the root of all sin. When we do not give time each day to earnest and believing prayer, we are saying that we can cope with life without divine aid. It is human arrogance at its worst. Jesus knew that he had to pray[2] and did so, gladly, necessarily and effectively. To be prayerless is to be guilty of the worst form

[1] 1 Tim. 6:13. [2] Mt. 14:23; Mk. 1:35; Lk. 5:16.

of practical atheism. We are saying that we believe in God but we can do without him. It makes us careless about our former sins and heedless of our immediate needs. This letter urges us to come into the presence of a God who welcomes us and a Christ who understands us. To neglect the place of prayer is to rob ourselves of immense and timely resources. For the Christian the throne of grace is the place of help.

In presenting his exposition of Christ's priesthood, our writer here points out that it was necessary for Jewish high priests to have three basic qualifications, the first Godward, the others manward. First of all, he must be *called by God*. He was selected from amongst men and appointed as a candidate for the priesthood, because it was genuinely believed that it was God's will for him so to 'act on behalf of men in relation to God'. Then he must also be *sympathetic*. He had to 'deal gently with the ignorant' (those who did not know the way) and the 'wayward' (those who knew it but ignored it). In addition to these two main requirements, our author points out that the priest of Old Testament times had to be *aware of his own needs*. He could serve others compassionately and helpfully because 'he himself is beset with weakness'. Whenever he was tempted to pronounce harsh judgments, place intolerable burdens, or make excessive demands on other people, he would remember that he too was exposed day after day to the same hazards. Their dangers were his also.

But Jesus was the most compassionate of all priests. He was appointed by his Father to this eternal ministry (5:5) and wore our frail flesh, being made for a little while lower than the angels (2:9). He can be of far greater help to us than any human priest because, whilst it is true that they sympathized, they also sinned. Many of them were holy and devout spiritual leaders,[3] but they were not sinless. Jesus committed no sin, but he was constantly exposed to its sinister attractions and subtle suggestions. 'The sinlessness of Jesus therefore does not turn on the absence of human frailty, but in a constantly renewed victory over temptation' (Héring). Jesus certainly did not need to offer a sacrifice for his own sins as the Old Testament priests did, but because he went through

[3] Mal. 2:4–7; Lk. 1:5–6.

so much bitter and hostile temptation, he can the more effectively meet our own deep spiritual needs.

3. A submissive priesthood (5:4–8)

4*And one does not take the honour upon himself, but he is called by God, just as Aaron was.*

5*So also Christ did not exalt himself to be made a high priest, but was appointed by him who said to him,*

'Thou art my Son,
today I have begotten thee';

6*as he says also in another place,*

'Thou art a priest for ever,
after the order of Melchizedek.'

7*In the days of his flesh, Jesus offered up prayers and supplications, with loud cries and tears, to him who was able to save him from death, and he was heard for his godly fear.*
8*Although he was a Son, he learned obedience through what he suffered.*

This letter unites the majestic themes of Christ's deity and humanity, his dignity and humility. The submissive resignation of Jesus is portrayed here with a keen eye for both historical detail and spiritual interpretation. The writer takes us into the garden of Gethsemane, to the moment of our Lord's greatest crisis. If there was any time in life when Jesus felt utterly alone, it must have been then. It is obviously appropriate to remind these early Christian people of such desolation. They would not face a greater grief and, even if they were tested to the very limits of human endurance, he would be near to them as one who had fully entered into human anguish and strain. But in order to achieve this complete union with us, Jesus had to submit himself entirely to God. His submission is here expounded by reminding the readers of Christ's relationship to the Father.

a. His appointment by God

Before the incarnation, in his pre-existent communion with the Father, Christ did not count his equality with God a thing to be grasped, but gladly came into this world and took the form of a servant.[4] Neither did he grasp the exalted office of the divine high priest. He waited submissively for the appointment of God to this eternal mission and was thus 'designated' (5:10) as *a priest for ever*. At this point our writer makes further use of two psalms[5] to emphasize Christ's eternal Sonship and his continuing priesthood, his relationship with God and his identification with men. In the course of one of these quotations Melchizedek makes his first appearance in the letter, the priest-king of Old Testament times and a significant figure for the Qumran community. But we shall postpone our discussion of him and return to the one he foreshadowed.

b. His dependence on God

In the garden Jesus prayed and wept *to him who was able to save him* from such an awful experience of death. Jesus was not afraid of physical death as such, for to say that would be to make him less than many other men and women who, through the centuries, have faced death confidently and courageously. But their death was not remotely like his. In the moment of his supreme agony he carried our sins to the cross, he was despised by those for whom he was making such a sacrifice and, worst of all, the Father's face was turned away from his only Son. No wonder his *prayers and supplications* were made that night with *loud cries and tears*.[6] Faced with such a humanly terrifying prospect and such a divinely necessary sacrifice, he came into the presence of a holy God as he knelt in the garden on the night of his arrest. He could no longer look to his friends for help. Although he had asked for their companionship and practical support, they slept as he prayed. In that hour his soul was 'very sorrowful' and he could find real comfort only at the throne of his Father. He did not for a moment doubt God's ability to save him from death. He cast himself upon a God who was able to save him. But he was not saved! Was even the prayer of Jesus unanswered? Surely it was answered, not by relieving Christ of the agony of the cross, but by giving him strength for it and peace in it. In those crucial moments help came. God sent his

[4] Phil. 2:6–7. [5] Pss. 2:7; 110:4. [6] Mt. 26:36–46.

own messenger to strengthen him.[7] And peace came too. It is grammatically possible to translate verse 7: '. . . and being heard was set free from fear.'

c. His reverence for God

It is perhaps more natural, however, to translate verse 7 as the RSV does: . . . *he was heard for his godly fear.* It was because of his own deep awe and reverence for his Father that his prayer was heard, even though it did not issue in his immediate physical deliverance. In this way he can more readily sympathize with his people when they are bewildered, even as they pray. In these spiritually daunting and humanly terrifying moments he did not resist the sovereign purposes of God. In sincerity before his Father he gave voice to his human distress: 'If it be possible, let this cup pass from me,' but in surrender he also added his words of complete resignation: 'Nevertheless, not as I will, but as thou wilt.' Gethsemane is the most moving example of that 'humble submission' (NEB) which characterized his whole life.

d. His obedience to God

Although he was a Son, he learned obedience through what he suffered. This is not meant to imply that Jesus learned obedience as one who had no previous knowledge or experience of it. The incarnation itself was an act of loving obedience (10:7). Even as a youth, that mattered to him more than anything else.[8] His ministry among people was marked by obedient surrender to God's will. Never at any point did he seek to please himself.[9] His dominant ambition was to obey, serve and glorify his Father so that at the end, with serene confidence, he could say, 'I glorified thee on earth, having accomplished the work which thou gavest me to do.'[10] In other words, he was *always* obedient and in the moment of his deepest agony he continued and maintained that same attitude of submission to his almighty sovereign and Father. In that garden 'he learnt that prayer can meet with an answer

[7] Lk. 22:43. [8] Lk. 2:49, 52.
[9] Jn. 4:34; 5:30; 6:38; Rom. 15:3. [10] Jn. 17:4.

very different from that which is requested . . . he took his obedience up to death (Phil. 2:8), to the point beyond which it could be taken no further' (Montefiore).

4. An effective priesthood (5:9–10)

[9]and being made perfect he became the source of eternal salvation to all who obey him, [10]being designated by God a high priest after the order of Melchizedek.

He was willing to suffer, and through the Gethsemane experience and what followed he demonstrated the greatest and most costly obedience. But what is meant by the writer's assertion that *being made perfect* he became the source of our salvation? It certainly does not mean that before Gethsemane and the cross he was *imperfect*, any more than the preceding verse meant that prior to such experience he was *disobedient*. The word 'perfect' here obviously does not refer to his moral perfection. It repeats the idea found earlier (2:10) that by his life, death and exaltation Christ became 'fully qualified' as our saviour.

This epistle has already noted the six essential qualifications required of God's Son in order for him to become man's priest. He had to be appointed by God, identified with men and sensitive to human need, victorious over sin, obedient to the divine purpose and willing to die to effect man's deliverance.[11] His final qualification was that of his victorious exaltation to the right hand of God when he was 'crowned with glory and honour' (2:9). This is what our writer means when he says that 'once perfected' (NEB) he became the author of eternal salvation. The obedient Son saves those who will respond to his redeeming message with obedient hearts and minds. Completely qualified, he is *designated*, clearly 'named by God' (NEB), to all mankind as the high priest of our completely adequate and eternally relevant salvation.

Before we leave this passage with its moving description of Christ's total submission, we need a further reminder that obedience was not only necessary for him; it is expected also

[11] Heb. 5:5; 2:17–18; 4:15; 5:8; 2:14.

of us. Salvation is for those *who obey him*. It is important for us to see that when Jesus surrendered himself entirely to God's will, he obeyed not only in order to honour God but also to help us to see what obedience is all about. In his exposition of this passage, Calvin says: 'He did this for our benefit, to give us the instance and the pattern of His own submission . . . If we want the obedience of Christ to be of advantage to us, we must copy it.'

These verses are particularly important at a time when some Christians may find themselves tempted to bypass the constant discipline Christ demands in favour of the 'instant' or 'immediate' holiness offered by some exponents of the Christian life. This is the 'instant' age; if a thing is to be had, it must be had *now*. The idea goes something like this: The promises are there, claim them at this very moment and the prize is yours, whether it is instant sanctification, instant power, or instant healing. We live in an impatient society and the idea of humble submission, patient waiting and steady perseverance does not make a ready appeal. But the way of Christ was the way of persistent obedience. All his life was given to it. He strongly resisted the temptation to have it effected in a spectacular and supernatural moment.[12] He resolutely pursued the will and purpose of God. He knew that it could not be achieved in a magical minute.

Moreover, he made it clear to his followers that his way was to be their way. There was no other. The only possible route to holiness of life was by way of the cross. When the disciples expressed their horror about *his* cross, he told them about *theirs*. 'If any man would come after me, let him deny himself and take up his cross and follow me.'[13] The act of taking up the cross may well occur initially and decisively at a precise moment of time. In that sense there is a crisis. But following after Christ and denying oneself is a daily, painful, costly reality that cannot be achieved by a sudden crisis, but only by a lifetime of constantly renewed dedication and obedient responsiveness to all that God requires of his people and equips them to do.

[12] Lk. 4:9–12. [13] Mt. 16:24.

5:11 – 6:8

9. Pastoral problems

It must be plain to us already that the author of our letter has compassionate pastoral concern. Physically he is at some distance from this church and longs to come to them (13:23), but spiritually he is as close to them as he can possibly be. In this section we have another parenthesis or digression, a further pastoral 'aside'. At the end of 5:10 he has stated that the eternal priesthood of the Lord Jesus is 'after the order of Melchizedek'. His reference to this Old Testament character leads him to reflect on this congregation's inability to benefit by the 'solid food' of deep Christian teaching. So he digresses to discuss three closely related spiritual problems confronting some of his readers. In studying these verses we shall find that we are considering issues which have a strangely modern ring about them.

1. The problem of ignorance (5:11–14)

11*About this we have much to say which is hard to explain, since you have become dull of hearing.* 12*For though by this time you ought to be teachers, you need some one to teach you again the first principles of God's word. You need milk, not solid food;* 13*for every one who lives on milk is unskilled in the word of righteousness, for he is a child.* 14*But solid food is for the mature, for those who have their faculties trained by practice to distinguish good from evil.*

The writer of Hebrews is convinced that his readers' ignorance stems from laziness (5:11). How can he begin to explain what it means for Christ's priesthood to be 'after the order of Melchizedek' when they have lost their appetite for Christian truth? Instead of giving their best mind to sound doctrine and its practical application, many of these early Christian readers have become *dull of hearing*. The word really means 'sluggish'; it is used in the Septuagint of 'slothful men' who refuse to tackle hard work, and occurs again later in this letter describing 'sluggish' people who need a good shake-up (6:12). It here describes those who develop a 'couldn't care less' attitude to the study of holy Scripture, and have failed to give themselves to a regular, methodical, and painstaking study of its teaching and its relevance in everyday life.

Secondly, he has observed that their ignorance has led to ineffectiveness (5:12). Turning their backs on strenuous study and diligent application to spiritual teaching, they remain like babies when they ought to be adults, pupils when they might be instructors, Christians in need of help when they could be offering it to others. Paul says something similar about the Corinthians.[1] It is not merely that they do not benefit personally but, even more serious, other people are denied the help which they might have received from them had they been strong and resourceful believers.

Thirdly, he knows that spiritual ignorance results in carelessness (5:13–14). The people who have not begun to master the ABC of the Christian life (first principles, *cf.* 6:1) can hardly hope to enrich the lives of others. Their own faith is far too insecure to be able to communicate confidence and assurance to other people. They cry for babies' milk when they ought to have passed on to a more varied and substantial diet. But what is most serious about their spiritual ignorance is that, being unfamiliar with God's word, they do not know his mind on important doctrinal, ethical and spiritual issues. His truth is a word of *righteousness* and those who master its message learn how *to distinguish good from evil.* This does not come to anybody without effort. These spiritual *faculties* have to be trained (*gegymnasmena*) as in a gymnasium,[2] an idea that returns later in the epistle (12:11), also in the context of discipline.

These Jewish Christians had certainly not intended to get

[1] 1 Cor. 3:1–2. [2] 2 Tim. 4:7; *cf.* 2 Pet. 2:14.

into this indolent, useless state, but this is clearly what has happened to them. When he says that their spiritual hearing has *become* dull, he uses the perfect tense; it describes the abiding result of a past act. However well intentioned they may have been at the beginning, this is what they have allowed themselves to become. It is a warning no believer can ignore. Many people casually drift into a low standard of Christian life simply because they minimize the importance of Christian instruction and disciplined Bible study. Quite possibly on most days they quietly ponder a few verses and say a quick prayer, but it does not occur to them that this is not nearly enough. Failing to acknowledge their need of it, they slowly lose their desire for it. Somehow or other, however busy he or she may be, every Christian needs to find a regular opportunity for serious study of the Bible.[3]

2. The problem of immaturity (6:1–3)

Therefore let us leave the elementary doctrine of Christ and go on to maturity, not laying again a foundation of repentance from dead works and of faith toward God, ²with instruction about ablutions, the laying on of hands, the resurrection of the dead, and eternal judgment. ³And this we will do if God permits.

'Solid food is for the mature' (5:14). Ignorance leads to immaturity. First, we must establish ourselves in *the elementary doctrine of Christ* and then acquire an appetite for the more solid food (5:12) of other aspects of Christian teaching. We must *go on to maturity.* The solid foundation of Christian truth is of immense importance but, once that is well and truly laid, there is no need to go on repeating that process, *laying again* a further foundation. Six basic aspects of Christian teaching are enumerated here. They may well have been regarded in this particular church as the essential features of catechetical instruction for young converts.

[3] See, *e.g.*, Graham Claydon, *Time with God* (IVP, 1979), and Bible study courses such as P. Lee, G. Scharf and R. Willcox, *Food for Life* (IVP, 1977) and A. M. Stibbs (editor), *Search the Scriptures* (IVP, ⁵1967).

a. Repentance from dead works

The message of repentance was an essential aspect of the teaching of John the Baptist, the Lord Jesus, and the apostles.[4] When, through his servant John, Christ gave his final message to the church, he called upon his people to repent.[5] In many New Testament contexts the call is to repent by turning from personal sin, but here, doubtless because of its Jewish background, the call is to repent from *dead works*, from man's futile attempt at self-salvation.

b. Faith in God

Merely to leave *dead works* is not likely to accomplish anything; it is a purely negative act. The positive aspect of faith demands forceful emphasis. It is *repentance from* and *faith towards*. Paul says a similar thing when summarizing his evangelistic ministry in mid-first-century Ephesus.[6] Repentance and faith are inseparable elements of the Christian gospel. It is not only that the old has to be abandoned; the new must be appropriated.

c. Baptism or washings

Technically the term is in the plural, *baptisms*; possibly a reference to the importance of correct teaching about baptism, especially in view of the variety of teaching which is reflected even in the New Testament. For example, the difference between John's baptism and Christian baptism might well have troubled young Jewish converts to Christianity.[7] Or it could be a reference to religious washings prevalent among Jews, and the essential difference between these lustrations, or ablutions (it is the same word as in 9:10) and the 'one baptism' of the Christian church.[8]

[4] Mk. 1:4, 14–15; Acts 2:38; 3:19; 5:31.
[5] Rev. 2:5, 16, 22; 3:3, 19.
[6] Acts 20:21. [7] Acts 18:25; 19:1–5.
[8] Acts 8:36; 9:18; 10:47–48; Eph. 4:5.

d. Laying on of hands

This simple form of Hebrew prayer symbolism became part of the Christian initiatory rite.[9] It was obviously related to the gift of the Holy Spirit. The reference here may even be to ordination for ministry.[10]

e. Resurrection of the dead

One gets the impression from 1 Corinthians 15 that some first-century Christian congregations had difficulties about the resurrection and its highly important implications for believers. The particular churches known to our writer believed in good teaching about the future. Death is not the end; it merely marks the physical conclusion of our only opportunity to live for God in *this* world. For believers, the best of all is yet to be.

f. Eternal judgment

'It is appointed for men to die once, and after that comes judgment' (9:27). Resurrection and judgment were clearly linked in the teaching of Jesus and in early Christian doctrine.[11] The future implications of the faith were an essential aspect of early Christian instruction. The doctrinal and spiritual importance of all these topics cannot be denied, but the author regards these foundational truths as *basic* Christian knowledge. It has been observed by some scholars that these six *elementary doctrines* can be paralleled in Judaism. Perhaps some of these first-century readers were retreating back into these aspects of faith which, in some measure, Christians had in common with their Jewish neighbours. To *go on to maturity*, these believers must develop an appetite for more 'solid food' (5:12, 14) which their leaders have endeavoured faithfully to impart in the past (13:7) and which our author intends to expound in the remaining chapters of his letter.

[9] Nu. 27:18–19, 23; Dt. 34:9; Mk. 6:5; Acts 8:17–19; 19:6.
[10] 1 Tim. 4:14; 5:22; 2 Tim. 1:6.
[11] Jn. 5:26–29; Acts 17:31.

3. The problem of apostasy (6:4–8)

[4]*For it is impossible to restore again to repentance those who have once been enlightened, who have tasted the heavenly gift, and have become partakers of the Holy Spirit,* [5]*and have tasted the goodness of the word of God and the powers of the age to come,* [6]*if they then commit apostasy, since they crucify the Son of God on their own account and hold him up to contempt.* [7]*For land which has drunk the rain that often falls upon it, and brings forth vegetation useful to those for whose sake it is cultivated, receives a blessing from God.* [8]*But if it bears thorns and thistles, it is worthless and near to being cursed; its end is to be burned.*

There are clear hints at this point and elsewhere in the letter that doctrinal ignorance and spiritual immaturity have led to serious disasters in this church. Some believers, who made an apparently excellent beginning in their Christian lives, are now not merely chronic invalids or spiritual casualties, but have become fierce opponents of the Christian gospel. Understandably, some members of this church may have become worried about the destiny of apostates, and the writer finds it necessary in the course of his pastoral involvement to say something about those who have not only drifted away (2:1), or fallen away (3:12), but have with hardened hearts (3:12–13) become active rebels against the way and work of Christ. In describing these sad apostates the letter mentions three characteristic features: they despise God's gifts, they reject God's Son, and they forfeit God's blessing.

a. They despise God's gifts (6:4–5)

Long before their fall, these apostates had been the eager recipients of God's generous bounty. For one thing, they had received the gift of *his transforming light.* At the beginning of their Christian lives they had been miraculously and mercifully *enlightened.*[12] The bright light of Christ's illuminating presence had shone into every dark corner of their hearts and minds. Were they now returning to the dark, deliberately

[12] 2 Cor. 4:4, 6; Eph. 1:18.

choosing a Christless way of life?[13]

They had also received the gift of *his enriching provision*. All the blessings of heaven had been theirs to take and taste,[14] to receive and enjoy. At one time, possibly years before, they had 'experienced how good the gospel is' (Moffatt). It is interesting that the metaphor of light is followed by that of food.[15] Jesus is the gift of God sent from heaven. He had been like manna in the wilderness, essential sustenance for the journey, the only satisfying 'food' of life.[16] Once they had delighted in such goodness; now they could only despise it. Once that spiritual appetite is lost, how difficult it is for someone to be brought to repentance.

Furthermore, they had received the gift of *his enabling Spirit*. Once we come to Christ we become *partakers*, or 'sharers', in the Holy Spirit. By God's astonishing generosity these believers had become 'sharers' of the Spirit's life, participants in the Spirit's work, and partakers of the Spirit's gifts. Yet now they forcefully and totally disown this 'Spirit of grace' (10:29). It was through his persuasive ministry that they had been brought to repentance and faith in the first place. How can they hope to amend their ways and be led back to God if they reject the only one who can bring them home?

In the past these believers had also received the gift of *his incomparable word*. They had *tasted the goodness of the word of God*. More than once we have noticed how important the word of God is to the author of this letter. So far every chapter in the epistle has had something to say about holy Scripture and our response to it. But now these apostates no longer see Christ in the pages of the Old Testament, or continue to hear him speak through the treasured reminiscences of his own life story, or through the inspired teachings and writings of his apostles. Once to have 'escaped the defilements of the world through the knowledge of our Lord and Saviour Jesus Christ' and then completely and consistently to spurn him, surely makes a renewed repentance impossible. There is no other way by which sinful people can return to God but by Christ.[17]

[13] Jn. 3:19–21. [14] Ps. 34:8. [15] 1 Pet. 2:3, 9.
[16] Jn. 6:27, 31–35, 47–51.
[17] 2 Pet. 2:20; Heb. 10:20; Jn. 14:6.

These apostates had, in earlier days, received the gift of *his strengthening power*. They had experienced in their own lives *the powers of the age to come*. The mighty powers (*dynameis*) of another world had broken in upon their weak lives, transforming their frailty into adequacy, their impotence into strength. To have been 'sharers' in the Holy Spirit's work was to have received his incomparable word and experienced his unrivalled power. And now they had trampled these treasures beneath their feet. Peter says it would have been better for such rebellious apostates 'never to have known the way of righteousness'.[18] This letter says it is quite impossible to restore such people to repentance if they commit apostasy. Of their own stubborn volition they have set themselves against the only one who can bring them back. They have abandoned his way, despised his truth, and spurned his life. Whilst such persistent hostility is maintained, genuine repentance is certainly impossible. Apostasy of this kind sets up a form of spiritual atrophy. As F. F. Bruce says, 'God has pledged Himself to pardon all who truly repent, but Scripture and experience alike suggest that it is possible for human beings to arrive at a state of heart and life where they can no longer repent.'

b. They reject God's Son (6:6)

Once, they turned to the cross of Christ in anguish and found in the moment of their overwhelming guilt a pardon too wonderful for words. Like the first followers of Christ, they proclaimed the Lord Jesus as their only Saviour and Lord. But now they denounce him and *hold him up to contempt*, as did the lawless and godless mob who derided him on that first Good Friday. This highly compressed verse indicates the seriousness of their offence. They disown his deity. It is *the Son of God* they are crucifying afresh, the Son who reveals the Father and sustains the universe. Moreover, they do not simply refuse to subscribe to an essential aspect of Christian belief; they abuse Christ. They despise his beauty. They *hold him up to contempt*, publicly rejecting the one who had given his life for their redemption. Having once adored and wor-

[18] 2 Pet. 2:21.

shipped him, they now view him as the priests, scribes and crowds did at his passion, as one 'despised and rejected by men'.[19]

c. *They forfeit God's blessing* (6:7–8)

The author brings this pastoral warning to a close by using a vivid parable drawn from agricultural life and probably dependent on familiar Old Testament Scripture. Deuteronomy 29:18–28 describes the fate of anyone who 'turns away . . . from the Lord our God'. Such a person walks in the stubbornness of his heart and produces 'a root bearing poisonous and bitter fruit'. An apostate of this kind cannot be pardoned, his sin being likened to 'a burnt-out waste, unsown, and growing nothing, where no grass can sprout'. Or it could be an oblique reference to the highly relevant prophetic word in Isaiah 5:1–7, the story of a vineyard which, because it failed to produce the expected fruit, was 'trampled down' and made a waste where 'briars and thorns shall grow up'. The parable which concludes this section confronts the reader with a stark choice. The suggestion is that both types of land, good and bad, genuine and apostate, have received *the rain that often falls upon it.* The blessings of God's rich goodness have come to both, but one produces useful vegetation and *receives a blessing from God*, whilst the other bears only useless and even harmful thorns and thistles. It receives God's present curse and anticipates his future destruction (12:29).

It is probably true to say that these warnings here and elsewhere in Hebrews have caused more unnecessary anxiety to believers than almost any other verses in the New Testament. Aware of moral failure or spiritual apathy, thoughtful people the world over have been haunted by these passages, some driven to despair at the thought that, having neglected or forsaken Christ, they have forfeited for ever the blessings of the gospel. This teaching has not only troubled distressed backsliders; it has baffled professedly dispassionate theologians. Those who are committed to a Reformed or Calvin-

[19] Is. 53:3.

istic doctrine of grace rightly emphasize God's sovereignty in our salvation and have been careful to point out that once a person is saved, he is always saved. Those who favour an Arminian interpretation of salvation do not deny that the truly saved person will ultimately be saved, but emphasize endurance. They rightly stress the importance of human responsibility, pointing out that we are not celestially manipulated robots making our way along predetermined routes totally outside our control. Theologians from both schools of thought adduce appropriate Scriptures. The Calvinist naturally rejoices that we are kept by the power of God, whilst the Arminian reminds us that we are also to keep ourselves in the love of God.[20]

These difficulties of interpretation, however, are not simply the preoccupation of theologians; many pastors have been genuinely bewildered by this teaching in Hebrews. They are only too deeply aware of people in their own congregations who appeared to begin the Christian life with fine promise and immense spiritual potential. But these professed believers, with such a rich spiritual life-expectancy, have since turned their backs on Christ, are now plainly embarrassed by their 'conversion' experience and openly disavow their baptismal profession or the promises made at confirmation. The minister or evangelist is bound to ask himself whether such people were really 'born again' spiritually. Thoughtful church members find themselves similarly troubled by such passages. They genuinely want to help people who have drifted away from their earlier spiritual moorings and have either allowed themselves to be carried away by strongly secularist currents into alien waters, or have deliberately rejected all their previous Christian commitment. Most Christians know of people who were once warm-hearted believing colleagues, but are now adrift without anchor or aim. Were such people ever 'saved', one naturally asks? If they are now plainly indifferent or even forcefully opposed to Christian things, what is their eternal destiny?

There have been innumerable attempts to provide an adequate explanation of these verses. It is not our purpose to rehearse them, though that is not meant to be either dismissive

[20] 1 Pet. 1:5; Jude 21.

of other views or ungrateful for some exceptionally helpful suggestions which have come from them. It is possibly best to summarize a few conclusions.

It is important, first of all, to say that these verses present us with *a genuine problem*. Some expositors have tried to overcome the difficulty by suggesting that the prospect of genuine believers slipping into apostasy is purely hypothetical. In other words, the author is putting up a purely imaginary situation: 'If such believers ever opposed Christ it would be impossible to renew them to repentance, but then such a thing could not possibly happen.' I am naturally diffident about rejecting a view sincerely held by many scholars, but find myself in agreement with Philip Hughes when he says that the danger of apostasy here 'is real, not imaginary; otherwise this epistle with its high-sounding admonitions must be dismissed as trifling, worthless and ridiculous. Certainly, in our author's judgement, the situation is one of extreme gravity. He is addressing readers whose loss of confidence and whose flagging will to perservere in the Christian race (10:35f.; 12:3, 12) point alarmingly to the possibility of their dropping out of the contest altogether, and in doing so of placing themselves beyond all hope of restoration.'

Secondly, these warning passages present us with *a particular case*. Naturally, there are lessons here for modern Christians and unbelievers alike, but these sayings must not be divorced from their first-century context in this Jewish-Christian community with its special dangers and difficulties. Our first task in interpreting Scripture is to discover what it meant to its first readers and then move from that to present application. The main purpose of this letter was to urge these Jewish Christians not to allow themselves, under pressure of persecution, to abandon the distinctively Christian aspects of their faith and slip back into its purely Jewish elements. To do this would mean that they had taken their stand with the Jewish attitude to Jesus, that he was a blasphemer, not Messiah, worthy of execution of the worst possible kind. The form of apostasy envisaged here is surely on a par with the serious 'blasphemy against the Holy Spirit' warning in the ministry of Jesus, the sin of ascribing the good, God-inspired, healing minstry of Christ to the work of demonic forces. It is to describe what is Christ's work as the devil's work.[21] These believers were in danger of identifying themselves with Christ's persecutors that first Good Friday, who deliberately rejected him and cried, 'Crucify him.'

We are not here dealing with the sincere believer who is depressed about his spiritual failure, or the backslider who has temporarily lost interest in the things of God. We are here confronted with fierce opposition to Christ and his gospel, public rebellion against Christian things and a determination to bring Christ's work to an end. The force of their Christ-rejection is vividly expressed in the tenses which are used here to describe their activity. Such people 'keep on crucifying' (present tense) for themselves the Son of God, and 'keep on putting him to open shame' (present tense again). If such people are resolutely determined to respond in this way to the message of Christ's love and forgiveness, then certainly it is 'impossible to keep on repeatedly leading them (present tense) afresh into repentance'.

Thirdly, there is *a serious warning* here. In other words, this passage and its parallels in this letter should not be hastily dismissed as though they merely dealt with a first-century situation without modern counterparts. As we have already indicated, similar warnings are found elsewhere in Scripture, especially in the teaching of Jesus. It is quite possible that these fierce opponents, although formerly having all the visible signs and marks of truly committed Christians, were not genuinely born again by God's Spirit. They may have convinced others that they were believers and at one time even persuaded themselves that they belonged to Christ, but their so called 'conversion' proved to be spurious and counterfeit. Just as some of the seed in the famous parable told by Jesus[22] fell into some ground to produce merely temporary growth, so it was with these apostates. Initially the seed had all the signs of healthy life, but when subjected to tests of various kinds it did not continue its promising growth. The seed of God's word had not reached into the depths of their hearts and minds. Jesus said that such people receive the word *immediately* with joy but, because they have no root in themselves, when persecution arises on account of the word they

[21] Mt. 12:22–32. [22] Mt. 13:3–9, 18–23.

are said to value, then *immediately* they fall away. Similarly, those who initially make better progress can easily be arrested in growth by the destructive weeds and thorns of anxiety and materialism. Worry and greed are enemies of the word; they betray a failure to trust in God's fatherly care. Moreover, these warnings are not simply found in the parables of Jesus. They are to be discerned in the New Testament's many vivid character studies. All sorts of people said 'Lord, Lord,'[23] and confessed their allegiance to Christ when first they met him, but they did not go on, and some actively turned against him – Judas, Demas, Simon Magus. Without indulging in morbid introspection, it is appropriate for all believers to examine themselves to see whether they are 'in the faith' (2 Cor. 13:5 NIV) and whether they are 'living the life of faith' (NEB).

We need also to remind ourselves that our spiritual security does not depend on a clear recollection of the moment of our conversion. Many people cannot point to a date and such a thing does not matter anyway. Some are brought to Christ suddenly and dramatically, but for others it is a slow, gradual process when the response to Christ may take place over a period of time, like the gradual opening of a flower. Jesus said, 'You will know them by their fruits.'[24] That surely is the clue. We depend for our salvation not on our love for God but his love for us, not on our commitment to him but his pledge to us, not on our hold on him but his grasp of us.[25]

Finally, we need constantly to remember that, forceful and relevant as these words are, because they are but a fragment of Scripture's total message, they can present us with only *a partial truth*. If we are to be built up in our faith, then it is of the greatest importance to store our minds with the truths of God's word. That will mean that whenever we come across a bewildering passage in the Bible, we shall attend carefully to what it has to say and then make sure that we compare scripture with scripture. Many distorted notions are promulgated because a verse of Scripture is wrested from its original context and then pressed into service in order to support an unbalanced idea which other verses in the Bible would deny. Alongside warning passages of this character one must also

[23] Mt. 7:21. [24] Mt. 7:16. [25] 1 Jn. 4:10, 19; Jude 24.

set the clear unequivocal teaching of Scripture concerning the eternal security of a Christian believer. This very letter contains such assurances. The author goes on here to emphasize that, although he is issuing these warnings, he is 'sure of better things' (6:9) in their case. He is confident that they belong to Christ's house and are partakers of his blessings. They have received a kingdom which cannot be shaken and as they endure in the Christian life they will certainly be equipped with everything good.[26] The many promises of the New Testament provide Christians with abundant evidence of their eternal inheritance in Christ. Their steady continuance and increasing love for Christ will prove the reality and genuineness of the work which God has wrought within them. Some experience of doubt can disturb the life of any Christian, but in such circumstances we do well to remember the words of that seventeenth-century saint, Samuel Rutherford:

> Sinners are anchor-fast and made stable in God. So that if God do not change (which is impossible), then my hope shall not fluctuate . . . Oh God be thanked that our salvation is coasted, and landed, and shored upon Christ, who is Master of winds and storms![27]

[26] Heb. 3:6, 14; 12:28; 13:20;21.
[27] Letter to John Stuart, Provost of Ayr (1637), in A. Bonar, *Letters of Samuel Rutherford* (Edinburgh, 1891), p. 372.

6:9–20

10. Confident of better things

It is hardly likely that a large number of Jewish Christians had become guilty of the kind of apostasy which the author has just described. The letter assures this church that the writer is certain that far *better things* are characteristic of their work and profession. Though he has had to write in strong terms about their waywardness, he is confident that such disobedience and rebellion are not widespread, and he now turns from his ministry of warning to that of encouragement. What are the *better things* that belong to salvation with which he heals their wounds? The passage expounds the greatness of God and his goodness to his believing children.

1. God is just (6:9–10)

9Though we speak thus, yet in your case, beloved, we feel sure of better things that belong to salvation. 10For God is not so unjust as to overlook your work and the love which you showed for his sake in serving the saints, as you still do.

The note of serious admonition is not allowed to obscure the opposite aspect of the same truth. If God's righteous justice is such that man's spiritual rebellion must not be ignored, then it is equally true that in the light of that same justice man's devoted service will not be overlooked.

The famous triad of faith, hope and love are all mentioned in this chapter.[1] At this point the author commends his read-

[1] Heb. 6:10–12, 19; *cf.* 1 Cor. 13:13; 1 Thes. 1:3.

ers' love which has been expressed in the rich quality of their service. He takes a moment to describe its exemplary character.

He notices, first of all, that it is *devoted* service. He is grateful for their *work*. They must not imagine that God is not interested in such things, or that their labour has not been noticed in heaven. As a gifted pastor the author does not dwell solely and negatively on the worthless 'thorns and thistles' (6:8) stored up for judgment. He knows that it is possible to exaggerate the defection of the few and minimize the love of the many. The apostates may only have been a tiny minority and most of his readers have not only served acceptably in the past, but continue to do so. Such love and loyalty will not be forgotten.

He is also aware that his readers have brought *practical* service to the work of the local church. To love is to do. The members of this church are later urged to stir up their fellow believers to 'love and good works' (10:24). Such devotion makes demands. In expounding this verse, John Calvin had this to say:

> We are not to spare ourselves from labour if we want to do our duty to our neighbours. We are not to help them financially only, but with advice, and by our efforts and in all kinds of ways. We must show great zeal, and put up with many annoyances, and sometimes undergo many hazards. Whoever wants to engage in the tasks of loving must be prepared for a laborious way of life.

The author is certainly aware that it has been *persistent* service. They have not only worked faithfully in the past, but have brought the quality of steady and reliable continuance to their service. How many really valuable forms of Christian work have been abandoned before there was time for fruit or success? We easily grow weary. These believers worked steadily and demonstrated tireless love towards the saints. He is grateful for all they have done in former days, but comments on their present ministry: *as you still do*. Here he admires persistent, compassionate service; later he commends steady, faithful continuance (6:11–12).

Looking to the future, he is sure that what they have done

for Christ will be *rewarded* service. Not all Christian work is immediately fruitful. In such moments they must take heart, that though the service is unnoticed by many, it is not ignored by God. *God is not so unjust as to overlook your work.* There is no need for us to be afraid of the idea of reward. It figures quite prominently in the teaching of Jesus.[2] As Montefiore says, 'Love brings its own reward, both now and in the future.'

Perhaps its most exemplary quality is that it has been *glorifying* service. All their work for the saints has been *for his sake*. It will certainly be rewarded, but the idea of reward has not motivated it. It has been done solely for the sake of God, or 'for his name', and that simply means 'for his glory'. That was the leading ambition of Christ's life,[3] and it must be ours also if we are to be acceptable servants. Work for Christ which is done entirely for the glory of God cannot possibly be overlooked by God.

2. God is generous (6:11–15)

11*And we desire each one of you to show the same earnestness in realizing the full assurance of hope until the end,* 12*so that you may not be sluggish, but imitators of those who through faith and patience inherit the promises.*

13*For when God made a promise to Abraham, since he had no one greater by whom to swear, he swore by himself,* 14*saying, 'Surely I will bless you and multiply you.'* 15*And thus Abraham, having patiently endured, obtained the promise.*

Our writer turns now from love to the other qualities of hope and faith. These also require persistence and continuance. The *same earnestness* which has been manifest in love at the beginning must now be expressed in faith and hope to the end. This church has known fierce hostility and aggressive opposition (10:32–34). The promises of God are of supreme importance in crises like these. In his love, God makes a pledge to his people that things will be different and better. His promises sustain them through these dark days, but they must be received, proved and inherited.[4]

[2] Mt. 25:34–40; Mk. 9:41. [3] Jn. 4:34; 17:4.
[4] Heb. 11:33; 11:11; 6:12.

Abraham is chosen as a single example, though he is one amongst many. He was not idle or slothful in the practical outworking of his believing experience, but steadily maintained *the full assurance of hope* right through his difficult life, until in the end *through faith and patience* he inherited the promises. Through persistent faith in a God who could not fail, and the promise that would not change, he pressed on in unwavering continuance. It would have been all too easy to have given up, but he relied on what God had clearly said and would certainly not withdraw: *Surely I will bless you and multiply you.* When God made his promise to his servant Abraham, everything seemed so impossibly bleak. God kept talking about his multitudinous descendants, but in point of fact he did not have a single child by his wife Sarah. Yet they went on persistently believing the rich promises of a faithful God (10:23; 11:11) rather than the comfortless doubts of their own hearts. And then it happened! Isaac was born. The promise was fulfilled. Years later, on the day when he almost lost his son, the gracious promise was renewed. God said, *I will bless you and multiply you*, and that was a word to be believed. Ultimately he was brought to the place where he did not need to cling on to the simple word of God's generous promise; there was God's gift before his eyes! God had been true to his word. In his justice our love is remembered; in his generosity our faith is rewarded.

3. God is dependable (6:16–20)

[16]*Men indeed swear by a greater than themselves, and in all their disputes an oath is final for confirmation.* [17]*So when God desired to show more convincingly to the heirs of the promise the unchangeable character of his purpose, he interposed with an oath,* [18]*so that through two unchangeable things, in which it is impossible that God should prove false, we who have fled for refuge might have strong encouragement to seize the hope set before us.* [19]*We have this as a sure and steadfast anchor of the soul, a hope that enters into the inner shrine behind the curtain,* [20]*where Jesus has gone as a forerunner on our behalf, having become a high priest for ever after the order of Melchizedek.*

These verses encourage our own faith and stimulate our hope. Three clearly identified ideas are presented here with great literary skill and pastoral artistry. Believers rely on God's word, God's nature and God's Son. All three are utterly dependable.

a. God's dependable word

It is all right for someone to make a promise, but how can we be sure that it is worth believing? People sometimes confirm the reliability and assert the integrity of their promises by adding an oath to the promise. Throughout the centuries God has done that for his people in order to encourage their fragile faith. He has given them his promise and then confirmed it by an oath. He obviously cannot swear by someone greater than himself, so he swears by himself.

b. God's dependable nature

It is of no use whatever for a dishonest or unreliable person to make a promise or swear by anything. The words would be empty and valueless. But God swore by himself and he will not fail. He does not vacillate.[5] The *heirs of the promise* looked to God for a fulfilment of his word and were not disappointed, simply because promise and oath were based on the secure foundation of God's holy and righteous character. It is quite impossible that God should prove false. We believe God's promises simply because *he* makes them.

c. God's dependable Son

We do not belong to this world. Like Abraham, we are pilgrims or refugees seeking a homeland (11:14; 13:14). The hope is set before us. It is like a strong dependable anchor, *sure and steadfast*. By the end of the second century the anchor had become a highly meaningful Christian sign. Clement of Alexandria, an outstanding teacher in the early church, mentions the anchor as an appropriate device for a Christian's ring: 'And let our seals be either a dove or a fish . . . or a

[5] Nu. 23:19; Mal. 3:6; Jas. 1:17.

ship's anchor.'[6] It is sometimes found on early Christian epitaphs as a symbol of secure hope. The imagery here is highly compressed, and can appear unhelpfully complex if one tries to visualize it – a ship's anchor being flung to the heavens so that it passes *behind the curtain*. Such mental gymnastics are hardly necessary. Its message about Christian hope is basically simple and persuasively direct.

Our hope is in what Christ has done. By his life, death, resurrection and ascension Jesus has achieved a momentous and eternal victory. He has gone into the holy presence of God as the *forerunner*. This term (*prodromos*) was used in Greek literature to describe the function of a small party of soldiers sent fully to explore the way ahead prior to the advance of an army. Christ is our *prodromos*. He has gone ahead of us.[7] He prepares our way to glory (2:10). With such a leader who has opened the way through his own sacrificial death (10:20), there is no room for anxiety regarding his future purposes or doubt concerning his former promises. With such an anchor *here* and such a priest *there*, we must not fear and we need not fail.

Conclusion

This passage has specially important things to say to ministers, pastors and Christian workers. We now turn to look at the practical implications of this passage as we apply its teaching to the day-to-day responsibilities of any man or woman in a position of Christian leadership.

a. We must be generous in our encouragement

The writer of this letter is only too well aware of the dangers to which his congregation is exposed in its first-century setting. He has already mentioned the immaturity of some and the apostasy of others, but he does not allow these serious failures to distort his view of this church. He is aware of *better things* in the lives of these believers. We must take care not to neglect the ministry of encouragement. With a commendable desire to see a congregation at its best, any pastor

[6] Clement of Alexandria, *Paidagogus* III. 11. [7] Jn. 14:2–3.

or minister is in danger of constantly exhorting his people to new heights of spiritual experience and severely rebuking them when he considers them to have been unresponsive. The note of challenge is certainly necessary, but constant reproof is wearisome. In explaining these verses, Calvin makes this helpful comment:

> Certainly anyone who wants to be a good teacher ought to treat his pupils in such a way as always to encourage rather than discourage them. There is nothing that has a greater effect in alienating us from listening to teaching than to see that we are thought of as hopeless.

b. We must be balanced in our preaching

Deeply concerned about the spiritual dangers to which these believers were exposed, the author of the epistle might well have been forgiven if he had concentrated almost exclusively on the hazards and their perilous consequences. But in point of fact he recognizes the importance and necessity of a balanced presentation of Christian truth. Any minister who preaches regularly to the same congregation needs to ensure that he declares 'the whole counsel of God'.[8] Without careful study and diligent work it is easy for the preacher to produce a severely distorted account of Christian truth. The peril can be avoided only by a commitment to Scripture as a whole and not to those parts of it which make the greater appeal to us. This is why it is important for a pastor to exercise an expository ministry. In explaining, week by week, the message of a book of the Bible, the expository preacher will naturally cover a whole range of subjects he might be tempted to ignore or which are unlikely to occur to him in more haphazard preparation.

c. We must be exemplary in our living

However warm and encouraging the pastor may be, and however balanced his preaching, the passage calls him to consistent behaviour. Like its first readers we are urged to be *imitators*

[8] Acts 20:27.

of those pilgrims who have gone on ahead, who by their faith and endurance have inherited the promises of God. Our author has illustrated his point by a direct reference to one of his favourite biblical characters, Abraham. Commendable conduct is possibly the most eloquent exposition of our faith. The teaching of sound doctrine is important to the author of this letter (5:11–14), but he knows only too well that if we strive to imitate those who have gone before and by God's grace follow the example of Christ,[9] our presentation of Christian doctrine will be not only eloquent but persuasive.

[9] Mt. 11:29–30; Jn. 13:14–15; 1 Pet. 2:21.

PART II
CHRIST'S WORK

7:1–19
11. That intriguing man Melchizedek

For this Melchizedek, king of Salem, priest of the most high
God, met Abraham returning from the slaughter of the kings
and blessed him; 2and to him Abraham appointed a tenth part
of everything. He is first, by translation of his name, king of
righteousness, and then he is also king of Salem, that is, king
of peace. 3He is without father or mother or genealogy, and
has neither beginning of days nor end of life, but resembling
the Son of God he continues a priest for ever.
4See how great he is! Abraham the patriarch gave him a
tithe of the spoils. 5And those descendants of Levi who receive
the priestly office have a commandment in the law to take
tithes from the people, that is from their brethren, though
these also are descended from Abraham. 6But this man who
has not their genealogy received tithes from Abraham and
blessed him who had the promises. 7It is beyond dispute that
the inferior is blessed by the superior. 8Here tithes are received
by mortal men; there, by one of whom it is testified that he
lives. 9One might even say that Levi himself, who receives
tithes, paid tithes through Abraham, 10for he was still in the
loins of his ancestor when Melchizedek met him.
11Now if perfection had been attainable through the Lev-
itical priesthood (for under it the people received the law),
what further need would there have been for another priest
to arise after the order of Melchizedek, rather than one named
after the order of Aaron? 12For when there is a change in the
priesthood, there is necessarily a change in the law as well.
13For the one of whom these things are spoken belonged to
another tribe, from which no one has ever served at the altar.

[14]*For it is evident that our Lord was descended from Judah, and in connection with that tribe Moses said nothing about priests.*

[15]*This becomes even more evident when another priest arises in the likeness of Melchizedek,* [16]*who has become a priest, not according to a legal requirement concerning bodily descent but by the power of an indestructible life.* [17]*For it is witnessed of him,*

'Thou art a priest for ever,
after the order of Melchizedek.'

[18]*On the one hand, a former commandment is set aside because of its weakness and uselessness* [19]*(for the law made nothing perfect); on the other hand, a better hope is introduced, through which we draw near to God.*

We have now reached the part of this letter which modern readers sometimes find a little difficult. It makes use of occasionally unfamiliar imagery and relies on a form of argument which seems strange to us. Our difficulties arise, first, because this character, Melchizedek, is not one of the best known of Old Testament personalities. Furthermore, this device of using a somewhat remote Old Testament character as a type of Christ is not a regular feature in modern Christian exposition, especially when we look carefully at the way the writer develops his argument and uses the biblical material.

The first thing we have to face is that, although this particular use of typology may not be common today, it was thoroughly familiar to our author and to many of his contemporaries. We must try to enter into their thought world, and in doing so we shall realize how helpful this form of interpretation was to them. The occasional intricacy of his argument must not be allowed to obscure the commendability of his aim. He genuinely desires to magnify Christ and do it in such a way as to help his contemporaries to understand the superiority of Christ's priesthood when set alongside the Levitical priesthood. The priesthood of Jesus was *after the order of Melchizedek* and as such is contrasted sharply with the Jewish priesthood which was *after the order of Aaron.* One was eternal and effective; the other temporary and imperfect, now *set aside because of its weakness and uselessness.*

Here again we have a forceful illustration of the author's

confident and helpful approach to the Old Testament. It is not simply a graphic account of God's dealings with his covenant people over the centuries. Old Testament Scripture is essentially Christ-centred. As we have seen earlier, it eagerly anticipates his coming, it describes his earthly ministry, vividly relates the precise circumstances and eternal benefits of his death for mankind, and looks beyond itself to the eventual fulfilment of its finest hopes. Its historical development, spiritual value and moral lessons are all fully appreciated by our author, but he comes to its arresting narratives as a man equipped by the Spirit of God to discern a further message. It is a book about Christ. The Son of God dominates the word of God in both Testaments. The marks of Christ are clearly impressed on all its pages for those who have the eye to see them.

Therefore, we must look at the Genesis account[1] of the incident used here by our author. It simply relates the story of Abraham's return from a military encounter with some Canaanite kings. Fresh from the scene of victory and laden with the battle spoil, Abraham is met by a king named Melchizedek who offers bread and wine to the victor (the only detail which our author does not mention, despite its potential typological value). Melchizedek implores God's blessing on Abraham and also praises God for Abraham's success. Abraham offers him a tenth of the spoil; thereupon Melchizedek disappears from the narrative. The only remaining mention of his name in Old Testament Scripture is in a highly important psalm[2] also used by our writer.

We must note that this Melchizedek event narrated in Genesis has both historical importance and a spiritual message. It relates to the gratitude of Abraham for God's help at a difficult moment in his life and the superiority of Melchizedek who, publicly acknowledging the greatness of God, invoked the divine blessing on Abraham and accepted tithes from him. The king-priest of Salem makes it clear that the God who created the world protects his children. But, accepting that message, the author of our letter goes beyond it to its additional and even more significant meaning.

Our author's main purpose in using the story is to em-

[1] Gn. 14:17–20. [2] Ps. 110:4.

phasize Christ's superiority over the Aaronic priesthood. It is quite possible that some of these Jewish Christians, in danger of forsaking the local church, were missing some of the traditional legalism and the cultic features of their one-time Jewish faith. Our author is at pains to say that Jesus is superior not only to the angels and to Moses, but also to Aaron and the priesthood which traditionally stemmed from the tribe of Levi. His earlier references to Christ as *a priest for ever after the order of Melchizedek*[3] now lead to an exposition of Christ's superiority. His key theme is conveyed in those words, priest *for ever.* It is the eternal and unique aspect of Christ's priestly work which excites him as he makes typological use here of five related ideas. He refers to Melchizedek's status, authority, name, uniqueness and superiority.

1. Melchizedek's status (7:1)

He was a priest and so is Christ. The idea of a priest-king may seem rather unfamiliar to us, but it was not at all unknown in the ancient world. The concept of Christ as priest dominates the central section of this letter. Although precise references to Christ's title as priest are confined to this letter, there are indications elsewhere in the New Testament of the priestly work of Jesus. His present ministry of intercession is mentioned by both Paul and John.[4]

2. Melchizedek's authority (7:1)

He was a king and so is Christ. The kingship theme has already been introduced in the author's superb exposition of Christ's regal splendour and work in chapter 1. His saving achievement complete, he is seated at the right hand of the Majesty on high, worshipped, enthroned and crowned with glory and honour. Our Lord's dual titles of king and priest are highly appropriate, for as Hughes reminds us, 'As king he is just, and as priest he justifies all who trust in his atoning sacrifice.'[5]

[3] Heb. 5:6, 10; 6:20. [4] Rom. 8:34; 1 Jn. 2:1–2.
[5] Rom. 3:26; 5:8–9.

3. Melchizedek's name (7:2)

He is *righteousness* and *peace*, and so is Christ. Our author takes the name Melchizedek to mean *king of righteousness*, and Salem,[6] where he was said to rule, means *peace*. The two characteristics are as relevant and appropriate as the two titles for, as Bruce observes, 'peace with God is based upon the righteousness of God'.[7]

4. Melchizedek's uniqueness (7:3)

It is at this point that some find it difficult to identify with our author's method of interpretation. He makes special mention of the fact that in Genesis we are given no ancestral details when Melchizedek's name is mentioned, a little surprising in view of the numerous genealogies found in that book. The author does not wish for a moment to imply that because Melchizedek's human parents are not mentioned they did not exist. The main point here is that in Scripture nothing is said of these things. So 'in the silences as well as in the statements' Melchizedek is 'a fitting type of Christ' (Bruce). This priest-king is in this sense timeless and as such he resembles the Son of God who *continues a priest for ever*. We ought to observe that he does not, as in some typology, use Melchizedek to illustrate the virtues of Christ, but moves his thought in the opposite direction. It is not Jesus who resembles Melchizedek, but Melchizedek who resembles the Lord Jesus. 'Melchizedek thus was the facsimile of which Christ is the reality' (Hawthorne).

5. Melchizedek's superiority (7:4–10)

Abraham was certainly a key figure in Judaism, the father of the race, but for all his greatness he offered tithes to, and received a blessing from, the priest-king and, says our author, *the inferior is blessed by the superior*. Here again we find the

[6] Salem was probably Jerusalem; such was the view of the Jewish historian, Josephus, which was, according to Jerome, supported by most early Christian writers. The parallelism of Ps. 76:2 clearly suggests this identification.

[7] Rom. 1:17; 5:1, 18–19.

argument a little unusual, though the intention is clear. The Levites are descended from Abraham and, he argues, all Abraham's progeny were represented in Abraham when he offered the spoil to Melchizedek. At that time Levi was *still in the loins of his ancestor when Melchizedek met him*, so it was as if Levi and all his tribe paid tithes to this priest-king.

Now, he proceeds, Jesus is a priest not from the Levitical line and *after the order of Aaron*, but *after the order of Melchizedek*. If the ministry of the Levitical or Aaronic priesthood had been spiritually effective, it would have been quite unnecessary for God to have sent another priest after Melchizedek's order rather than Levi's. Jesus did not belong to the tribe of Levi but to the tribe of Judah, and that tribe was not entitled to present its male members for the Jewish priesthood (7:13–14). The necessary authentication for Christ's priesthood is not a legal requirement like physical membership of a specified tribe, but his vindication and attestation by God at his resurrection. *By the power of an indestructible life* he lives eternally and can thus serve as our effective and only mediator, *a priest for ever*. The old Jewish order of priesthood is thus set aside because of its inadequacy, *its weakness and uselessness* and its imperfection, *for the law made nothing perfect*. The saving work of Christ has introduced *a better hope* and it is by this way, and this way alone, that we draw near to God.

Jewish opponents were likely to hurl angry questions at their Christian contemporaries, especially those who had come from a Jewish background. They would naturally insist on knowing precisely why Christ's priesthood and sacrifice are considered superior to those found in Judaism and hallowed by constant use over many centuries. Our author now turns to this question: Why is Christ's work unique? The relevance of his argument is not a first-century affair. It is of the greatest possible importance to twentieth-century men and women facing surprisingly similar problems, and at the same disadvantage. Like them, we are sinners, without strength, without hope and without God in the world.[8] It is the writer's purpose to devote the main central section of the letter to an exposition of this theme.

[8] Rom. 5:6; Eph. 2:12.

7:20–28

12. A superior priesthood

In this passage some of the leading ideas of the letter are gathered together and expounded with persuasive and attractive conviction. It might be helpful for us briefly to recall the background. Some readers had begun to feel wistful about the traditional and familiar religious ceremonials of Judaism and seriously questioned whether they had been right in abandoning it all when they became Christians. In this section the writer wants to assure them that in Christ they have what he has earlier described as 'a better hope' (7:19). Jesus exercises a 'more excellent ministry' than any Jewish priest. He mediates a far better covenant, far superior to the old 'since it is enacted on better promises' (8:6).

The priesthood of Christ is here claimed to be infinitely preferable to anything these Jewish Christians had known in their unconverted days. Its superiority is based on its oath, its guarantor and its priest.

1. Its oath (7:20–21)

[20]*And it was not without an oath.* [21]*Those who formerly became priests took their office without an oath, but this one was addressed with an oath,*

'The Lord has sworn
and will not change his mind,
"Thou art a priest for ever."'

On three occasions in chapter 7 the writer stresses that Jesus is 'a high priest *for ever*' (7:3, 17, 21) quoting Psalm 110:4 as an authority for his conviction. He cites this Psalm because it contains God's oath that this distinctive priesthood 'after the order of Melchizedek' will be permanent and changeless. *The Lord has sworn and will not change his mind.* Nothing could be more definite. The first part of the oath declared the supreme fact, *The Lord has sworn*, and it must be remembered that in Hebrew thought, when God said something it was done.[1] It was not a mere word; it had in itself the power to initiate the event. The second part of the oath declared its reliability: *and will not change his mind.* The Lord will not go back on his word. So, when in eternity the Lord took upon himself for us this priestly work 'in the service of God' (2:17), the permanence of his ministry ('a priest for ever') was confirmed by God's oath. The Lord God said it would last *for ever*, so it certainly will.

2. Its guarantor (7:22)

This makes Jesus the surety of a better covenant.

If God has said it, that surely is enough; but in order to encourage these Jewish Christians to commit themselves unreservedly to the finished work of Christ, he introduces us to a new picture, that of Jesus as the surety or guarantor of a better covenant. We ought to look a little more closely at those three key words, *better*, *covenant* and *guarantor*.

Better is a key word in the letter. At the beginning the author declares that Jesus has a better (RSV 'more excellent', same word) name than angels (1:4), for he is 'the Son of God'. Motivated by deep pastoral concern, the writer dreads the thought that some of the members of this church might go back to something inferior, temporary and partial, when in Christ there is 'a better hope', 'a better covenant', with 'better promises'. The once-for-all offering of Christ's life is a 'better sacrifice'. In time of persecution some lost their homes and property, but rejoiced that in heaven they had a 'better possession'. They set their hope not on those earthly, material things which might be plundered by aggressive neighbours; their eyes were fixed on a 'better country'.[2] Even if their 'hard struggle with sufferings' exceeds verbal abuse and physical

[1] Gn. 1:3; *cf.* Lk. 7:6–9 [2] Heb. 7:19, 22; 8:6; 9:23; 10:34; 11:16.

affliction (10:32–34) so that they are compelled to lay down their lives for Christ (12:4), still they would not be distressed. They know that in him they will 'rise again to a better life' (11:35). When they are up against opposition and violence, their confidence is not in their material goods or moral effort, or even their spiritual integrity; they rely entirely on the blood of Christ which has something far 'better' to say than Abel's blood (12:24). It speaks graciously to them of security, purification, pardon and access,[3] and so they are supremely content.

Covenant is another word which is prominent in the writer's thought, though this is the first time that it makes its appearance in the letter. In chapters 8 and 9 this word covenant, or testament (*diathēkē*), is to dominate the exposition. The word is used in two senses in this letter. More commonly *diathēkē* signifies the covenant of God with us. In Old Testament times agreements were made, for example, between two kings fixing the conditions of peace or the allocation of their territories. In these circumstances some form of mutual acceptability was always necessary. But in God's covenant with us it is not entirely satisfactory to translate the term as 'agreement', for in God's *diathēkē* the initiative is not with us but with God. In his merciful goodness God deigned to enter into a covenant with us through the work and merit of his Son. In this letter the *diathēkē* is described as a 'better', 'new', and 'eternal' covenant.[4] The author intends to develop this covenant theme later and we will defer any further discussion of its meaning and implications until then.

Surety or *guarantor* (*engyos*) is an interesting word which makes its only New Testament appearance in this verse. Westcott observes that a surety 'for the most part pledges himself that something will be: but here the Ascended Christ witnesses that something is: the assurance is not simply of the future but of that which is present though unseen'. In the Greek text the name 'Jesus' stands in the most emphatic place, right at the end of the sentence, 'the guarantor is Jesus'. Once again the human name of Christ is given prominence. Our guarantor is one who knows our need, having lived amongst us, but he now sits in God's presence as our surety. In

[3] Heb. 9:12, 14, 26; 10:19–22. [4] Heb. 8:8, 13; 9:15; 13:20.

classical literature the *engyos* was a person who guaranteed that a legal obligation would be carried out. In this letter we see that in heaven Jesus 'now acts as the guarantor and representative of those who are still on earth awaiting the rest promised to the people of God'.[5]

3. Its priest (7:23–28)

[23]*The former priests were many in number, because they were prevented by death from continuing in office;* [24]*but he holds his priesthood permanently, because he continues for ever.* [25]*Consequently he is able for all time to save those who draw near to God through him, since he always lives to make intercession for them.*

[26]*For it was fitting that we should have such a high priest, holy, blameless, unstained, separated from sinners, exalted above the heavens.* [27]*He has no need, like those high priests, to offer sacrifices daily, first for his own sins and then for those of the people; he did this once for all when he offered up himself.* [28]*Indeed, the law appoints men in their weakness as high priests, but the word of the oath, which came later than the law, appoints a Son who has been made perfect for ever.*

In point of fact there are three portraits of Christ in this section of the letter. Jesus is our present guarantor, our eternal priest and our effective sacrifice. At this stage our attention is directed to Christ's priestly office and especially to its superiority over the Jewish priesthood. Five significant aspects of his person and work are shown in these verses. We are invited to consider Christ's permanent achievement, limitless power, present ministry, sinless character and perfect offering.

a. His permanent achievement (7:23–24)

Over the centuries the Jewish people had been served by thousands of priests. However dedicated a priest might be in the exercise of his special work, death put an abrupt end to

[5] C. Brown (editor), *Dictionary of New Testament Theology*, 1 (Paternoster, 1975), p. 372.

his ministry. But Jesus is the *permanent* holder of this priestly office because *he continues for ever.* For this reason 'he is able for all time to save those who draw near to God' (7:25). Perhaps some of these Christians were only too ready to acknowledge the power of Christ in the days of his earthly ministry when the living truth was 'declared at first by the Lord' so convincingly, or the spiritual blessing which attended the mission of the apostles in the church's earliest days when 'signs and wonders' attested the apostolic gospel (2:3–4), but things had settled down since then. For some, the persecution had intensified. Nobody doubted the earlier manifestations of Christ's saving activity, but could he save people *now*? It is 'for all time', says the author. What he achieves for us is done for ever.

b. His limitless power (7:25a)

It is also possible to translate these words *for all time* (*eis to panteles*) as 'completely' (NIV), 'fully', or 'absolutely' (NEB). The phrase is doubtless a further reference to the far-reaching effects and unlimited adequacy of Christ's saving work. His power knows no limits and his life knows no end. He is able to save his people fully and completely. Nothing is necessary to supplement their salvation. They are not saved by a little believing plus a little doing. He achieves it absolutely by his victorious work and, moreover, he can save them now. The tense of the verb is of the greatest importance here. It is present tense (*sōzein*), reminding us, as Westcott says, that 'support comes at each moment of trial'.

c. His present ministry (7:25b)

Although this letter has so much to say about Christ's redemptive work on the cross in the past, 'once and for all', it also emphasizes his present work for his people. His saving mission complete, he now supports and sustains us through his intercessory ministry. Day by day and hour by hour Christ prays for us. We ought to pay special attention to this aspect of Christ's present work, especially in the light of this letter's Jewish background.

The rabbis maintained that intercession on behalf of people

was a ministry entrusted to the angels and especially to Michael the archangel. Here, yet again, Christ is portrayed as one who as priest exercises an intercessory role far superior to the angels in the Jewish tradition. He intercedes for us meaningfully for, unlike the angels, he has first-hand experience of our trials. He intercedes for us compassionately, for, unlike the angels, he knows exactly what we need. He intercedes for us effectively, for, unlike the angels, he has the power to meet our need.

During his earthly ministry Jesus prayed for his friends.[6] The early Christian people rejoiced at the thought that his effective intercessory ministry was not confined to his life on earth; it is continued in heaven.[7]

d. His sinless character (7:26)

Even the most devout priests who served under the old covenant were transgressors. Although required by their office to lead pure and sinless lives,[8] they were, like others, sinners by nature. The former priesthood stressed the importance of outward cleansing and ritual purity, but Christ's priesthood is effective because of his inward moral purity and his sinless perfection. His life among people and his present glory are described in a series of majestic adjectives. Christ lived a *holy* life;[9] it was set apart completely for God's work and so was fully pleasing to the Father. He lived a *blameless* life; it was completely guileless, never at any point disappointing as far as its moral perfection is concerned.[10] He lived an *unstained* life; nothing remotely impure ever marred its sinless beauty. He lived a *separated* life; although he moved freely and lovingly among us, he was entirely given over to God's will and so was in no sense compromised by his constant contact with sinners. He now lives an *exalted* life; he has passed through the heavens to the throne of God. It is God's final seal of perfect approval; that beautiful life was fully acceptable to his Father and his saving sacrifice fully effective for us.[11]

[6] Lk. 22:32; Jn. 17:9, 15. [7] Rom. 8:33; *cf.* Is. 53:12.
[8] Mal. 2:4–7. [9] Acts 2:27; 3:13–14.
[10] 1 Pet. 2:22. [11] 1 Pet. 3:18–22.

e. His perfect offering (7:27–28)

Jesus was not only the perfect priest; he was the perfect sacrifice. In this letter Christ is priest, sacrifice, altar and even the 'curtain' which was rent on that first Good Friday so that everyone might have direct access to God.[12] The Jewish priest offered the blood of bulls and goats both for himself and for his contemporaries (9:6–7). Christ *offered up himself*, not the blood of animals, and he did it all for others, not for himself. Moreover, their offerings had to be repeated constantly. *Daily* sacrifices may be a reference not to the annual Day of Atonement but to the sin offering[13] which, although not required as a daily offering, may well have been needed day by day. This particular sacrifice covered those inadvertent sins which, as Bruce points out, 'could well have been a daily hazard'. The sacrifice of Christ is unique in its permanence, its purity, its efficacy and its cost. *He did this once for all when he offered up himself.*

Under the law people had to be content with the service of weak priests who, like themselves, were frail and fallible; weak, because they were merely human, imperfect, and because they were inevitably sinful. Our high priest is by contrast pure and spotless, *made perfect for ever*, that is, completely efficacious. An Italian commentator on this epistle, Teodorico, describes the closing verses of this section as 'a hymn to the High Priest . . . as though an outburst of the joy of humanity which has at last found the high priest qualified to understand its weaknesses and to come to its aid: so far above us and so near to us; himself in need of no cleansing and able to cleanse and expiate all our guilt.'[14]

Conclusion

Amongst several practical implications which emerge in the course of these verses, we select two as worthy of special emphasis. As Christians, we recognize two characteristics or essential aspects of our believing experience: we trust God's word and appropriate Christ's work.

[12] Heb. 10:19; Mk. 15:38. [13] Lv. 4:1.
[14] I am indebted to P. E. Hughes for this reference.

a. We trust God's word

'The Lord has sworn and will not go back on his word, "Thou art a priest for ever" ' (7:21 NEB). We have already seen that Hebrews deals with two central themes, the word of God (chapters 1–6 and 11–13) and the work of Christ (chapters 7–10). God's word is completely trustworthy. He does not vacillate or change his mind.[15] In other words, our eternal salvation depends neither on our changeable feelings nor on our wavering experience. All our confidence is in the God who will not go back on his word. Christ is our priest *for ever*. We may disappoint him and from time to time fail him, but he does not cast us off. God is true to his word and for all time Jesus is priest to those who love and trust him. We are his brothers and we are his house. We belong to a kingdom which cannot be shaken. God is our compassionate Father (12:5–9, 28) and Christ is our changeless priest. In times of doubt and uncertainty we are urged by this letter simply to take God at his word and recall afresh that, although our feelings and circumstances may alter, he has sworn on oath that his Son is our priest *for ever*.

b. We appropriate Christ's work

No expositor can possibly exaggerate the sense of wonder which emerges again and again throughout this letter that at the cross, 'once and for all', Christ dealt with man's triple problem of sin, death and the devil. We are saved. But it is not simply a question of our spiritual past. Salvation in this letter is also a present, immediate and constantly renewed experience. He is always able to keep safe (*sōzein*) all those who come to God by him (7:25). Westcott observes that the thought here is 'the working out of salvation to the uttermost in those who have received the gospel'.

Quite unintentionally this present tense can be minimized in evangelistic preaching and experience. We are so concerned to expound 'the finished work of Christ' in its eternal dimension that we can neglect its continuing efficacy. We look to the past and some of us recall the very day we were 'saved'.[16]

[15] Is. 40:8; Mal. 3:6; Jas. 1:17.
[16] Rom. 8:24; Eph. 2:5; 2 Tim. 1:9; Tit. 3:5.

But the New Testament is equally insistent about our *present* salvation. When Paul wrote to the Corinthians he rejoiced in the gospel by which they were 'being saved',[17] even amidst all the corruption and immorality of a first-century Greek seaport. This saving activity is not restricted to the glorious moment of our conversion. Day by day he rescues his people. The 'pioneer' of our salvation brings us to the eternal glory by a saving route; we have been saved, we are being saved, and we shall be saved. Our present salvation is in Christ, but we must appropriate this blessing and *be what we are*. The author of this letter insists that Christ can save his readers from sin, fear, disobedience, apostasy and apathy. He is the author of their eternal salvation (5:9), which means that he is the source of their present salvation. He rescues us, not only in the moment of initial commitment, but day by day and moment by moment. We must constantly renew our trust in him, knowing that he will never fail us.

[17] 1 Cor. 1:18; 2 Cor. 2:15.

8:1–5

13. The heavenly sanctuary

The verses which now follow direct our attention from the necessity and nature of the Son's priestly work to the *sphere* where its effectiveness is recognized, acknowledged and confirmed as efficacious – in heaven. The Jewish priestly system was concerned about four great themes, the priesthood itself (expounded throughout chapter 7), the sanctuary (8:1–5), the covenant and sacrifice. The author turns next to the subject of the heavenly sanctuary.

1*Now the point in what we are saying is this: we have such a high priest, one who is seated at the right hand of the throne of the Majesty in heaven,* 2*a minister in the sanctuary and the true tent which is set up not by man but by the Lord.* 3*For every high priest is appointed to offer gifts and sacrifices; hence it is necessary for this priest also to have something to offer.*
4*Now if he were on earth, he would not be a priest at all, since there are priests who offer gifts according to the law.* 5*They serve a copy and shadow of the heavenly sanctuary; for when Moses was about to erect the tent, he was instructed by God, saying, 'See that you make everything according to the pattern which was shown you on the mountain.'*

The old priests ministered for God in an earthly tabernacle. It was inhibited by time and space. Christ's priesthood is superior because he ministers in the *true tent which is set up not by man but by the Lord.* The earthly tent was only a copy of the heavenly one. The writer knows that his previous argument is detailed, demanding his meticulous care in exposition, but he has now come to his 'main point' (8:1 NEB), or, as Coverdale translated it, 'this is the pyth'. In other words, everything leads up to this 'essential matter': we have an infinitely superior high priest and he ministers in heaven itself. The ministry he now offers is as intercessor, not as sacrificer. His sacrificial work was 'once for all' in history. His present work is to pray for us, and that he does, as we have seen, with compassionate understanding.

Some interpreters of this passage about the heavenly sanctuary trace some kind of dependence here on Greek thought, popularized in Alexandria, which, they suggest, is the author's geographical and cultural background. In other words, the Platonic concept of 'ideas' dominates the writer's thinking. The 'idea' was the immaterial form of an object which had 'copies' made from this heavenly pattern. But other expositors insist that there 'is no need to invoke Plato here; we are within the framework of Hebrew thought, Biblical thought of Promise and Fulfilment'.[1] By presenting his readers with this vivid word picture of the heavenly sanctuary, our author is turning their gaze away from that order of priesthood which was merely earthly, temporary and passing, belonging to the realm of shadow, to the real sanctuary beyond the immediate reach of mere man. He insists that if Christ were still on earth in human form he would certainly not exercise his ministry as a Levitical priest for, belonging to the tribe of Judah, he did not qualify for such office (7:14). Such priests were still officiating in Judaism, the writer says,[2] so when we speak of the priestly ministry of Christ we are certainly not referring to the old order of priesthood. We are discussing a ministry which takes place in the realm of eternal reality. The earthly tent was portable and exposed to change, but this sanctuary is established in the heavens (9:24). It cannot be plundered or destroyed. In AD 70 Jerusalem's famous temple was destroyed by the Roman armies. This letter asserts that we have a better sanctuary; it is eternal and imperishable, securely set in the heavens.

The 'main point' of this passage is, once again, the person and work of Christ, and three issues are of particular relevance

[1] F. C. Synge, *Hebrews and the Scriptures* (London, 1959), p. 25.

[2] An argument used to support an early date for this letter, prior to the destruction of the Jerusalem temple in AD 70.

for us in the contemporary world. The verses before us focus attention on his exalted person, his eternal ministry and his present work.

1. Who he is

The 'pyth' of all this is that Christ is now our exalted and triumphant Lord, *seated at the right hand of the throne of the Majesty in heaven*. These words are a typically Hebraic way of saying that Jesus is now for ever with God, his Father, in the place of sovereignty and authority. Like Melchizedek of patriarchal times, he is both king, having ascended to the eternal throne, and priest, now serving as *a minister in the sanctuary*. The ascension idea recurs throughout this letter like the main theme of a great symphony; variations are introduced, but only to give further expression to the rich cadences and majestic tones of the most memorable music ever heard. He is the exalted Lord, the Son of God. All this is of the greatest possible importance to us at a time when some of our contemporaries are prepared to make room for Christ, but a reduced Christ, a Christ who matches their ideals rather than one who determines them. Malcolm Muggeridge has spoken forcefully of those who are ready enough to cheer Jesus to the skies 'as a superstar, elect him with a huge majority to be the Honourable Member for Galilee South, sign him up with the urban guerillas and adapt his Sermon on the Mount to be a Sermon on the Barricades'.[3] What emerges in the thinking and writing of some moderns is a Jesus totally unlike the majestic, exalted Christ of the letter to the Hebrews. He is a Christ who cannot save; a projection of human imagination and not the Christ of inspired Scripture. It may sound as though Christ is being preached, but he is not. They are partial Christologies and therefore not only unsatisfying, but totally misleading. In one of his sermons, John Donne made an assertion perhaps more relevant today than when he preached it in the seventeenth century: 'Hee that confesses not all Christ, confesses no

[3] M. Muggeridge, *Christ and the Media* (Hodder & Stoughton, 1977), p. 39.

Christ.'[4] Strong sayings like that, and the rich testimony of millions throughout the centuries, need to be set alongside the humanitarian Christologies of some contemporary theologians with their fascination for a Christ without deity and therefore without power to help.

2. What he does

In addition to being the exalted Son of God, seated on the eternal throne, he is *a minister in the sanctuary*. What does that mean? Our writer says that he ministers to mankind in *the true tent which is set up not by man but by the Lord.* Over the centuries there have been a variety of interpretations regarding the *true tent* (*skēnē*) and its nature. Some, like John Chrysostom and John Owen, assert that the tent here refers to the body of Christ; the phrase refers to his earthly ministry. It links this verse with a later reference in this letter to 'the greater and more perfect tent' (9:11) and recalls the biblical imagery about Christ's body and ours as a tent.[5] To these expositors the true tent is the human body of Christ in which he ministered on earth and in which, supremely by dying, he accomplished our redemption. Others suggest that the tent is the church, a view maintained by the great nineteenth-century commentator, B. F. Westcott, in his monumental commentary on this letter. Some insist that the tent here refers to the individual believer. The sanctuary, or tent, which Jesus enters is the soul of the believing man or woman.[6] Even the virgin Mary has been suggested as the true tent, whilst others, equally speculative, offer the idea that the tent refers to the heavenly regions through which the ascended Christ made his journey.

The most natural reading of the text is that our writer here refers simply to the eternal or heavenly realm where he is seated at the right hand of God. It is here that Christ serves as our *minister* and it is appropriate at this point briefly to

[4] E. M. Simpson and G. R. Potter, *The Sermons of John Donne*, 7 (University of California Press, 1954), p. 266.

[5] Jn. 1:14; *cf.* 2 Cor. 5:1, 4; 2 Pet. 1:14.

[6] For example, F. F. Bruce who (commenting on Heb. 9:11) links this verse with the earlier reference to believers as the 'house of God' (3:6) and to Stephen's sermon in Acts 7:48–50.

discuss the nature of his ministry on our behalf. The word 'minister' (*leitourgos*) denotes the activity of the priest. In Old Testament times the priest's responsibilities extended far beyond the work of sacrificing. He served God's people as their intercessor, example and instructor,[7] and it is clear from the New Testament that Christ now ministers as our priest in these ways also.[8] The priest offered sacrifices on behalf of the people and also for his own needs, but Jesus has already offered that one, final and complete sacrifice. It cannot be presented again.

Perhaps we ought to note here that some of this epistle's ideas about the heavenly ministry of Jesus have been used to support the concept of the 'eucharistic sacrifice' whereby, in some sense, the sacrifice of Christ's death is perpetually offered or presented for man's redemption. Verse 3 of this passage is sometimes used in support of the idea that if Jesus is not offering a sacrifice now, he cannot possibly fulfil the priestly function: *it is necessary for this priest also to have something to offer.* Consequently, his present role must be that of a priest who constantly offers a sacrifice for us. Roman Catholic theologians have regarded the eucharist as some kind of extension in contemporary experience of what happened in history on that first Good Friday. By means of the Mass sacrificially offered in earthly sanctuaries, the faithful are mystically and sacramentally united with Christ in his eternal sanctuary. It is hard to think how this view can be substantiated from this epistle with its repeated assertion that Christ died once for all. Alan Stibbs has a helpful illustration of what is meant here:

> Admittedly the act of offering was necessary to constitute Christ a priest in fact, and not only in name, just as the act of child-bearing is necessary to constitute a woman a mother. But that truth does not mean in the case of motherhood that henceforth, to those who resort to her as mother, such a woman is always giving them birth. Her act of child-bearing is for them not only an indispensable but also a finished work. What they now enjoy are other complementary ministries of motherhood, which lie beyond

[7] See Mal. 2:5–7 for a vivid description of the priestly ideal.
[8] Rom. 8:34; 1 Pet. 2:21; 1 Jn. 2:6; Jn. 14:26.

the child-bearing. Similarly with Christ's priesthood His propitiatory offering is not only an indispensable but also a finished work.[9]

3. How he serves

Christ is the *minister* of his people; what does he *offer* for his people? Utilizing passages in Hebrews, such as this one, many Roman Catholic writers have insisted that the perpetual priesthood of Christ is given unique expression in every celebration of the Mass. It is suggested that in heaven Jesus 'presents His five wounds and pleads the efficacy of the work He accomplished on Calvary; while on earth He continues and applies his Sacrifice in the holy Mass thus remaining a priest for ever.'[10] *The Constitution of the Sacred Liturgy* of Vatican II (1:7) claims that Christ is 'always present in His Church especially in its liturgical celebration . . . Rightly then the liturgy is considered as an exercise of the priestly office of Christ.' But there is no direct support whatever in this epistle for teaching of this kind. Christ's priestly sacrifice cannot in any sense be 'continued'. On the contrary, Hebrews frequently asserts that the sacrificial work of Jesus is essentially unrepeatable and his priestly ministry is certainly not focused in the sacramental life of the church as far as New Testament writers are concerned. The tense and mood of the verb used here in verse 3 preclude any idea of a continual offering. It is an aorist subjunctive. The NEB has a footnote rendering for this verse which conveys the sense perfectly: 'this one too must have *had* something to offer.' The offering has already been made, by the shedding of Christ's blood; the benefits of that offering are available to his people every moment of every day. Christ now ministers as our intercessor. He offers prayer continually to God for all his people. It is clear that the help he offers to us now is that of available pardon and abiding security, vividly illustrated in this passage by the concepts of sacrifice and sanctuary.

[9] A. M. Stibbs, *The Finished Work of Christ* (IVP, 1952). For a full discussion of this subject see 'Excursus III: The Blood of Jesus and His Heavenly Priesthood' in Hughes pp. 329–354.

[10] W. E. Addis and T. Arnold, *A Catholic Dictionary* (London, [17]1960), p. 158.

First, the fact of sacrifice: our priestly minister has procured our forgiveness. Haunted by a sense of remorse and failure, thousands the world over have searched for some assurance of cleansing. Pilate plunged his guilty hands into a basin of water. Lady Macbeth grieved that all the perfumes of Arabia would not eradicate her great sin. The teaching of Hebrews is that such guilt can be banished through Christ and his sacrifice, man's iniquity can be taken away and his sin purged.[11] He 'entered' there for us to 'appear' on our behalf in order 'to put away sin by the sacrifice of himself'. His work complete, he made that heavenly appearance 'once for all at the end of the age'. He inaugurated a completely new age as he offered his own blood.[12] The sacrifice was offered *once* and it was presented *once* by God's Son who appeared in that heavenly sanctuary doing for us then something we were unable to do for ourselves. Believing in that perfect atoning work means that sin's stain is eradicated for ever.

Secondly, the message of the sanctuary: our pardon was obtained on earth, but its continuing effects belong to the secure realm of heaven. The sanctuary concept is yet another rich theological idea. It has profound pastoral implications for our author and immediate practical relevance for us. This eternal sanctuary was designed not by man but by the Lord. It was 'not made with hands . . . not of this creation' (9:11). The key thought here is that our salvation is beyond the reach of that cynical and destructive opponent who taunts us about this aspect or other of our belief. Christ has appeared there for us. It cannot be undone.

Here is a clear word to any Christian in despondency or despair. We may feel crushed, dejected, bewildered or broken, but our eternal salvation has never depended on our vascillating moods or our changing circumstances. Christ has entered the heavenly sanctuary; 'once and for all' he offered his blood for us. There he has appeared for us and now he is praying for us. We are ever remembered at that throne and our names are enrolled in heaven. This is our confidence. Our faith is grounded not in what we are or what we have done, but ever and always in what he is, God's perfect Son, and what he has done through his perfect, eternal sacrifice.

[11] Is. 6:7. [12] Heb. 9:12, 24, 26.

8:6 – 9:14
14. The better covenant

The covenant idea lies at the root of all Jewish religious thought. It was natural for the author of Hebrews to make reference, sooner or later, to this rich theological concept. A little earlier in the letter (7:22) the covenant theme was first introduced when Jesus was described as the 'surety' or 'guarantor' of a better covenant (*diathēkē*). At this point the theme is more carefully developed and thoroughly applied by suggesting three reasons why the new covenant can well be described as better than the old. The writer expounds the better covenant in terms of its promises, its necessity and its effects.

1. Its promises (8:6–13)

6*But as it is, Christ has obtained a ministry which is as much more excellent than the old as the covenant he mediates is better, since it is enacted on better promises.* 7*For if that first covenant had been faultless, there would have been no occasion for a second.*

8*For he finds fault with them when he says:*
'The days will come, says the Lord,
when I will establish a new covenant with the house of Israel
and with the house of Judah;
9*not like the covenant that I made with their fathers*
on the day when I took them by the hand
to lead them out of the land of Egypt;
for they did not continue in my covenant,

and so I paid no heed to them, says the Lord.
10*This is the covenant that I will make with the house of Israel*
after those days, says the Lord:
I will put my laws into their minds,
and write them on their hearts,
and I will be their God,
and they shall be my people.
11*And they shall not teach every one his fellow*
or every one his brother, saying, "Know the Lord,"
for all shall know me,
from the least of them to the greatest.
12*For I will be merciful toward their iniquities,*
and I will remember their sins no more.'
13*In speaking of a new covenant he treats the first as obsolete. And what is becoming obsolete and growing old is ready to vanish away.*

But . . . Christ; the words introduce the prospect of a completely different kind of relationship. Something dramatically new has happened in Jesus. The writer shows that even in Old Testament times the covenant which God made with his people at Sinai was regarded as a purely temporary agreement. In passing, it is important for us to note that there is an earlier covenant of patriarchal times, namely the one made with Abraham which, as Paul vigorously maintains in his letter to the Galatians, is permanent and lasting. This Abrahamic covenant is one of promise and faith, not (as the Mosaic) of law and works. The Abrahamic covenant abides but, from Jeremiah's time onwards, the Jewish people knew that the Mosaic covenant was not permanent, for that prophet promised a new one. Our author quotes Jeremiah's new-covenant passage in full and, not content with that, quotes part of it again in chapter 10. The Mosaic covenant was certainly inadequate and the temporary nature of its purpose is not hidden. Yet our author does not want any Jewish reader of this letter to regard Christianity as a completely new religion; it is an essential realization of the Old Testament promise. The Lord Jesus is the direct and only fulfilment of all the sacrifices and ceremonial and priesthood of the old covenant.

Why is this new covenant necessary? Three reasons are

offered. The old covenant is regarded as imperfect, powerless and obsolete.

a. The old covenant was imperfect

If that first covenant had been faultless, there would have been no occasion for a second. It is important to note that the author does not mean that God's *moral* law has been abolished. Far from it. That law, embodied in the commandments, is still essential and relevant, and demands the obedient response of everyone,[1] whilst an even higher standard is expected of believers.[2] What is meant here is that the old ceremonial laws of Judaism about sacrifices, lustrations and the like, have all been superseded by Christ.

Any first-century Jewish Christian reading this letter would certainly be aware of the striking similarities between Jeremiah's time and his own. Centuries before, this tender-hearted prophet peered into a dark and gloomy future for Judah. The Babylonian armies would certainly come as he predicted, marching through Judean territory and capturing its leading cities. Eventually Jerusalem's strong walls would be broken down and its beautiful temple left a heap of charred ruins.[3] But Jeremiah looked beyond all that to a time of restoration and renewal when a new covenant would be made with the house of Israel. Likewise, first-century Palestinian Judaism had recently encountered a series of horrors quite as terrible as their nation had suffered in the sixth century BC. The Roman armies had fulfilled a role similar to that which the Babylonians had exercised in Jeremiah's day. Jerusalem had been devastated and its temple destroyed. The Jews had been scattered, feeling an acute sense of desolation and despair. On both occasions people were relying on outward things, on their sacrificial system, on the presence of the temple, on the ark of the covenant and cultic regulations.[4] But Jeremiah looked to a time when things would be different. He portrayed a new covenant. The law will not be con-

[1] Mt. 5:17–19; Rom. 7:7–12. See J. R. W. Stott, *Christian Counter-Culture* (IVP, 1978), pp. 70–81.

[2] Mt. 5:20–48. [3] 2 Ki. 25:9–10.

[4] Je. 3:16; 6:20; 7:1–7, 21–23; 9:25.

cerned solely about external features; it will be written on the heart.

b. The old covenant was powerless

A better covenant was necessary because the old covenant could only point the way forward; it could not provide man with the power to meet its requirements. They *did not continue in my covenant.* The old covenant was to give way to something far superior. The old law was but a signpost to direct man; the new covenant supplies the power to make the journey.

c. The old covenant was obsolete

In speaking of a new covenant he treats the first as obsolete. It had been in existence for a long time and served some important divine purposes, but now it is near destruction or is vanishing away. The new covenant which Jeremiah predicted has now come to rich fruition in Christ and his work for us. Five features of Jeremiah's new covenant are worthy of special note. The blessings of the better covenant are conciliatory, inward, universal, generous and assured.

First, it is *conciliatory.* This better covenant is to be made *with the house of Israel and with the house of Judah* (8:8). During the reign of Rehoboam the kingdom, which had been united under Saul, David and Solomon, became divided into two parts, Israel and Judah. They became alienated and estranged. Hughes draws attention to this neglected aspect of Jeremiah's new covenant. Bringing together 'those who had been divided by bitterness and hostility', it symbolized the reconciliation effected under the better covenant by Christ.[5]

Secondly, it is *inward.* Writing this new covenant in our minds and hearts means a great deal more than memorizing it.[6] The old covenant was external. It was engraven on stone tablets. The new is within us; it forms part of our very souls. It was not a new covenant in its promise (*I will be their God*), for the old covenant offered that same intimate relationship.[7]

[5] Eph. 2:14–16; *cf.* Gal. 3:27–29. [6] Dt. 6:6–9.
[7] Ex. 6:7; Lv. 26:12.

It was new in its ability to enable us not only to learn God's instructions but to obey them.

Thirdly, the better covenant is *universal*. In Old Testament times God's people were dependent on a long succession of human teachers, who regarded this covenant message as the exclusive possession of the Jewish people. But under the new covenant this restrictive and possessive hold on the truth would be a thing of the past. *All shall know me, from the least of them to the greatest.*[8]

The new covenant was, fourthly, *generous*. *I will be merciful toward their iniquities.* This new covenant promises the forgiveness of sins. The old covenant did not provide for the forgiveness of *all*, but God's promised pardon is actually written into the terms of the new covenant.

Finally, the better covenant is *assured*. The old covenant was naturally limited, temporary and partial, but the new covenant is unrestricted in its power, eternal in its duration and complete in its effects. God makes definite promises to his people and binds himself in honour to blot out their transgressions. Here are the better promises. The 'I wills' of God rob uncertain, doubting man of his timidity, reticence and fear. God says, '*I will* make this covenant', '*I will* engrave my laws in their hearts', '*I will* be their God', '*I will* manifest myself to them all', '*I will* make myself known to the least as well as the greatest', '*I will* be merciful', '*I will* forget their sins'. All the tentativeness and hesitancy of the earlier days have gone. Man can now be sure: *All shall know me.*

2. Its necessity (9:1–10)

1*Now even the first covenant had regulations for worship and an earthly sanctuary.* 2*For a tent was prepared, the outer one, in which were the lampstand and the table and the bread of the Presence; it is called the Holy Place.* 3*Behind the second curtain stood a tent called the Holy of Holies,* 4*having the golden altar of incense and the ark of the covenant covered on all sides with gold, which contained a golden urn holding the manna, and Aaron's rod that budded, and the tables of the covenant;* 5*above it were the cherubim of glory oversha-*

[8] *Cf.* Jn. 10:16; 11:51–52; Eph. 2:13–18; 1 Jn. 2:2.

dowing the mercy seat. Of these things we cannot now speak in detail.

Although the old covenant is a vanishing shadow, our writer does not dismiss it hastily, casually or unappreciatively. He recognizes something of its former glory, even when he is explaining its partial worth. Westcott observes: 'He seems indeed to linger over the sacred treasures of the past . . . there was, he says, something majestic and attractive in the Mosaic ordinances of worship.' Christians do not doubt that; rather when they acknowledge the beauty and meaning of the law, they understand the gospel better. At the beginning of this chapter, therefore, the writer turns to a description of the tabernacle or earthly sanctuary,[9] concluding his brief account of its furnishings with the tantalizing comment that he cannot stay to discuss these items in any detail. Would he like to have given some enriching typological interpretation of these historical details? We can only guess at what he might have said. Throughout the centuries commentators have provided the author of Hebrews with ideas he might have introduced at this point, though most interpretations reveal more of the expositor's ingenuity than the message of Scripture. Appropriately, at this point, Calvin issues a warning:

> Since nothing is enough for inquisitive men the apostle cuts out any opportunity for subtleties . . . in case too much discussion of these things might break the thread of his argument . . . philosophizing beyond reasonable bounds (as some do) is not only futile but also dangerous . . . we must show discretion and moderation in case we desire to know more than it has pleased God to reveal.

Our writer's passionate desire is to expound the gospel against the background of law, the new covenant in the light of the old, all its incompleteness contrasted with the present secure blessings. He goes on to mention three limitations of the old covenant. A bettter covenant was necessary because the old could offer only restricted access, partial cleansing and limited pardon.

[9] *Cf.* Ex. 25 and 26.

[6]*These preparations having thus been made, the priests go continually into the outer tent, performing their ritual duties;* [7]*but into the second only the high priest goes, and he but once a year, and not without taking blood which he offers for himself and for the errors of the people.* [8]*By this the Holy Spirit indicates that the way into the sanctuary is not yet opened as long as the outer tent is still standing* [9]*(which is symbolic for the present age). According to this arrangement, gifts and sacrifices are offered which cannot perfect the conscience of the worshipper,* [10]*but deal only with food and drink and various ablutions, regulations for the body imposed until the time of reformation.*

a. Restricted access

The information he has given about the structure and furnishings of the tabernacle provides a useful prelude to a description of the annual Day of Atonement. In the course of this festival the high priest went beyond the outer tent, where ordinary priests served, into the Holy of Holies. His admission to this most sacred place was restricted to one day a year when he took blood to sprinkle over the mercy seat in order to atone *for himself and for the errors of the people.* In those days *the way into the sanctuary* was not yet opened for all. The very presence of that outer tent symbolized the restricted way and limited ministry of the old covenant. A heavy curtain kept ordinary priests out of the inner sanctuary. This arrangement would certainly have to be changed to something better if the access was to be made available to all. As long as that division existed between the outer and inner tent, the way was *not yet opened.* It is regarded by our writer as *symbolic for the present age*, 'an illustration for the present time' (NIV). In Christ the way has been opened for all (10:19–20). The era of restricted access is gone for ever.

b. Partial cleansing

But our writer knows that the real barrier between man and God is not merely a physical one. The heavy curtain is symbolic. The problem is not purely external; it is internal, within our hearts and minds. The real trouble is what Bunyan described as 'a wounded conscience'. The old covenant did all it could possibly do. But it could not bring help to man at a point where it was needed most desperately, in his conscience. All the sacrifices and gifts in the world could not ease the most seriously disturbed part of man's inner life. The better covenant offered full and complete inward cleansing.

c. Limited pardon

Under the old covenant man's conscience was certain to be troubled because many sins simply could not be forgiven through the sacrifical system. Even these provisions were effective only for Israel's sins of ignorance; they related only to sins which had been committed unwittingly. No atonement was offered here for transgressions and offences which were of a deliberate nature. Man was seriously troubled by the fact that he had sinned not only inadvertently, through carelessness or ignorance, but consciously and rebelliously. What could the law do about people like us who are, in Forsyth's words, 'not even stray sheep, or wandering prodigals merely; we are rebels taken with weapons in our hands'?[10] Can anything be done for the blameworthy sinner, overwhelmed with remorse, longing for release from the oppression and tyranny of unrelieved guilt?

The reader with a disturbed conscience is likely to find more help in Hebrews than almost anywhere else in Scripture. Here is the message of eternal forgiveness. God promises it (8:8–12). The word of assurance in the new covenant, spoken centuries before the coming of Christ, sounds in our own ears with comfort and hope: 'I will be merciful . . . I will forgive.' God declares it and Christ obtains it. His sacrifice procures the cleansing and release for which we long. Hebrews reminds us repeatedly of the assurance of pardon. God's people enjoy the privilege of undeserved remission and eternal security. Their sins are remembered no more and their names are enrolled in heaven.[11] This is the staggering message of a better hope, of a new covenant and an eternal redemption.

[10] P. T. Forsyth, *Positive Preaching and the Modern Mind* (London, 1949), p. 38.

[11] Heb. 8:12; 12:23.

3. Its effects (9:11–14)

[11]*But when Christ appeared as a high priest of the good things that have come, then through the greater and more perfect tent (not made with hands, that is, not of this creation)* [12]*he entered once for all into the Holy Place, taking not the blood of goats and calves but his own blood, thus securing an eternal redemption.* [13]*For if the sprinkling of defiled persons with the blood of goats and bulls and with the ashes of a heifer sanctifies for the purification of the flesh,* [14]*how much more shall the blood of Christ, who through the eternal Spirit offered himself without blemish to God, purify your conscience from dead works to serve the living God.*

The author now turns from the frustration caused by the limited effectiveness of the ceremonial laws to *the good things that have come*. Christ has entered the eternal sanctuary, *the greater and more perfect tent* in the heavens, taking the blood, not of some sacrificial animal, but his very own. What are the spiritual effects of this new covenant and its better sacrifice offered by Christ himself? This covenant procures our redemption, purifies our conscience and sanctifies our service.

a. It procures our redemption

In this central section of the letter its message is expounded with the aid of another series of vivid contrasts. The old covenant and the new are set side by side in order to bring out the defectiveness of the old and the superiority of the new. The beauty and dignity of the earthly tabernacle are portrayed alongside the glory and majesty of the heavenly sanctuary.[12] That which is merely external is contrasted with that which is internal.[13] That which is only temporary and impermanent, merely operating 'until the time of reformation' in Christ, is forcefully contrasted with that which is lasting and eternal.[14] The blood of involuntary animals is set alongside the voluntary sacrifice of God's Son.[15] The repetitive, incomplete sacrifices are contrasted with the finality of

[12] Heb. 9:1–5; *cf.* 9:24.
[13] Heb. 9:10, 13; *cf.* 9:14.
[14] Heb. 9:9–10; *cf.* 9:12.
[15] Heb. 9:12–14.

Christ's death.[16] Promise is set alongside fulfilment. The annual reminder of man's sin is introduced along with the once-for-all promise of God's will to forget it.[17] The priests who *stood* in God's presence to serve are mentioned along with the eternal priest who *sits* at God's right hand having accomplished our salvation; their incomplete ministry is contrasted with his finished work.

In 9:12 one of these great contrasts is presented with pastoral artistry as well as theological insight. The writer wants to help the man or woman with a troubled conscience. Under the law one could never be sure of forgiveness. The sacrifices had to be repeated, since they could 'never take away sins' in any final sense, but Christ has come to secure for us by his death an eternal redemption (10:11; 9:12). It covers man's immense needs as a sinner, tomorrow's sins as well as those of yesterday. In this moment, by virtue of that sacrificial death, the truly penitent person can be saved immediately and eternally. Throughout the years such people have acknowledged their pardon and security with deep thanksgiving, not in a cocksure form of spiritual arrogance, but with unspeakable gratitude and a sense of unpayable debt:

> Bearing shame and scoffing rude,
> In my place condemned he stood;
> Sealed my pardon with his blood:
> Hallelujah! what a Saviour![18]

The writer's mention of *redemption* recalls the slave market. The word he uses (*lytrōsin*) depicts the release or liberation of the captive. The imagery has a rich Old Testament background.[19] Eternal liberation procured in history and offered now by Christ is the experience of freedom from the penalty and power of inward sin. Its distinctive nature is in danger of being obscured in some contemporary theological interpretations of liberation, which deliberately overlook the radical exposure of human sinfulness vividly portrayed not only in Scripture but on the pages of every daily newspaper throughout the world. Nothing matters for them more than the pre-

[16] Heb. 9:25–26. [17] Heb. 10:3, 17.
[18] P. Bliss, 'Man of Sorrows'.
[19] Lv. 25:48; Nu. 18:16; Ps. 111:9; 130:7.

sent and the need for change. Hugo Assmann from Brazil says he is attracted by the remark of one he describes as a 'committed Christian' who said, 'The Bible? It doesn't exist. The only Bible is the sociological bible of what I see happening here and now as a Christian.'[20] But any theology which ignores or dismisses the primary question of biblical authority is not merely suspect but misleading and dangerous.

Some forms of black theology, motivated by an understandable desire for racial freedom, are a serious distortion of the apostolic gospel as it is clearly expounded in the New Testament. Of course, racial discrimination is wrong, wherever it is found. But one must not react to such offensive oppression by producing 'another gospel'. A leading exponent of black theology, James H. Cone, insists that we 'cannot solve ethical questions of the twentieth century by looking at what Jesus did in the first. Our choices are not the same as his.' He says: 'The idea of heaven is irrelevant for Black Theology. The Christian cannot waste time contemplating the next world (if there is a next).' 'Revolution is not merely a "change of heart" but a radical black encounter with the structure of white racism, with the full intention of destroying its menacing power. I mean confronting white racists and saying: "If it's a fight you want, I am prepared to oblige you." This is what the black revolution means.'[21] All Christians who take the Bible seriously will agree with Cone that the oppression and discrimination which he opposes are evil. But Paul (once an extremely violent zealot) insists that evil can by overcome only by good,[22] not by dismissing Christ's peace-loving example and our eternal hope.

This glance away from Hebrews to some forms of contemporary theological exposition is important. It is clear that such teaching is directly opposite to the main theme of this letter. Here is the unmistakable assertion that in effecting man's redemption by the sufferings of Christ, and by no other way, God did what he knew to be not simply the best solution to the human dilemma, but the only one. The quest

[20] H. Assmann, *Practical Theology of Liberation* (Search Press, 1975), p. 161.

[21] J. H. Cone, *Black Theology and Black Power* (Seabury Press, New York, 1969), pp. 139, 125, 136.

[22] Rom. 12:17–21.

for freedom is right, natural and desirable, but New Testament teaching makes it abundantly evident that man's most serious form of imprisonment is that which, unless overcome, will lead to his eternal separation from the God who gave his only Son for our redemption.

b. It purifies our conscience

Those who had become ceremonially unclean, suffering from some form of defilement and condemned by the law, could, through the provisions of the old covenant, obtain outward cleansing and ceremonial acceptance before God. Those sacrifices certainly achieved *the purification of the flesh*, but *how much more* does the blood of Christ meet man's need. Man needs not ritual cleansing, but a purified, healed and clear conscience. He wants peace with God and peace from God,[23] and the law could not achieve this. The writer of this letter is clearly aware of man's inmost spiritual problems. He has written earlier about the law's inability to ease man's troubled conscience (9:9). Here he is concerned about man's unclean or defiled conscience, which is cleansed by Christ, purified from *dead works*. Our writer rejoices in the fact that man's evil conscience can be 'sprinkled clean' through Christ's work (10:22), not through the sacrificial system (10:2).

In his pre-conversion days, anyone sensitive to the rigorous demands of the law can be in acute mental pain because of his troubled conscience. He calls to God for help, and this epistle, possibly more than anywhere else in the New Testament, gives the answer to his cry. The blood of Christ is God's answer to man's disturbed conscience. He can be cleansed and know he is forgiven. For all its sophisticated ceremonial rites, first-century Judaism knew no experience of freedom and release from the consciousness of sin. Christians who had been converted from a Jewish background could rejoice in a clear conscience through Christ's effective sacrifice.

[23] Rom. 5:1; Col. 1:20.

c. It sanctifies our service

Pathetically mistaken about the things that please God and can bring satisfaction to himself, man has devoted his energies to the pursuit of *dead works*. This may be a reference to ceremonial works; dead, because they are not able to inspire spiritual life; or, as is more likely, works of any kind which belong to the way of corruption and are devoid of true life from God. They probably refer to man's futile attempts to secure by his puny efforts his own present satisfaction and ultimate salvation. But important as this deliverance is, it is but the negative side of Christ's great achievement. The two aspects of this redeeming work, negative and positive, are both important: '*from* dead works *to* serve the living God'. Westcott is right when he comments on this verse:

> Purity is not the end but the means of the new life. The end of the restored fellowship is energetic service to Him Who alone lives and gives life. The thought of performing certain actions is replaced by that of fulfilling a personal relation.

Conclusion

This passage has introduced the reader to some inspiring teaching about the better covenant. That is its dominant theme, but there is also an important sub-stratum of truth here about the Christian life. It reminds us of our many privileges, challenges our spiritual inertia and stirs us to renewed commitment.

a. Christians are attentive learners

The new covenant is written on the Christian's heart and mind. Its transforming knowledge is available to all (8:10–11). From his own study of the Scripture, the writer knew the message of the prophets,[24] as well as the furnishings of the tabernacle and the Day of Atonement ritual, food and

[24] Heb. 8:8–12; *cf.* Je. 31:31–34.

drinks laws, and ceremonial cleansing.[25] Once more we are here reminded that in order to be able to use holy Scripture effectively, we must study it attentively. Bible study is essential not only for our spiritual growth, but for other people's spiritual welfare as well.

b. Christians are sincere penitents

The Lord has no favourites from a privileged class or background. Social circumstances have no bearing whatever on God's grace. It is for all, 'from the least of them to the greatest' (8:11). When our sins and iniquities are confessed, God pledges himself to forget them. We are incapable of making up our minds to forget. If we determine to forget anything, it is only likely to impress the fact more deeply on our memories. But God says, 'I will be merciful toward their iniquities, and I will remember their sins no more' (8:12). God remembers his mercy and forgets our sins. It is the devil who tries to remind us of both our former sins and our present weakness.

c. Christians are submissive servants

Serving the living God is not to be understood as undertaking some occasional duty, or even regular responsibility in Christian work. The word used (*latreuein*) depicts 'the service of a sacred ministry of complete surrender' (Westcott). It is adoring and worshipful service; the same word is found in John's description of the eternal city where 'his servants shall worship him'.[26] It is also grateful service; glad that we are no longer the slaves of sin, we serve God in gratitude. The redeemed of the Lord do not only 'say so',[27] but offer something more than words, important as they are in witness and worship. Gratitude for our redemption must also express itself in willing surrender to God's will and loving devotion to God's work.

[25] Heb. 9:1–10, 13. [26] Rev. 22:3. [27] Ps. 107:2.

9:15–22
15. The eternal legacy

We have already seen in this letter that in his persuasive exposition of the eternal and unrepeatable work of Christ, our author uses a series of vivid word-pictures to impress upon his readers the 'better things' of the gospel. In order to press home his message about the superiority of Christ and the benefits of the new covenant, he employs some forceful illustrations in this section which serve to emphasize these benefits: the first is legal and the others are biblical. The first is drawn from everyday life, the remainder from the pages of Scripture.

1. A legal illustration (9:15–17)

15*Therefore he is the mediator of a new covenant, so that those who are called may receive the promised eternal inheritance, since a death has occurred which redeems them from the transgressions under the first covenant.* 16*For where a will is involved, the death of the one who made it must be established.* 17*For a will takes effect only at death, since it is not in force as long as the one who made it is alive.*

In these verses our writer takes advantage of the double meaning found in an important word he has already used in this letter: *diathēkē*, 'covenant'. This word can also be translated as 'testament', and it is exactly the same word as that used in secular Greek literature to describe a will or a legacy. Some scholars think that the term *diathēkē* should still be translated 'covenant' even in these verses we are discussing, but the reference to the necessary death of the one who makes the *diathēkē* and the word about the *promised eternal inheritance* certainly make the legal illustration of a 'last will and testament' far more appropriate at this point. Moreover, to translate *diathēkē* as 'will' or 'testament' here is far less forced than maintaining the covenant idea in these verses. The author's reference to our inheritance introduces us to the idea of Christ's last will and testament, the legacy he bequeathed through his death by the shedding of his own blood. We can see three aspects of 'bequest' here: the testator who makes the will, the legatee who benefits from the will, and the inheritance which the beneficiary receives on the death of the testator.

a. The gracious benefactor

How does the eternal testator express his generosity to needy man?

First, by *the exercise of his love.* Christ is here described as *the mediator* (*mesitēs*) of a new covenant, an idea we have already met in the previous chapter of the letter where Christ's ministry is described as 'much more excellent' than anything known under the old covenant, 'as the covenant he *mediates* is better' (8:6). The word denotes the activity of an arbitrator, 'one who mediates between two parties to remove a disagreement or reach a common goal'.[1] This title of Christ (*Mesitēs*), so important in this letter,[2] emphasizes the humanly impassable gulf between God and man, and yet at the same time indicates God's merciful compassion and his longing for reconciliation with man. Christ comes as God's *Mesitēs* to bring a righteous God and his aggressively disobedient children together, to break down the huge barriers between God and man, and to open up the way into God's holy presence.

But the *Mesitēs* is also generous in *the gift of his life*. God gave his Son and Jesus gave his all. Jesus effected this reconciliation by the shedding of his blood. In love he gave himself for us on the cross and bore our sins. These verses make the point that until the testator dies the benefits of the will cannot possibly be made available to the legatee. The death of the testator must be established beyond all doubt.

[1] AG, pp. 507–508. [2] Heb. 9:15; 12:24; *cf.* 1 Ti. 2:5.

At many points this letter insists that Christ died and died for us, offering himself for our redemption (9:12, 14).

b. The grateful beneficiary

Man is a pauper before God, unable to meet the demands of a pure and holy God with his own cheap and useless 'righteous' efforts. It is only when we recognize our need, see ourselves as we really are and allow him to remove the flimsy curtain of our moral pretence, that we can be brought to the place where we receive his help.

In his destitution and need, man hears the merciful and generous call of God. It is *those who are called* who receive the inheritance. Those who have responded to this 'heavenly call' (3:1) know only too well that God did not call them as a reward for, or in response to, their special merit, religious devotion or moral achievements. It is all of grace. Moreover, we must remember that in the New Testament the call is something far more than invitation, though the term is used in the gospels to describe an invitation to a wedding reception or a private dinner.[3] It also figures in Greek and New Testament literature as the summons to a law court. In other words, when interpreting the word 'call', the invitation idea perfectly conveys the concept of generosity, but the idea of summons must also be present. It is God who calls and not simply a benevolent host. In responding to such a summons we are brought to the place of pardon and wealth.

c. The generous bequest

The sharers in this heavenly call are here told of the legacy that will come to them. The three words are rich in meaning. It is a promised, eternal inheritance: 'promised' describes its certainty, 'eternal' its quality, and 'inheritance' its content.

Consider first the *certainty* of the inheritance. This generous bequest is *promised.* Here the author is introducing us yet again to one of his favourite words and ideas. Throughout his letter he is at pains to point out that the gift of God's grace through Christ's work does not depend upon anything

[3] Mt. 22:3; Lk. 14:8; Jn. 2:2; 1 Cor. 10:27.

we do, but upon what he says. If it is a *promised* inheritance, then it is as good as ours, because the God who does not lie has declared it on oath (6:17–18), swearing by himself that we shall receive it. In that case, we shall.

What of the *quality* of the inheritance? It is *eternal*, another important word in Hebrews.[4] It cannot waste away or be taken away. It is not exposed to the ravages of time. Hebrews was written to Christians on the verge of persecution and suffering. But, although their opponents rob them of earthly possessions and even physical life, their heavenly inheritance and eternal life were alike imperishable. Their treasures had not been laid up in the banks and repositories of the Roman world, but in the place where Jesus had told them to deposit their true riches, in heaven itself.[5]

And what of the *content* of this bequest? It is God's *inheritance*, promised to and reserved for God's people. The idea of inheritance which appeals most to our author is that of the inherited place which God has prepared, the land of promise. But all the blessings are not reserved for the future. Hebrews also delights in the present inheritance. The 'last days' are here, the new age has begun. In Christ we have entered 'the world to come' and 'the powers of the world to come' are already very much in evidence.[6] This immediate inheritance of believers is specially emphasized here when he refers to our *present* redemption. His death *redeems* man *from the transgressions under the first covenant*. We have already noticed that redemption (*apolytrōsis*) is a slave-market word. Until Christ comes we are slaves to sin, but through his work we are released from this tyrant's captivity so that we are set at liberty, free to serve God as his righteous slaves.[7] These blessings are ours now. The testator has died and once that death has taken place the priceless benefits of that legacy are ours.

2. Two biblical illustrations (9:18–22)

18*Hence even the first covenant was not ratified without blood.* 19*For when every commandment of the law had been declared*

[4] Heb. 5:9; 6:2; 7:24; 9:12, 14–15; 13:20.
[5] Mt. 6:19–21. [6] Heb. 1:2; 2:5; 6:5.
[7] Rom. 6:16, 18, 22: Gal. 3:13; Eph. 1:7; Col. 1:14.

by Moses to all the people, he took the blood of calves and goats, with water and scarlet wool and hyssop, and sprinkled both the book itself and all the people, [20]saying, 'This is the blood of the covenant which God commanded you.' [21]And in the same way he sprinkled with the blood both the tent and all the vessels used in worship. [22]Indeed, under the law almost everything is purified with blood, and without the shedding of blood there is no forgiveness of sins.

The main theme in these verses can be summed up in the words, *not . . . without blood.* The reference to the essential death of the great testator reminds our writer of the way Christ died. His blood was shed.

It is necessary at this stage to comment on the meaning of 'the blood' of Christ, found frequently throughout this letter and elsewhere in the New Testament. It is an unmistakable reference to the sacrificial death of Christ, and needs to be seen (as our author is about to present it) against the background of the Old Testament. There are far more references to the 'blood' of Christ in the New Testament than to the 'cross' or 'death' of Christ. Several modern scholars have followed the late-nineteenth-century interpretation offered by B. F. Westcott, that when the New Testament makes use of this term, it is meant to indicate the release of life. Westcott says that in the biblical idea of sacrifice 'two distinct ideas were included': 'the death of the victim by the shedding of its blood, and the liberation, so to speak, of the principle of life by which it had been animated, so that this life became available for another end'. Westcott goes on to say that 'the Blood of Christ represents Christ's Life.'

Alan Stibbs, however, has shown that in biblical thought blood shed 'stands . . . not for the release of life from the burden of the flesh, but for the bringing to an end of life in the flesh. It is a witness to physical death, not an evidence of spiritual survival'.[8] In this letter to the Hebrews, the phrase

[8] A. M. Stibbs, *The Meaning of the Word 'Blood' in Scripture* (IVP, 1947), p. 12; see also L. Morris, 'The Biblical Use of the Term "Blood"', *Journal of Theological Studies*, 3, 1952, pp. 216–227, for a survey and evidence that in Old Testament usage 'blood' signifies 'life violently taken rather than the continued presence of life available for some new function, in short, death rather than life' (*ibid.*, p. 223).

'resist to the point of shedding your blood' (12:4) plainly means to die rather than compromise. When this letter refers to the 'sprinkling' of the blood of Christ, it means 'the extension to the persons sprinkled of the value and the benefits of the death of which it is the token'. It refers essentially to our 'application of, and the participation in, the saving benefits of the death of Jesus'.[9] The 'shedding' of Christ's blood refers to the once-for-all sacrificial death of Christ; the 'sprinkling' to our benefit from that death. Our writer is at pains to illustrate the necessity of the 'shed' and 'sprinkled' blood at two great moments of Jewish religious history. In this way he drives home his main point that without the shedding of Christ's blood there can be no purification for sinful mankind.

First, in Old Testament times the covenant was *ratified* by blood (9:18). The first covenant given through Moses had to be 'inaugurated' (NEB) by the shedding of blood. At that inauguration the blood was sprinkled over the congregation and thus they became the people of the covenant.[10] Similarly, says our author, blood was sprinkled on the book of the covenant. Both people and book, congregation and covenant, had the mark of the cross upon them. This theme was given special prominence by the Lord Jesus. As he took the cup at the Last Supper, he referred to his forthcoming sacrifice, the outpoured life, as 'the blood of the covenant'; it was to be 'poured out for many for the forgiveness of sins'.[11]

Secondly, the sanctuary was *sanctified* by blood (9:21). That first sanctuary, the desert tent of meeting, used by the Hebrew people during their wilderness journey, had to be cleansed by the sprinkling of blood so that all its furnishings were purified.[12] Under the old covenant nothing was considered as purified unless it had upon it the mark of the shed blood, and our writer sees this as a type or parable of spiritual life. Apart from the sacrificial death of Jesus, the shedding of Christ's blood, there is no forgiveness of sins.

[9] A. M. Stibbs, *The Meaning of the Word 'Blood' in Scripture*, p. 28.
[10] Ex. 24:6–8; 1 Pet. 1:2. [11] Mt. 26:28.
[12] Ex. 24:6; Lv. 8:15, 19; 16:14–16.

Conclusion

Harassed by their opponents and threatened by persecution, these first-century Jewish Christians were in danger of falling away (3:12) or of slipping away (2:1) from the moorings of Christian truth. Under the law they appeared to have had so much. Priests had served as their mediator, the sacrificial system had offered some spiritual security, and as Jews they had believed themselves part of God's chosen people, destined to an assured future. In his pastoral concern our writer emphasizes three assured facts. In Christ we have a forgiveness which covers our past (9:22), a mediator in the present, and an inheritance in the future which no-one can take away (9:15).

These three issues are not confined to the first century; we face them too. In times of crisis and despair our contemporaries suffer from the problem of loneliness. Hemmed in by our circumstances, sickness, bereavement, the breakdown of a marriage, the collapse of business, or the end of a career, we can be terribly lonely. In moments such as these we long for companionship. We cry desperately for the help of almighty God. But if we are not believers how can we approach the holy and righteous God? We need a mediator. Longing for companionship and understanding in our distress and, worst of all, feeling isolated in the presence of a holy God, we too need someone who will go between man and God. It must be one who is not remote but alongside us.

Moreover, modern man is also confronted by the problem of death. This writer shares with his readers a message of serene confidence about the future. The teaching of this epistle not only had great things to say to its first readers; its message has striking relevance in the contemporary world. Verse 15 reminds us that Jesus Christ is the answer to man's problem of guilt, loneliness and death. Our past sin is forgiven: *a death has occurred which redeems.* Our present access is assured: Jesus is *the mediator of a new covenant.* Our future inheritance is imperishable: *those who are called . . . receive the promised eternal inheritance.*

9:23 – 10:18

16. The unique sacrifice

We come now to the last of the five main themes presented by our writer in this important central section of the letter (7:1 – 10:18). After expounding Christ's work as a superior priesthood (7:1–28) in the heavenly sanctuary (8:1–5), he has discussed the inauguration of the better covenant (8:6 – 9:14) and the inheritance which comes to believers through Christ's eternal legacy (9:15–22). He now develops a theme which has been introduced many times in the earlier passages of the letter, that of Christ's perfect sacrifice. He believes that *the offering of the body of Jesus Christ* (10:10) is unique in its purpose, nature, cost and effect.

1. Its divine purpose (9:23–24)

23*Thus it was necessary for the copies of the heavenly things to be purified with these rites, but the heavenly things themselves with better sacrifices than these.* 24*For Christ has entered, not into a sanctuary made with hands, a copy of the true one, but into heaven itself, now to appear in the presence of God on our behalf.*

In the divine intention this sacrifice of Christ has a threefold purpose. The writer here discusses what Christ has purified, where he has entered, and why he has appeared in the presence of God for us.

a. What Christ has purified (9:23)

Our writer has just explained that in Old Testament times the tabernacle furnishings had to be cleansed and consecrated by the sacrificial blood. He reminds us that such sacrifices were merely earthly copies, and the heavenly realities which they represent cannot possibly be cleansed by the blood of animals.

But what does the author mean when he says that *the heavenly things themselves* need *better sacrifices* than those made possible by the offering of calves and goats? William Manson offers a helpful interpretation of this verse when he reminds us that our author is writing to Jewish Christians 'who perhaps missed in the spiritual worship of Christianity the *many* holy sanctions and consecratory rites of the old religion'. This letter assures its readers that 'Christianity has its own sublime, though invisible, sanctions imparted by a greater Sacrifice . . . we can well imagine him saying that the book of the New Covenant (the eternal gospel written in heaven, for the New Testament was not yet in being), the Christian sanctuary (the heavenly Zion, cf. 12:18–24), and the New Israel (the Christian Church, including the company of the redeemed in heaven) have all been consecrated by the blood of Christ. The stamp of the Cross is on all of them.'[1] In other words, the gospel we proclaim is marked by the sprinkled blood of this perfect sacrifice. There is no 'good news' if Christ's saving death is not 'publicly portrayed'[2] before people. When we come before God in prayer, the sanctuary we enter is 'by the blood of Jesus' (10:19) and the community to which we belong is made up of those who have experienced the cleansing of that blood (12:24).

b. Where Christ has entered (9:24a)

Christ has entered . . . into heaven itself. God's redemptive purpose for mankind is complete through this perfect offering. Once each year on the Day of Atonement, devout worshippers waited patiently as the high priest entered the Holy of Holies on their behalf (9:7). Simply to know that the high

[1] Manson, p. 140. [2] Gal. 3:1.

priest had *entered* and was acting for them as well as for himself brought them immense comfort. His work, however, was never complete. But the fact that Christ has entered *into heaven itself* is an indication of his *finished* work. Here is the same truth as that declared in the letter's opening paragraph: 'When he had made purification for sins, he sat down at the right hand of the Majesty on high.' The assurance that our great high priest has 'passed through the heavens' encourages us to believe that by that death his redemptive mission has been brought to a triumphant conclusion. In the moments of his final anguish on the cross, Jesus cried, 'It is finished.' He entered heaven as an outward visible sign that his eternal achievement was finished and complete.

c. *Why Christ has appeared* (9:24b)

'But', one may ask, 'does all this simply belong to the past? How can this fact of history help me now?' The text reminds us that he entered *into heaven itself*. Certainly that is history. But the verse goes on to assert that he entered as part of the divine purpose *now to appear in the presence of God on our behalf*. The idea of the appearance of Jesus is given special prominence in this part of the letter. At the incarnation Christ *appeared* on earth in the presence of mankind to put away sin (9:26). Here we are told that, with his saving work complete, he appeared in heaven in the presence of God, though with man's needs upon his heart. Eventually he will make another appearance at his return, not on that occasion to deal with sin as at the incarnation, but to appear in triumph for 'those who are eagerly waiting for him' (9:28). He has appeared, he now appears and he will appear. As surely as we know, beyond all shadow of doubt, that he has appeared on earth, so, just as certainly, we know that he appears in heaven. He now represents our present needs before God. His sacrifice atoned for our sin. The one who now appears in the eternal sanctuary *on our behalf* is the mediator who has acted for us in the past, the surety for us who guarantees our acceptance in the present, and the pioneer who has gone before us into the future. In his fulfilment of the divine purpose, Christ accomplished by his sacrifice what the sacrifices of the old covenant were never intended to achieve.

Those sacrifices were limited and local. His sacrificial offering was extensive and eternal.

2. Its unrepeatable nature (9:25 – 10:4)

25Nor was it to offer himself repeatedly, as the high priest enters the Holy Place yearly with blood not his own; 26for then he would have had to suffer repeatedly since the foundation of the world. But as it is, he has appeared once for all at the end of the age to put away sin by the sacrifice of himself. 27And just as it is appointed for men to die once, and after that comes judgment, 28so Christ, having been offered once to bear the sins of many, will appear a second time, not to deal with sin but to save those who are eagerly waiting for him.

10:1For since the law has but a shadow of the good things to come instead of the true form of these realities, it can never, by the same sacrifices which are continually offered year after year, make perfect those who draw near. 2Otherwise, would they not have ceased to be offered? If the worshippers had once been cleansed, they would no longer have any consciousness of sin. 3But in these sacrifices there is a reminder of sin year after year. 4For it is impossible that the blood of bulls and goats should take away sins.

When Hebrews describes the work of Christ, it insists, again and again, that it is *once for all* (*hapax*). One of the essential features of the Old Testament sacrificial system was its unfinished nature. Such sacrifices were *continually offered year after year* (10:1). They served as a necessary reminder of man's sin *year after year* (10:3). And in doing just that they performed a most important and necessary function. Whenever the sacrifices were offered, man realized his spiritual need. Although these animal offerings could not fully meet such need, they pointed *inward* by exposing man's sin, and *forward* to a time when adequate provision would be made for man's pardon and reconciliation.

Our writer reminds his readers that such provision has most certainly been made. The period of anticipation is now over and Christ *has appeared*. The high priest had to go into the holy place year after year, but this perfect offering of Jesus is not a repetitive sacrifice. He has appeared *once for all* at the end of the age. This word *hapax* is repeated again in verse 28: 'Christ, having been offered *once* to bear the sins of many'. In the old covenant sacrifices the priest offered animal blood. He went into the sanctuary *with blood not his own*; no priest offered himself. But our great high priest has offered *the sacrifice of himself*. This *once for all* sacrifice of Christ needs no repetition because it is so completely effective; it produces spiritual results of a kind impossible through the offering of animal sacrifices.

By his sacrifice Christ has done two things with our sin. He has put it away and he bears it away. This is first expressed in legal terms (it is annulled) and then in priestly terms (it is carried away as an offering is carried up to the altar).

a. Sin's power is annulled for us (9:26)

Our high priest has *put away sin by the sacrifice of himself*. The word used here, *athetēsin*, 'put away', 'abolish' (NEB), 'do away with' (NIV), literally means that Christ came 'for the disannulling of sin'. It is the same word as that used in 7:18 when our writer says that the law concerning priesthood was 'set aside (*athetēsis*) because of its weakness and uselessness'. In other words, by Christ's death it is not only that the devil is deposed and the power of death overcome, but also that sin is vanquished. Jesus came to rob sin of its tyranny and its suffocating stranglehold on man. Obviously, sin is still at large in the world, just as death and the devil are still active, but all three have been robbed of their former hold on man. In Christ we are free from their enslaving power.

b. Sin's penalty is removed from us (9:28)

Christ died 'to bear' or 'take away' (NIV) our sin. This verb is commonly used in the Septuagint to describe the priest's task in bringing the sacrificial victim and laying it on the altar.[3] The language and ideas used here, therefore, deliberately recall this priestly action, and are used in this sense elsewhere in the epistle.[4] Its New Testament parallel is found in Peter's words that Christ carried our sins up to his cross.[5]

[3] Lv. 14:20. [4] Heb. 7:27; 13:15. [5] 1 Pet. 2:24.

'Christ "carried to the Cross" and there did away with sin and sins' (Westcott). Moreover, in God's redemptive purpose sin has been carried away by Christ in the same way as the Levitical scapegoat bore away the iniquities of the Israelite people into the wilderness. Symbolically the high priest had to lay both his hands on the scapegoat as he confessed the sins of the congregation: 'and he shall put them upon the head of the goat, and send him away.'[6] As was the case for these Hebrew people, our guilt is 'taken away',[7] and our sin is purged.

Surely there is also another picture here, drawn from prophetic literature. Our writer deliberately intends to recall in this verse the famous Servant Song passage from Isaiah where it says that 'he bore the sin of many'. Almost identical phraseology is used here in Hebrews and in Isaiah 53:12. When Christ took our sins to his cross, he took upon himself the penalty and punishment due to us because of them. He 'suffered the "curse" of them . . . which is separation from God: and endured their penal consequences'.[8] All this has already been achieved for us in the unrepeatable sacrifice of Christ at his cross. The tense of the verb 'to bear' (*anenengkein*) implies something done once for all. It is his finished work. We cannot add to it by our works; we can only trust in it by his grace.

In these verses the first and second advents of Christ are united. *He has appeared . . . to put away sin* (9:26). He *will appear . . . to save those who are eagerly waiting for him* (9:28). F. F. Bruce helpfully suggests that even this may have its origin in the priestly background of the writer's argument. 'The Israelites who watched their high priest enter the sanctuary for them waited expectantly for his reappearance; that was a welcome sign that he and the sacrifice which he had presented had been accepted by God . . . So our author thinks of Jesus as going into the heavenly holy of holies, to reappear one day in order to confirm finally to His people the salvation which his perfect offering has procured for them.' Westcott had expressed the same idea by emphasizing that here our writer has pointed out that he 'once for all was offered (9:28);

[6] Lv. 16:21–22. [7] *Cf.* Is. 6:7.

[8] E. G. Selwyn, *The First Epistle of Peter* (London, 1955), p. 180; *cf.* Dt. 21:23; Gal. 3:13.

and in due time, coming forth from the Divine Presence, He will proclaim the consummation of His work'.[9]

Once again the letter emphasizes that nothing of this spiritual magnitude and sense of completion was offered to Jews under the law. Those *who are eagerly waiting for him* know that when he comes *to save* it will be to complete their salvation. No salvation of that kind was available to people under the law; its most faithful adherents knew nothing of the pardon, certainty and peace, which those first-century Christians possessed. The law was but a *shadow* (10:1) and not the true form or image (*eikōn*). These old covenant sacrifices are not only shadows; they are ineffective, they cannot 'make perfect' (*teleiōsai*) or bring to spiritual maturity or completion those who *draw near*. In the teaching of this letter Christ's work is brought to perfection or completion (2:10; 5:8) and this results in the completion of the perfect work of God in the heart and life of the believer. The law 'made nothing perfect'; sacrifices 'cannot perfect the conscience of the worshipper'. But by his sacrifice, Jesus 'has perfected for all time those who are sanctified'.[10]

Our author states that it is *impossible* for the sacrificial blood of animals to effect the total cleansing which man needs (10:4). He here rejects not only the sacrificial system of Old Testament times as an adequate way of cleansing, but clearly, by implication, writes the same judgment, 'impossible', over every other religious system as a means of present forgiveness and eternal salvation. This claim takes us to the heart of a difficult subject, one which demands an appreciation of other people's deeply held religious convictions as well as a concern for their eternal destiny. But the issues cannot be baulked. What does our author have to say to us in contemporary society, surrounded as we are by a multiplicity of competing religious ideas? Topics of this kind cannot now be left to our missionary friends working overseas. Adherents of all the world's main religions are to be found in most western cities. Islam is now reckoned to be the second biggest faith in Britain, as it is also in Europe. The impact of other religions is widespread and, in many cases, effective. How does a Chris-

[9] Westcott, p. 303. [10] Heb. 7:19; 9:9; 10:14.

tian reconcile the uncompromising message of Hebrews with the challenge of other faiths?

It needs to be said that the Christian who wishes to witness to adherents of other religions will become, first of all, a careful listener. He will not rush in, hastily judging and condemning the treasured views of others. He will seek to understand and respect the convictions of someone he genuinely desires to befriend and not simply to convert. Love will demand that he listens so that the doctrines held by his Jewish, Muslim, Buddhist, Hindu or Sikh neighbour are not grossly misunderstood and misinterpreted.

Secondly, the believer will want to go on to commend whatever he recognizes as good in the religion of his friend. It will hardly compromise the distinctive qualities of Christianity if we acknowledge the positive qualities to be found in other faiths. For example, as R. W. F. Wootton has reminded us, we 'may well find much to admire in the Hindu's reverence for life and search for peace, in the Buddhist's longing for enlightenment and moral excellence and in the Sikh's practical goodness to those in need, and be challenged in our own faith and practice thereby'.[11] We have noted that the author of Hebrews writes appreciatively about Judaism even though he cannot recognize it as *the* way of salvation. Its laws expose our sin (10:2–3), its history illustrates our dangers (chapters 3–4) and its heroes exemplify our faith (chapter 11).

Thirdly, it may be possible for the dialogue to focus initially on man's basic problems of guilt, fear, loneliness, moral failure, meaninglessness, insecurity and the like. Other religions may represent 'a variety of human attempts to explain the phenomena of life, to reach out after ultimate reality and to construct some system of thought . . . which will satisfy man's needs'.[12] With some kind of common ground in the basic needs of humanity the Christian may attempt to build bridges much in the same way as the apostle Paul did at Mars Hill, starting with the literary heritage and vague beliefs of his Greek neighbours, before going on to mention their frustrations and then God's distinctive revelation in Christ.[13]

[11] P. Sookhdeo (editor), *Jesus Christ The Only Way* (Paternoster, 1978), p. 74; see also P. Sookhdeo, *Asians in Britain* (Paternoster, 1977).
[12] J. N. D. Anderson (editor), *The World's Religions* (IVP, 1975), p. 232.
[13] Acts 17:16–31.

Although the Christian believer will not *rush* insensitively to the distinctive doctrines of his faith, he will not be ashamed to declare them, though always in the spirit of love and genuine concern. He has no need to be embarrassed about the uncompromising nature of his faith. Other religions, with the possible exception of Buddhism, are just as definite and dogmatic. But we will surely recognize that in presenting our gospel it may be necessary for us to reserve certain truths until our friend is in a position to receive them. Discharging a salvo of 'proof-texts' will only cause our unconverted friend to take up defensive positions. He needs to be understood, loved and helped.

Ultimately, however, we will come to the uniqueness of Christ and this letter is, at this point, important authority for Christian faith and practice. We shall be compelled in the end to confess, graciously but firmly, that eternal life cannot be found outside Christ. It is, to use our author's word, *impossible* for the blood of bulls and goats to take away sins and it is just as impossible for man to achieve his salvation by the five pillars of Islam, or by Hindu resolutions of renunciation, or by Buddhist ethics, or by Sikhism's patterns of self-salvation. The passage we have considered forcefully underlines man's desperate spiritual need. His sin must be 'put away'. Christ 'has appeared' on earth, God's Son, to effect that saving miracle *by the sacrifice of himself*. It cannot possibly be that though his death was necessary for the salvation of some, most could equally attain it by other means. Our author is convinced that such a view is *impossible*. Man is not only needy; he is condemned (9:28). Christ will appear a second time, not then as the incarnate redeemer but as eternal judge. By that 'single sacrifice for sins' (10:12) men and women can be saved immediately and for ever. The religious pluralism of contemporary society, with its competitive ideas of salvation, must not be allowed to obscure the distinctiveness and assurance of the Christian gospel. New life for all is in Christ alone but, as our writer is about to show, it was procured at the greatest price.

3. Its immense cost (10:5–10)

5*Consequently, when Christ came into the world, he said,*
'Sacrifices and offerings thou hast not desired,
but a body hast thou prepared for me;
6*in burnt offerings and sin offerings thou hast taken no pleasure.*
7*Then I said, "Lo, I have come to do thy will, O God,"*
as it is written of me in the roll of the book.'
8*When he said above, 'Thou hast neither desired nor taken*
pleasure in sacrifices and offerings and burnt offerings and sin
offerings' (these are offered according to the law), 9*then he*
added, 'Lo, I have come to do thy will.' He abolishes the first
in order to establish the second. 10*And by that will we have*
been sanctified through the offering of the body of Jesus Christ
once for all.

In these chapters the new covenant is proved from prophecy and the quotation from Jeremiah 31 is repeated to bring this main central section to a close (10:16–17). At this point, however, our writer turns from prophecy to psalmody and in a moving passage puts the eloquent words of Psalm 40 into the mouth of the Lord Jesus at his incarnation. The words of Jeremiah 31 expound the better covenant; the words of Psalm 40 explain the better sacrifice. The verses here record a conversation of great beauty. Jesus is addressing the Father. He is saying that God does not now require the repetitive and impersonal sacrifices of the old covenant. God took far greater pleasure in the surrendered life of one eager to do his will. Once again the writer is using Old Testament Scripture, honoured by Jews and Christians alike, as a proof that something far better has taken place by Christ's sacrifice than could have been accomplished by *sacrifices and offerings and burnt offerings and sin offerings*.

But whatever does this Psalm mean when it says that these sacrifices were neither desired by (10:5) nor pleasing to God (10:8)? Surely God instigated the sacrificial system of the Old Testament? Undoubtedly what is meant here is the same kind of thing as is proclaimed most eloquently by a number of Old Testament prophets. Jeremiah, for example, said that in the day when the Hebrew people were brought out of Egypt,

God did not give instruction about sacrifices until he had first issued this prior command: 'Obey my voice.' In other words, sacrifice is no substitute for obedience. No offering is acceptable to God if it is not an expression of loving devotion.[14] He cannot be bought by gifts. He looks for covenant love, righteous behaviour and a contrite heart.[15] As Westcott puts it: 'In themselves . . . the sacrifices gave no pleasure to God. Their value was in what they represented.'

In quoting Psalm 40 our writer has followed his usual custom of citing the Septuagint version, where there is a variant reading. It does not translate the Hebrew of Psalm 40:6 as 'thou hast given me an open ear', but as 'a body didst thou prepare for me'. Some expositors have seen in the 'open ear' of Psalm 40:6 a reference to the boring of the slave's ear in Exodus 21:6 and Deuteronomy 15:17, a symbol of willing obedience on the part of a servant who, because he loves his master, does not want to be released from his service. Whether it has this background or not, the 'open ear' and the 'surrendered body' amount to the same. Christ has opened his ear to God's word and surrendered his body for God's work. It was his constant desire to fulfil in deed what had been written of him in the word. The 'book roll' was the scroll of the law. Christ knew that this law perfectly recorded God's appointed purpose for his life and he was determined to bring it all to completion. Such fulfilment was possible only through obedience. He surrendered his body for God's saving plan. Christ came to do God's will and *by that will we have been sanctified.* Once again our writer is leading us to Gethsemane ('Not my will, but thine') and underlining the immense cost of our sanctification. That pure and spotless body (7:26) was offered for us *once for all.* Yet again that affirmation (*ephapax*) comes dramatically at the end of the sentence to give it special emphasis. Moreover, *once for all* may refer here not only to the sacrifice which has been offered, but the sanctification it has effected. Something more is achieved by Christ's death than the removal of guilt. *We have been sanctified.* And the verb is in the *perfect* tense. It is actually done. Our sanctification is perfectly accomplished by Christ for all time.

[14] Je. 7:21–23; 1 Sa. 15:22; Ho. 6:6.
[15] Mi. 6:6–8; Is. 1:10–20; Ps. 51:16–17.

4. Its sanctifying effect (10:11–18)

Earlier in the letter we have noticed that, whilst Paul wants the world to know how man can be *right with God*, our author thinks about how man can be *clean before God*. These ideas of purification and sanctification have their background in the Old Testament tabernacle and temple, so important in this letter. In Jewish faith certain things, people and days were *hēgiasmenoi*, purified, not just so that they would be clean, but 'clean for God's use', 'set apart' as 'holy' and for his work alone. In these verses we are reminded that our sanctification has been achieved by Christ's work and is attested by the Spirit's word.

a. Christ's finished work (10:11–14)

11*And every priest stands daily at his service, offering repeatedly the same sacrifices, which can never take away sins.* 12*But when Christ had offered for all time a single sacrifice for sins, he sat down at the right hand of God,* 13*then to wait until his enemies should be made a stool for his feet.* 14*For by a single offering he has perfected for all time those who are sanctified.*

In the concluding sentences of this main doctrinal section we are confronted again with these arresting contrast-pictures which have formed the main substance of the writer's argument throughout the letter. The priests of the old covenant stood (10:11) in God's presence, their task unfinished. But Christ is seated, his work complete (10:12). They presented their sacrifices repeatedly. He offered a single sacrifice, effective *for all time*. The priestly sacrifices could *never take away sins*, but his offering was *for sins* and for our sanctification. A few verses earlier our sanctification was presented as an accomplished fact, 'we have been sanctified' (10:10). Here (10:14 and in 2:11) sanctification is portrayed as a continuing process, '. . . by one sacrifice he has made perfect for ever those who are *being made holy*' (NIV).

But apparently there are those who will not take advantage of this sanctifying work. Instead of becoming his purified worshippers whose sins have been taken away, they choose to be his resistant *enemies*. Possibly this repeated allusion to

Psalm 110:1 (*cf.* 8:1) has been introduced here to remind the readers that not all are Christ's friends. It may be anticipating a serious passage later in this chapter (10:26ff.). Such apostates will discover how fearful a thing it is to fall into the hands of the living God (10:29–31).

b. The Spirit's reiterated word (10:15–18)

15*And the Holy Spirit also bears witness to us; for after saying,*
16*'This is the covenant that I will make with them*
after those days, says the Lord:
I will put my laws on their hearts,
and write them on their minds,'
17*then he adds,*
'I will remember their sins and their misdeeds no more.'
18*Where there is forgiveness of these, there is no longer any offering for sin.*

It is not simply that God has spoken in the past. As we turn to this word the Holy Spirit *bears witness to us* in the present. Once again he uses Jeremiah's new-covenant passage.[16] In chapter 8 he quoted it in expounding the essentially new things which have been accomplished by Christ. Here it amplifies the theme that it is not only new but perfect. The heart of this new relationship is focused on what we choose to remember (10:15–16) and what God chooses to forget (10:17).

We know that if this continuing process of sanctification is to be a reality in our lives, we shall need the Holy Spirit's constant reminder (10:15) of that indwelling word which is written in our minds. In Old Testament times the word of the law was external, written on tablets of stone, but God's new Israel treasure it in their hearts. The Spirit not only tells us what to do, but provides the strength to do it.[17]

The greatest message this word conveys to us is the assurance of forgiveness: *I will remember their sins and their misdeeds no more.* The writer has reached the end of his argument about the superiority of Christ's person and work. If, in Christ, we have a forgiveness of this range, certainty and efficacy, there is no need whatever for the continuation of the

[16] Je. 31:31–34. [17] Acts 1:8; Eph. 3:16.

former sacrificial system. The sacrifices are not merely superfluous; they depreciate and disparage the only sacrifice acceptable to God and effective amongst men.

Conclusion

In this passage the reader has been reminded of three things of practical importance in our daily Christian living: God's holiness, man's accountability and Christ's return.

a. God's holiness

We need this reminder in case we become morally careless. The function of the law in Old Testament times was to remind God's people of the sinfulness of sin.[18] The Day of Atonement was an annual reminder of man's need of cleansing. The law and its sacrifices exposed sin and showed people how desperately they needed forgiveness. Under the new covenant, the one offering of Christ similarly reminds man that he is a helpless sinner. But this sacrifice does not merely expose the nature of sin; it effects the removal of sin. In an age when moral standards are declining rapidly and ethical values are constantly exposed to ruthless scrutiny, the Christian needs continually to recall the immensity of his salvation. In the course of his daily devotional life he should turn his eyes to Calvary and visit the empty tomb. He should say: 'My sin took him there and that is where he was condemned for me. By that death I am not only cleansed but consecrated. I am set apart for God's service in the opportunity of this day, for Christ's glory and for the blessing of others.'

This kind of deliberate mental recollection is an essential part of our progressive sanctification. Without it the Christian may hardly notice that the world around him has so squeezed him into its own mould[19] that his standards and values are no longer distinctively Christian at all.

[18] Rom. 7:13. [19] Rom. 12:2 JBP.

b. Man's accountability

We need this reminder in case we become absorbed with material things. *After that comes judgment.* The judgment theme emerges time and again in the letter, bringing its own sense of urgency and seriousness.[20] In contemporary society all the emphasis is on the profits and pleasures of today. The prevailing attitude is that of the prosperous farmer in Christ's parable: 'You have ample goods laid up for may years; take your ease, eat, drink, be merry.' But God called that farmer a fool,[21] and Jesus reminded his hearers that to be saved we must prefer the riches of the next world to the treasures of this one. The Christian seeks constantly to sharpen the focus of this eternal perspective. He knows that a day is coming when everyone's work will be exposed.[22] In determining any course of action in life he pursues not merely things which gratify man, but those which glorify God.[23]

c. Christ's return

We need this reminder in case we become spiritually despondent. This passage assures us that Christ *will appear a second time . . . to save those who are eagerly waiting for him.* So often materialistic man seems to prosper. He not only shrugs his shoulders and demonstrates his apathy about spiritual things; sometimes he sets himself against Christ and the people of God. Believers remember that Christ is coming back. They do not allow themselves to become crushed and defeated. They know that one day it will all be different. The message of Christ's return delivers them from desperation and fills their minds with buoyant confidence.

[20] Heb. 10:27, 30–31; 12:14, 23, 25; 13:17.
[21] Lk. 12:19–20.
[22] 1 Cor. 3:12–15; 2 Cor. 5:8–10.
[23] Mt. 5:16; Col. 1:10; 1 Thes. 4:1.

PART III
OUR RESPONSE

10:19–39
17. A call to steadfast hope

'Therefore, brethren . . .' In these words, at the beginning of this new section, we are immediately reminded of our author's main purpose in sending this letter. It is a 'word of exhortation' (13:22) written out of a deep sense of pastoral concern. He knows only too well that his exposition of these impressive themes in the earlier chapters is not likely to achieve a great deal if it is to remain unrelated to their everyday lives. Without exception, all the New Testament writers link doctrine with deeds. In this they were following the example of the great Old Testament prophets who insisted on relating the great themes of Old Testament faith to the lives of men and women, kings and nations, pressing home the social, economic and political implications and obligations of their faith. Jesus himself, the greatest of all prophets, insisted on consistent behaviour as well as correct teaching. What is the use of acknowledging his lordship with our lips if it is not evident in our lives?[1]

From this point on, the writer builds on the rich doctrinal teaching of the earlier chapters, pressing it home by exhortation, encouragement, illustration and warning. So much has been done for his readers and is available to them, but in order to receive and appropriate these blessings they must enter in (10:19–22), hold fast (10:23–25), keep near (10:26–35) and press on (10:36–39).

[1] Lk. 6:46–49.

1. Enter in (10:19–22)

[19]Therefore, brethren, since we have confidence to enter the sanctuary by the blood of Jesus, [20]by the new and living way which he opened for us through the curtain, that is, through his flesh, [21]and since we have a great priest over the house of God, [22]let us draw near with a true heart in full assurance of faith, with our hearts sprinkled clean from an evil conscience and our bodies washed with pure water.

Our author has laid a secure doctrinal foundation in the minds of his readers. If Jesus is our high priest, then we must follow his steps into the holy place. By his life on earth he left us an inspiring example: he prayed, and we must copy him. Now he lives in heaven; he still prays (7:25), and we must join him. These verses explain how we must enter the holy place of prayer. It must be with confidence, gratitude and sincerity.

a. Enter with confidence (10:19)

Through Christ's work we have *confidence* or boldness[2] and this enables us to draw near 'in full assurance of faith' (10:22). Even in this practical section of the letter our writer continues to hint at the difference between the old covenant and the new. Our approach to God is confident and joyous; theirs was tentative and fearful. We are urged always to 'draw near'; they were frequently exhorted to keep their distance (12:20). Only the appointed high priest could enter 'the holiest of all' and even then only on one day a year; here *all* Christians (*brethren*) are urged to come in any moment of trial (4:16). If, however, they are to receive their necessary spiritual resources, they must come with 'full assurance of faith' or 'faith which has reached its mature vigour' (Westcott on 10:22). Faith can become strong and resilient, able to cope with the hazards and adversities of life, only if it is nurtured and nourished on the word of God; our faith is in the one who is faithful, who has made and keeps his promises (10:23).

[2] Heb. 3:6; 4:16; Eph. 3:12.

b. Enter with gratitude (10:20–21)

The cost of 'entering' has been repeatedly emphasized in the foregoing chapters, and it is not overlooked here. Christians need constantly to be reminded of the blood he shed, the way he opened and the work he does. These three aspects of his redemptive work should inspire our gratitude and ensure that the first words we utter whenever we 'enter the sanctuary' are those of adoration, worship and thanksgiving.

This way into the sanctuary is *new* because it was not as accessible to the ordinary worshipper until Christ came. It is *living* because, although he died, he is alive for ever (7:25). The way was opened *through the curtain* of *his flesh*. Just as the heavy temple curtain was torn from top to bottom on that first Good Friday,[3] so that pure and spotless body of Christ was rent for us. He shed his blood that the approach to God might not be barred as in earlier centuries, but open to all; through Christ's death the way is no longer obscured, but visible.

Moreover, Christians are grateful not only for what he has done, but for what he continues to do. He serves them now and ministers to their needs. At this moment he intercedes as *a great priest over the house of God*. Believers are accepted in him, helped by him and belong to him; *the house of God* recalls an earlier passage about the Christian community (3:1–6).

c. Enter with sincerity (10:22)

In Old Testament times the serving priest had to wash himself thoroughly and only then could he enter the holy place.[4] When Christian believers come into God's presence it is with a sense of concern not about external washing, but about heart purity. They must come with a *true* or sincere heart; it must be 'whole-hearted' (Moffatt) and not mechanical. The phrase *our bodies washed with pure water* is probably a reference to Christian baptism. It may well be a gentle though direct tilt at those Jews, and possibly Jewish Christians, who continued to place some reliance on continuing ceremonial

[3] Mk. 15:38. [4] Lv. 16:4; Ex. 29:4.

ablutions. Our writer may be insisting that Christians do not place their confidence in external ritual of that kind (9:10), but in a confession of Christ made once in the past at baptism (see 'confession' in the next verse) and in the continuous inward purification made possible and available by Christ's eternal sacrifice.

2. Hold fast (10:23–25)

[23]*Let us hold fast the confession of our hope without wavering, for he who promised is faithful;* [24]*and let us consider how to stir up one another to love and good works,* [25]*not neglecting to meet together, as is the habit of some, but encouraging one another, and all the more as you see the Day drawing near.*

Three closely related themes emerge here, each of which has already been mentioned in one form or another earlier in the letter.

a. Personal confession (10:23)

Once again, as earlier, the readers are exhorted to hold on resolutely to their initial confession of faith in Christ. This is a call not only to perseverance, but also to witness. In a society like ours where Christ is not loved or his standards honoured, where God's word is widely ignored and the Christian faith often dismissed as either incredible or unattractive, believers must 'be firm and unswerving' (NEB) in the confession of their hope.

b. Mutual encouragement (10:24–25a)

Since in the teaching of this letter Christians are brothers in the same family,[5] partners in the same enterprise[6] and members of the same household,[7] they have a responsibility not only to 'hold fast' themselves, but also to encourage their fellow believers to do the same. John Wesley often reminded the early Methodist people of the words of a friend: 'The

[5] Heb. 3:1; 13:1, 22. [6] Heb. 3:14.
[7] Heb. 3:6; 10:21; 1 Tim. 3:15; 1 Pet. 2:5.

Bible knows nothing of solitary religion.' In the teaching of this passage, the exhortation is not simply to the exercise of fellowship, but to the stimulation of compassionate activity in the work of Christ. Many early nonconformist congregations included these words in the covenant which members were required to sign on joining the local church: 'We engage to watch over one another in love.'

But is this an impossible ideal in the twentieth century? Aware of the selfish and materialistic pressures of contemporary society, and convinced of the need for a more distinctively Christian life-style, some believers have turned from the institutional churches to communities. The 'Jesus People' movement of the late sixties, the charismatic movement and the 1974 Lausanne call to 'radical discipleship' have all contributed to the popularization of community living. Derek Tidball[8] has shown that, although the biblical arguments for this type of communal life-style may not, on careful examination, be specially convincing, the practical reasons for this quest need to be considered. He observes that enthusiasts for communities focus their pragmatic arguments on the issues of resources and relationships. First, there is a financial asset, the saving of costs – no mean contribution in a materialistic age especially if the surplus money is then released for the crying needs of others. In addition, however, there is the spiritual and emotional asset. It is claimed that the community meets an immediate human need, the longing for fellowship, clearly recognized by the writer of Hebrews at this point in the letter.

Such thinking must surely challenge the contemporary church which can be just as materialistic and selfishly preoccupied as secular society. It is because some people have not found within our churches the warmth, care and concern for which they hoped that they have turned away from the organized or institutional churches to religious communities and house churches, some of them vibrant with a more intimate commitment to fellowship and caring. Despite the danger of authoritarian leadership tendencies, and the insularity and lack of evangelistic outreach in some of these groups, their supportive compassion surely challenges the churches to

[8] *Vox Evangelica*, 11, 1979, pp. 65–80.

a radical re-examination of their priorities and a willingness to change any activity if it fails to encourage the life of God's people as a loving, caring and serving fellowship.

At this point it is important to emphasize that the writer of Hebrews would hardly have encouraged separatist splinter-groups of any kind. We have noted earlier that some scholars believe the letter may well have been addressed to a group of believers in danger of isolating themselves from their fellow Christians in the local church. Its teaching reminds us that the church's defects present us with an opportunity for earnest prayer, careful thought, loving discussion and united action to correct the deficiencies and not run away from them. Calvin's observation on these verses is as important now as in the sixteenth century: 'There is so much peevishness in almost everyone that individuals, if they could, would gladly make their own churches for themselves . . . This warning is therefore more than needed by all of us that we should be encouraged to love rather than hate and that we should not separate ourselves from those . . . who are joined to us by a common faith.'

c. *Spiritual incentive* (10:25b)

Believers must engage vigorously in this ministry of encouragement, because their opportunities are at the same time both immense and limited. At present there are many avenues of service, but the *Day* is *drawing near* when we can no longer witness and serve in this way. When the Day is here rather than near, we shall all wish we had done so much more. In the light of Christ's return the writer issues the positive and negative injunction: believers must stir each other up and not absent themselves from the Christian meeting.

3. Keep near (10:26–35)

This passage reaches its climax in the writer's earnest appeal: *Do not throw away your confidence*. He has urged them to draw near, but he fears that some have gone away (10:26). He has two ways of recalling them all to vigorous and persistent faith. They must remember those who have fallen and those who have endured.

a. A warning – remember those who fell (10:26–31)

[26]*For if we sin deliberately after receiving the knowledge of the truth, there no longer remains a sacrifice for sins,* [27]*but a fearful prospect of judgment, and a fury of fire which will consume the adversaries.* [28]*A man who has violated the law of Moses dies without mercy at the testimony of two or three witnesses.* [29]*How much worse punishment do you think will be deserved by the man who has spurned the Son of God, and profaned the blood of the covenant by which he was sanctified, and outraged the Spirit of grace?* [30]*For we know him who said, 'Vengeance is mine, I will repay.' And again, 'The Lord will judge his people.'* [31]*It is a fearful thing to fall into the hands of the living God.*

Some professing Christians, known to the writer and readers of this letter, either had not been given or had not responded to the encouragement of their fellow believers. They began by drifting away from the moorings of truth (2:1), then they neglected to 'meet together' (10:25); gradually they had been lured on from spasmodic doubt to a persistent apostasy which expressed itself not only in unbelief, but in violent opposition to Christ and his people. Calvin points out here that in this passage we are not dealing with either the weak backslider or the penitent offender:

> The apostle describes as sinners not those who fall in any kind of way but those who forsake the Church and separate themselves from Christ . . . there is a great difference between individual lapses and a universal desertion of this kind . . . He says that there is no offering left for those who reject the death of Christ because such rejection does not come from some particular offence, but from a total rejection of faith.

These apostates have swept aside the eternal blessings of the triune God.

They have rejected God's truth (10:26–28). Whereas at one time they received the word eagerly and obeyed it instantly, they now go against its teaching, and *sin deliberately. Truth* is obviously the message of salvation which had been preached to them (2:3–4). The reference is probably to those Jews who had in earlier days made an open profession of faith in Christ but had not held it 'firm to the end' (3:14). Possibly under the pressures described a few verses later (10:32–34), they had abandoned their Christian faith and slipped back into Judaism. In the latter half of the first century the gulf between Jews and Christians began seriously to widen. In the beginning many devout Jews, including priests, were brought to personal faith in Jesus as Messiah and Saviour.[9] Then, religious rulers in general,[10] and Saul of Tarsus in particular,[11] brought fierce opposition against the church. Once converted, Paul used the synagogue as a base for his evangelistic work[12] but, overcome with jealousy, the Jewish leaders began to revile Paul and he was cast out of their synagogue and cities.[13] Problems soon arose in his newly established churches. Some Jews, who had acknowledged the Messiahship of Jesus, were teaching Christians that, although under grace, they were not free to dispense with the ceremonial law of Judaism.[14] The letters to the seven churches, written by John from Patmos, show that later, in some parts of Asia Minor, Jews were actively persecuting Christians.[15] When Hebrews was written, the clash of loyalties was already evident, and some Christians had returned to their Jewish ceremonies and others to reliance on 'dead works' (9:14). Under the old covenant the apostate was doomed to physical death (10:28),[16] but under the new those who reject its truth thereby choose a worse punishment, eternal death (10:27, 29).

They have spurned God's Son (10:29a). These apostates once acknowledged Christ's deity and trusted his work. They no longer believe him to be *the Son of God* and they actually profane the precious blood which he shed for them. If they have rejected Christ's sacrifice, there is no other offering which can avail and atone for their sin and rebellion. The word translated *profaned* clearly denotes the sustained rejection and violent antagonism of these apostates. It means that they trample the things of Christ beneath their feet. The same word occurs twice in the teaching of Jesus describing the

[9] Acts 6:7. [10] Acts 6:9–14; 7:54.
[11] Acts 8:1–3; 9:1–2. [12] Acts 13:14–44; 14:1; 17:1–4, 10–12.
[13] Acts 13:45, 50; 17:5, 13; 18:6–8. [14] Gal 3:1–5; 5:1–7; Phil. 3:2–9.
[15] Rev. 2:9–10; 3:9–10. [16] Dt. 17:2–6.

tasteless salt which is 'trodden under foot', and the pearls which swine 'trample . . . under foot' as useless things. This is how these apostates have come to regard Christ Jesus, the priceless treasure of his people.[17]

They have despised God's Spirit (10:29b). The Holy Spirit is here described as *the Spirit of grace* for, as Calvin observes, it is through his ministry alone that 'we receive the grace that is offered in Christ'. The word here translated *outraged* indicates the deepest kind of personal insult. God's gracious Spirit has in some cases met with a contemptuous reaction. He comes to the sinner in grace, but his merciful love is not always welcomed. Those who insult him are self-condemned and, denying the only way of forgiveness, make pardon impossible.[18] Such people ignore the teaching of Scripture, its warnings (10:30)[19] and appeals (3:7–13). Instead of penitently falling into the arms of the God who is their lover,[20] they choose to fall into the hands of a God who becomes their judge (10:31; 12:23).

b. An encouragement – remember those who endured (10:32–35)

[32]But recall the former days when, after you were enlightened, you endured a hard struggle with sufferings, [33]sometimes being publicly exposed to abuse and affliction, and sometimes being partners with those so treated. [34]For you had compassion on the prisoners, and you joyfully accepted the plundering of your property, since you knew that you yourselves had a better possession and an abiding one. [35]Therefore do not throw away your confidence, which has a great reward.

Our writer is far too gifted and devoted a pastor to concentrate for too long on negative, though necessary, warnings. His earlier warnings are always followed by compassionate encouragement and he does the same here. He invites his readers to look not only at the impenitent opposition of others, but also at their own firm reliance and perseverance. Fierce persecution had hit their community some time past when their faith in Christ was young and immature, just after

[17] Mt. 5:13; 7:6.
[18] Mk. 3:28–30.
[19] Dt. 32:35–36.
[20] Dt. 33:27; Lk. 15:20.

their conversion and baptism (10:32 *enlightened*). Even their homes were invaded by vandals and robbers, determined to expose them to every possible discomfort and insult. Yet in all these cruel circumstances they had certainly held fast to their confession 'without wavering' (10:23). Only good had come out of their troubles. What had been gained in the earlier persecution?

It had deepened their fellowship. Even if they had not suffered personally themselves, they had become *partners with those so treated*. The word *partners* is a familiar one (*koinōnoi*). Those who share by partnership with Christ in his sufferings also share inevitably and gladly in the sufferings of Christ's people. Such people will also be *partners* in Christ's coming glory.[21]

It had increased their compassion. During these troubles some appear to have been thrust into prisons, but fellow Christians, as their partners, pitied and cared for them (10:34), though it may well have been dangerous to identify themselves so openly with the trouble-makers. Prison visiting, as an act of practical Christian compassion, is mentioned later in this letter (13:3), once again in the context of partnership in suffering.

It had demonstrated their resilience. They *joyfully accepted* this plundering, looting and violence (10:34). No unbeliever could possibly have responded in that way to such dire trouble. A non-Christian may tolerate his troubles, but he cannot rejoice in them. Only Christ can enable a believer to do that. Jesus taught his followers to rejoice when persecution comes: 'Blessed are you when men revile you . . . rejoice and be glad.'[22]

It had sharpened their priorities. When bands of marauders broke into their homes, these persecuted Christians soon realized that the thieves could not steal the things which were of the greatest value to them. That is why they were joyful. They believed the word of Jesus that their reward was great in heaven. Such treasure[23] was *a great reward*. They must not *throw* away *confidence* of that kind as though it were useless. Our writer urges his readers to remember the lasting things.

[21] 2 Cor. 1:7; Phil. 3:10; 1 Pet. 5:1. In all these verses the same Greek word recurs.

[22] Mt. 5:11–12. [23] Mt. 6:20; 19:21.

Christians need to remember that adversity is rarely a vicious enemy; it is often a valuable ally. It reminds us of the imperishable things which matter most of all.

4. Press on (10:36–39)

36*For you have need of endurance, so that you may do the will of God and receive what is promised.*
37*'For yet a little while,*
and the coming one shall come and shall not tarry;
38*but my righteous one shall live by faith,*
and if he shrinks back,
my soul has no pleasure in him.'
39*But we are not of those who shrink back and are destroyed, but of those who have faith and keep their souls.*

In view of these former trials, present apostasy and future uncertainty, these believers have need of *endurance*. Moffatt translates this, 'steady patience is what you need'. This was no time for giving up (10:35), shrinking back (10:38–39) and dropping out like discouraged pilgrims or exhausted athletes (12:3). If these Christians will persistently pursue the *will of God* for their lives they will eventually receive *what is promised*. Once again, with his intense love of Scripture, our writer turns to God's truth. The word which apostates have rejected (10:26) is written not only for their warning (10:30), but for *our* encouragement.[24]

There is at least a hint here, though nothing more, that some of these Christians were discouraged because they had hoped and prayed for Christ's return. Why was his coming so delayed? They wanted the reward (10:35) there and then. But this prophetic word from Isaiah and Habakkuk[25] reminds them of his promise and insists that if they are to please him, then steadfastness is essential. The use of Habakkuk is interesting, for in the late seventh century BC, distressed by widespread godlessness and disobedience, that prophet had cried for help to the Lord God.[26] The divine reply was that Habakkuk was to be patient. It was all very relevant in the difficult circumstances of the first century. These believers,

[24] Rom. 15:4. [25] Is. 26:20 (LXX); Hab. 2:3–4. [26] Hab. 1:1–4.

tested and troubled, must remember that God's righteous ones live by faith (10:38). Our writer is about to define this faith and illustrate it. At this point he asserts its infinite worth. Those who possess it are not destroyed as apostates and infidels (10:29); they *keep their souls* or 'win through to life' (Bruce). They may lose a lot in this life, but, relying on Christ alone, they are not even remotely in danger of losing the only possession that matters, 'the life which is life indeed'.[27]

Conclusion

When we look back over the pastoral exhortation found in this passage, two features of its teaching about the person of Christ call for practical application in our own everyday lives. One relates to the future, the other to the present. They concern the Lord's promised return and his present ministry.

a. Christ's delayed return

The secularist pressures of the modern world insist on the importance of the immediate and the priority of the tangible. It is what you have *now* that matters; promises are valueless. But the believer refuses to be choked by this restrictive, futureless outlook. He lovingly believes in Christ, though he has never seen him.[28] He looks to the God who cannot be seen and presses toward the distant city, even though it is not visible on the immediate horizon (11:27, 10). It is natural for Christians to long for Christ's triumphal return. The postponement, however, is an essential aspect of God's sovereign purpose. Calvin rightly pointed out that 'the Church was so constituted from the beginning of the kingdom of Christ that the faithful ought to imagine the coming of the Judge as imminent . . . we should continually expect His second revelation and think of each day as though it were the last'.[29]

b. Christ's immediate help

In a society obsessed by the lust for possessions, in which people who have never had so much are hungry for more,

[27] 1 Tim. 6:19. [28] 2 Cor. 4:18; 1 Pet. 1:8.
[29] Commenting on Heb. 10:25.

the Christian rejoices in what he has in Christ, the spiritual treasures which can never be taken away. One of the believer's most priceless possessions is the promise of Christ's sufficiency. Luther was expounding Hebrews to his students in Wittenberg at a time (1517) when things were exceptionally difficult. Later that year he posted his Ninety-Five Theses on the door of the Schlosskirche and quickly realized that his request for a debate had antagonized many of the leaders of his day, political as well as religious. In this crisis the message of Hebrews came to him with startling relevance and deep assurance. Expounding this passage's invitation into the sanctuary (10:19) he says: '(Christ) crossed over first of all, and He smooths the exceedingly rough road . . . For he who relies on Christ through faith is carried on the shoulders of Christ.'

Believers today in many parts of the world know only too well that they belong to an ignored, despised or even persecuted minority; their faith is often held up to ridicule, even their matchless Lord is *profaned* and his deity denied by some who profess to believe in him. In times such as these Christians do well to recall Luther's words that they are 'carried on the shoulders of Christ'. For such people the place of prayer is the way to life, and the company of God's people a 'house' which, whatever the hazards, can only be enlarged and never destroyed.

11:1–16

18. Faith: its meaning and its heroes

We have now come to one of the most familiar chapters of the Bible. Even Christians who find some of the earlier teaching of this letter difficult to understand turn to this chapter for help, especially in times of crisis or when their own faith seems weak. And they do not go away disappointed. These courageous heroes beckon the reader on to daring exploits and encourage the contemporary believer by their persistent endurance. But it is important to recognize at the start that the chapter cannot be taken in isolation. Its teaching builds on what has gone before. The artificial chapter division has obscured the fact that this famous chapter must be read as a sequel to the previous verses. It is a vigorous exposition of what it means to have faith and obtain life.

1. The definition of faith (11:1–3)

The passage begins by explaining the nature and quality of true faith. Christian believers are those who 'have faith' (10:39), but for some it has been spasmodic or impermanent. Earlier passages in the letter have already indicated that not all who began in faith continued in faith. It is important therefore to interpret this intriguing word 'faith'. Our writer does not pretend to say all that can be said about it. He is defining faith here in relation to the particular situation in which this congregation found itself. We have no reason to doubt he was aware of other aspects of faith, for the word is used in the New Testament in a variety of senses and comes to have rich content. It can indicate the way we believe ('faith in Jesus') and what we believe. It can be used to indicate mere intellectual assent which even demons give to the fact of God's existence; or deep personal commitment, which only Christians can give.[1] But the interest in this chapter is deliberately restricted to the author's immediate discussion. The opening verses explain the kind of faith which is necessary for those who endure (10:36) and 'keep their souls' (10:39). Those with true faith accept God's word, win his approval and recognize his power.

a. Faith accepts God's word (11:1)

Now faith is the assurance of things hoped for, the conviction of things not seen.

In this chapter, as elsewhere, faith is man's response to what God has said. It takes seriously the message of God's revealed truth in holy Scripture. It does not merely agree with God's word, but acts upon it. Our writer narrows his interest to the two aspects of faith which are of immediate relevance to his readers, what might be described as the future reference and present function of Christian faith.

First, *it anticipates the future.* It does not place its reliance on that which is merely visible to our physical sight. It is *the assurance of things hoped for.* The 'faithful' characters arrayed in chapter 11 did not simply live for the passing moment; they realized that there was far more to life than the immediate and temporary scene. Life was a pilgrimage. They knew that there were better things ahead because, in one way or another, God had told them so. And they preferred to believe that word rather than the flimsy promises and facile assurances of the world around them.

Secondly, *it evaluates the present.* It would be wrong to imagine that the believer has no interest whatever in contemporary life. Indeed, the Christian looks far more closely at the immediate scene than the unbeliever. The person without any clear faith often accepts things simply as they are. If money comes his way, then it is obviously his to enjoy. If he is confronted with an opportunity for sensual pleasure, he

[1] Rom. 3:26; 10:8; Jas. 2:19; Jn. 1:12.

will take it, regardless of its immediate effects or ultimate consequences. He does not necessarily sit down to consider whether it damages him or hurts others; that is not his concern. But the man or woman of faith possesses *the conviction of things not seen*. Such people look beyond the situation as it can be perceived by natural vision or enjoyed by the physical appetites. They do not look simply at their circumstances; they discern the activity of the invisible God (11:27) in their present situation and are able to endure.

b. Faith wins God's approval (11:2)

For by it the men of old received divine approval

By exercising this kind of faith, *the men of old* gained that which matters most, the warm commendation of God. These 'elders' (it is the same word as that used in the opening sentence of the letter) received the word of God and in different generations made their own response to its message, thus receiving *divine approval*. Without this kind of faith man cannot please God (11:6) nor have the satisfaction of knowing that his life has the divine favour. For the Christian, pleasing God is of the greatest possible importance. He does not set his heart on gaining human approval; that can be dangerous. He longs that at this present moment he is earning God's approval and that in the end God will express it.[2]

c. Faith recognizes God's power (11:3)

By faith we understand that the world was created by the word of God, so that what is seen was made out of things which do not appear.

The writer has made several references to creation and now returns to this theme in order to emphasize faith's ability to discern God's majestic power in the created order. The letter began by asserting Christ's share in creation (1:2); it now turns to our understanding of it.

Only by faith can we accept the astonishing statement that

[2] Mt. 25:21; *cf.* Lk. 6:26.

'the visible came forth from the invisible' (NEB). Bruce says that when our author makes this statement 'the first chapter of Genesis is probably uppermost in his mind, since he is about to trace seven living examples of faith from the subsequent chapters of that book'. We have already seen that in referring to the Old Testament, he consistently uses the Septuagint. That version translates the beginning of the creation account in this way: 'The earth was invisible' (*aoratos*), the same word which is used later in this chapter to describe the 'invisible' God (11:27). God's incomparable power is such that he can call the universe into being when there is nothing from which it can be fashioned. He simply declared that it was to be, and once he said it, it was done.

2. Three righteous men (11:4–7)

We now come to what the seventeenth-century Puritan writer, Richard Sibbes, called 'a little book of martyrs'. This galaxy of saints is not arrayed simply in order to exalt their virtues; indeed all of them were sinners who made mistakes and at times grieved God. The Bible does not seek to mock us when it outlines the achievements of its great characters. It records the truth about them so that, amongst other things, we recognize that they were ordinary people who, by God's grace alone, were enabled to do extraordinary things. In selecting certain individuals by way of illustration, the writer begins by introducing Abel, Enoch and Noah.

a. Abel recognized his obligations before God (11:4)

By faith Abel offered to God a more acceptable sacrifice than Cain, through which he received approval as righteous, God bearing witness by accepting his gifts; he died, but through his faith he is still speaking.

Abel offered a sacrifice which was *more acceptable* than that presented by his brother Cain. Its acceptability was not simply that he made a blood offering and a valuable offering ('the firstlings of his flock'), but also that he gave a sincere offering. Abel offered a pure heart as well as the best gift. Cain could not overcome the powerful tyrant, sin, which was couching at his door.[3] Later, Jesus testified to Abel's purity of heart and John to Cain's sinful desires.[4] God bore witness to Abel's righteousness *by accepting his gifts*. Although Abel was murdered by his evil brother, *he is still speaking*; the story of his faithful achievement speaks to people in every generation, not only about the quality of their offering to God, but also their motivation. Is the outward offering of worship, money and service a genuine expression of our love and commitment? God sees not only the value of the sacrifice, but the heart of the giver. But Abel speaks to man still more clearly by reminding us of the most important offering of all, 'the sprinkled blood' of Christ (12:24) who, although he was murdered by the angry and jealous successors of Cain, was not like Abel, the helpless victim of sudden hate. His entirely voluntary sacrifice was both determined and approved by God.

b. Enoch maintained his walk with God (11:5–6)

[5]By faith Enoch was taken up so that he should not see death; and he was not found, because God had taken him. Now before he was taken he was attested as having pleased God. [6]And without faith it is impossible to please him. For whoever would draw near to God must believe that he exists and that he rewards those who seek him.

For the Christian believer devotion to God is more than the regular act of religious worship or the occasional presentation of some sacrificial gift. All life belongs to God and our righteousness has to extend to the whole of life. Those who possess true faith walk with God[5] day after day. The brief Genesis account of his long life contains the fascinating detail that Enoch did not always walk with God. There was a time, it appears, when the walk began. He 'walked with God after the birth of Methuselah'. It may not be too much to assume that the responsibilities of parenthood forced Enoch to recognize his serious moral and spiritual limitations, and in this experience of inadequacy he may have felt himself cast upon God for help. He came to realize that only if he walked with God could he be a good example to his children. By this kind of

[3] Gn. 4:1–7. [4] Mt. 23:35; 1 Jn. 3:12. [5] Gn. 5:22, 24.

daily reliance Enoch *pleased God*, and only by that same kind of dependent trust can believers of any generation please him.

Those who, like Enoch, wish to *draw near to God*, must encourage their faith to give constant expression to two great facts about God – his existence and his generosity. They must not merely believe intellectually *that he exists*, for without that faith would be meaningless. Belief in his existence means commitment to his presence and involvement in every part of our lives. In a thoroughly secular society, and because of our preoccupation with material things, it is easy for us to ignore God's existence and it is common for us to overlook God's grace. He is the rewarder of *those who seek him*. He does not merely reveal his existence to us, but proves his generosity. Those who seek him in everyday life can testify to his goodness.

c. Noah rendered his obedience to God (11:7)

By faith Noah, being warned by God concerning events as yet unseen, took heed and constructed an ark for the saving of his household; by this he condemned the world and became an heir of the righteousness which comes by faith.

Noah is a perfect example of the believer as defined in the opening verses of this chapter. He accepted God's word (*took heed*), he won God's approval (*became an heir of the righteousness which comes by faith*) and recognized God's power (manifest in *events as yet unseen*) in both judgment and salvation. Noah is a splendid example of the attentive believer, eager to hear what God is saying and ready to do what he commands. He not only received a warning, but built the ark. God said it, so Noah did it. Jesus himself stressed the necessity of the obedient response[6] and all who walk by faith recognize its importance. Moreover, Noah brought a daring response to God's word. The warning was about *events as yet unseen*. When he constructed an ark Noah gained not only the approval of God, but also the ridicule of men. Over the long years, as he built, the people gave voice to their blatant unbelief.

[6] Mt. 7:24–27.

God exercised his merciful patience and Noah offered his persistent obedience.[7] By it he achieved three important things, salvation, witness and righteousness. Through his obedience his household was saved whilst others perished. His action affected his neighbours. They regarded his obedience to God as an act of folly, but 'through his faith he put the whole world in the wrong' (NEB). In every generation Christian obedience has powerful evangelistic value. Men and women are influenced not only by what we say to them, but by the way we respond to what God says to us Moreover, by his obedience he became the possessor of *righteousness*, which is God's gift to the man who has faith in him.[8] His secret was in his total, unhesitating obedience to God's revealed word for, as Scripture testifies, Noah 'did *all* that God commanded him'.[9]

3. Abraham and his family (11:8–12)

8By faith Abraham obeyed when he was called to go out to a place which he was to receive as an inheritance; and he went out, not knowing where he was to go. 9By faith he sojourned in the land of promise, as in a foreign land, living in tents with Isaac and Jacob, heirs with him of the same promise. 10For he looked forward to the city which has foundations, whose builder and maker is God. 11By faith Sarah herself received power to conceive, even when she was past the age, since she considered him faithful who had promised. 12Therefore from one man, and him as good as dead, were born descendants as many as the stars of heaven and as the innumerable grains of sand by the seashore.

Noah's example of attentive obedience is followed by a detailed account of the obedience shown by faith's exemplar *par excellence*, Abraham. His place in this account of Old Testament worthies is to be expected, especially as he has already appeared in this letter (6:13–15) as an example of one who through faith and patience inherited the promises.

Abraham naturally occupies an important place in the Jew-

[7] 2 Pet. 2:5; 1 Pet. 3:20.
[8] Gn. 7:1; Ezk. 14:14; Rom. 3:22.
[9] Gn. 6:9, 22.

ish tradition as father of the race, but is also presented in New Testament teaching as the father of all who have faith. In this letter, for example, all who believe are regarded as 'descendants of Abraham' (2:16). In these verses the patriarch and his wife are introduced to illustrate five different aspects of faith. It is responsive, sacrificial, courageous, persistent and dependent.

a. Responsive faith

This is demonstrated by Abraham's eagerness to do what the Lord required of him: *By faith Abraham obeyed when he was called.* The Genesis account of Abraham's call emphasizes with stark clarity the patriarch's obedient response to the divine voice: 'Now the Lord said to Abram, "Go from your country . . ." So Abram went.'[10] In more than one context our writer is eager to point out that the obedience demonstrated by these great personalities of the Old Testament was surely due to their unwavering confidence in a God who speaks. These men and women were prepared to take God at his word because they knew it was a word of unrivalled authority, decisive importance, immense power and complete reliability.[11] Commenting on Abraham's obedience to God's call, Calvin says that the patriarch 'did nothing that was not by the command of God. This is surely one of the principles of faith that we do not move a step unless the Word of God shows us the way and shines before us like a lantern.'

b. Sacrificial faith

This is to be seen in Abraham's willingness to *go out* from all that was secure, prosperous, peaceful and enjoyable. The Genesis narrative mentions God's demand that Abraham leave his kindred and 'his father's house', and the patriarch was prepared to abandon all this. Luther commented on the cost of this obedience: 'In the first place, it was hard for him to leave his native land, which it is natural for us to love . . . Furthermore, it is hard to leave friends and their companionship, but most of all to leave relatives and one's father's

[10] Gn. 12:1–4. [11] Heb. 1:1–2; 2:1–4; 4:12; 6:12–18.

house.' Faith in God sometimes makes this kind of demand.

The sacrificial aspect of faith's work is also illustrated here in Abraham's willingness to make this journey *to a place which he was to receive as an inheritance*. Abraham responded to God's orders, and God, in his merciful goodness, added to the clear command a word of rich promise. Calvin observed that it is 'a rare trial of faith to leave what is in one's hand to go seeking for what is far off and unknown to us'. Abraham recognized that in responding to God's demands he must place his entire reliance on the God who not only called him, but would guide his steps, meet his needs and prepare his future. New Testament writers have a similar conviction about God's call to believers. We do not know every step of the way, but God has promised to equip us with everything good (13:21).

c. Courageous faith

Abraham began his travels *not knowing where he was to go*. It is important to notice what our author is emphasizing here. Abraham was not given the clear promise of his future inheritance when he was in Haran. He was sent out *to a place which he was to receive as an inheritance*. The biblical narrative makes it plain that this promise was not made to Abraham until he had actually entered Canaan itself. The Haran promise was that God would make of him a great nation and that he would be a blessing. Once he reached the land, then the Lord appeared to him and said, 'To your descendants I will give this land.'[12] 'The promise of the inheritance was not in the first instance an incentive to obedience; it was the reward of his obedience' (Bruce). Abraham was in his mid-seventies when he went out from his own country and it required heroism and courage to take God at his word. Similar courage is expected of all who 'walk by faith, not by sight'.[13]

d. Persistent faith

Abraham's persistence is given special prominence here. Even when he entered the land and received the promise of the

[12] Gn. 12:7. [13] 2 Cor. 5:7.

inheritance, it did not become his immediate possession. He possessed it only by promise, not in fact. The land was already inhabited by others. They lived in its cities while Abraham lived, like his sons and grandsons after him, *in tents*. Isaac and Jacob shared the same nomadic existence as *heirs* with Abraham *of the same promise*. They did not see the land as their own, but exercised persistent and confident faith knowing that God would be true to his word.

In times of tension and difficulty, Abraham looked backward as he recalled the moment when God had given his command and made his promise. When things seemed against him he looked upwards to a God who had promised to be both his protector and rewarder.[14] Baffled and bewildered, there were times when he derived great comfort as he *looked forward*, beyond the hazards and uncertainties of his life in tents to *the city which has foundations, whose builder and maker is God.*

e. Dependent faith

Abraham's dependence on God is linked here with the faith of his wife Sarah who, after an initial expression of doubt,[15] believed in the reliability of a God who not only keeps promises but works miracles. Even when she was *past the age* she conceived because, like her husband, she came to the place where her confidence was renewed in her faithful God (*cf.* 10:23). Humanly speaking, it was impossible for this old woman to bear her own child. She longed for her own baby, but only God could achieve such a miracle. And, relying upon him, she proved his dependability. To a man *as good as dead* the child of promise was given.

4. Faith's qualities (11:13–16)

At this point there is a momentary pause in the recollection of patriarchal faith, while the writer mentions five rich spiritual qualities manifested in the lives of these Old Testament personalities: their confidence, witness, quest, discernment and security.

[14] Gn. 15:1. [15] Gn. 18:12–15.

[13]*These all died in faith, not having received what was promised, but having seen it and greeted it from afar, and having acknowledged that they were strangers and exiles on the earth.* [14]*For people who speak thus make it clear that they are seeking a homeland.* [15]*If they had been thinking of that land from which they had gone out, they would have had opportunity to return.* [16]*But as it is, they desire a better country, that is, a heavenly one. Therefore God is not ashamed to be called their God, for he has prepared for them a city.*

a. Their confidence

All these characters *died in faith*, that is, under the rule of faith, with the promises of God deeply engraved on heart and mind, but without the joy of seeing their fulfilment. But such was their spiritual vision that, although they did not actually possess the promised gift of God, they knew that they had *seen it*. They *greeted it from afar* or 'hailed it with delight'; part of their abundant joy is contained in that phrase. It may have recalled for Jewish readers the experience of Moses *seeking a homeland* in Canaan, climbing to the top of the mountain Pisgah, only to behold it with his eyes and yet greet it as the promised possession of God's people.[16] These patriarchal leaders did not receive *what was promised*, whereas believers do receive what is promised (10:36). Calvin glories in the heroism of these Old Testament believers when their limited spiritual resources are contrasted with the wealth of privilege given to believers: 'God gave to the fathers only a foretaste of his favour, which is poured out generously upon us . . . yet they were satisfied and never fell from their faith . . . If we fail we are doubly without excuse . . . how great will be our idleness if we grow tired of believing when the Lord supports us with so many helps?'

b. Their witness

These people *acknowledged that they were strangers and exiles*. It was not simply an attitude of mind; they gave expression to it in their conversation with their contemporaries.

[16] Dt. 3:25–28.

They *speak* of their conviction regarding life on this earth as *strangers and exiles* and a better one in heaven. Faith refuses to be silent. It must share its testimony with others.

c. Their quest

These exiles *are seeking a homeland*, and it is clear from their lives that the object of their quest is not an earthly land at all, or they would have found their way to it. Their hearts were set on heaven, not on *the land from which they had gone out.* Heaven was their homeland, simply because it was the home of God and, as his children, his home must also be theirs. The 'aliens and exiles' concept frequently emerges in New Testament teaching with forceful clarity. Christian citizenship is in heaven; that is where believers have set their hope.[17]

d. Their discernment

They did not merely anticipate heaven, they evaluated the things of earth. Looking at the things that were 'seen', they quickly discerned that all the marks of transience, impermanence and perishability were upon them. They looked away from such material gains to something which was 'better', the heavenly home of the people of God. Once again, the key word 'better' has made a dramatic appearance in the letter. The man or woman of faith has the ability to distinguish between good and evil, eternal and temporal, permanent and perishable; this is one of the great features of Moses' life as recorded a few verses later in this chapter (11:24–28).

e. Their security

These pilgrims often experienced physical hardship, social ostracism, emotional tension and economic deprivation. Exiles were not viewed with favour in the ancient world. To reside in a country other than one's own carried a stigma in antiquity. But these pilgrims of heaven were marching towards home. *God is not ashamed to be called their God*, and he has prepared for them a city. Westcott[18] makes the fasci-

[17] Phil. 3:20; 1 Pet. 1:17; 2:11.
[18] Additional note on Heb. 11:10 on the social imagery in the epistle.

nating suggestion that our author's use of 'the city' imagery is deliberate and illuminating. Three concepts of the city were prevalent in the first-century world, Jewish, Greek and Stoic. In Jewish thought the city was the home of the *divine sovereignty*.[19] In Greek thought the city was the place of *special privilege*. It was not for all and sundry, but for a specially select company. The Stoic view was rather the opposite. It believed the city to be the focus of *universal hope*. The New Testament concept of the city of God makes use of the leading ideas of all three. By divine sovereignty, it is God's city. He dwells among his people (12:22). By special privilege it is the believers' city, yet in God's mercy he calls into it all who will believe in Jesus.

Conclusion

Some practical considerations force themselves on the attention of any serious reader of these verses. The vision and heroism of these great patriarchal figures have some important lessons for us and for our far more sophisticated and far less contented society. The description of these heroes of faith challenges our cowardice and rebukes our materialism.

a. It challenge our cowardice

These *strangers and exiles* have something to say to us about personal evangelism in the twentieth-century world. They made bold confession of their pilgrim attitude to life. They made it clear that they were seeking a homeland. Their outspoken witness is a challenge to our guilty silence. The majority of our contemporaries live as though this world is everything. They have no eternal dimension to their thinking whatever. Christians have the responsibility of reminding them, winsomely but directly, that there is a life beyond this one and that after death comes judgment (9:27). Taking its cue from the teaching and command of Jesus, this theme of man's accountability has a most important place in early Christian evangelistic preaching.[20]

[19] Ps. 48:2. [20] Mt. 16:27; Acts 10:42, 17:31.

b. It rebukes our materialism

It has something of pressing relevance to say to us about our present life-style as Christians. Those who know that the next world is a 'better' one do not waste their limited opportunity in this life by clutching greedily for the next material acquisition. Believers look to the city beyond and its abiding joys. In the early Christian centuries many believers read a work now known as *The Shepherd of Hermas.* It contained this highly relevant exhortation:

> You know . . . that as the servants of God . . . your city is far from this city. If then you know your city in which you are going to dwell, why do you here prepare lands and costly establishments . . . Take heed, then, make no further preparations for yourself beyond a sufficient competence for yourself as though you were living in a foreign country.[21]

Such words come to us in our affluent western society as a striking rebuke. They call us to a far simpler life-style and remind us that it is sinful to acquire so much when millions of others have so little. After all, in biblical teaching covetousness is markedly characteristic of the godless; it is hardly appropriate for Christians to lust for things. Jesus lived simply and for our sakes became poor. Inspired by this example, the early church did all within its power to meet the material needs of the hungry and destitute, and throughout the centuries many have been rebuked by the sacrificial life-style of truly committed Christians. In our time we are not likely to make any impact with the gospel if self-contented affluence becomes a feature of our lives rather than outgoing compassion. Whilst we reach out for more, 500 million men, women and children throughout the world are starving, and double that number are seriously undernourished. In developing countries one child in every four dies before reaching its fifth birthday.

Sider has said: 'World poverty is a hundred million mothers

[21] *Parables* I.1, 6 in K. Lake (editor), *The Apostolic Fathers, Loeb Classical Library* II, pp. 139–141.

weeping . . . because they cannot feed their children.'[22] Those who, in the teaching of this letter, claim that they too are *strangers and exiles on the earth*, must surely adopt a life-style which is both simple and sacrificial. This is, in Sider's words, 'crucial' if we are to 'symbolize, validate and facilitate our concern for the hungry'.[23] Scripture makes it clear that, when the needy cry for help, God looks to us for something more than our prayers.

[22] R. Sider, *Rich Christians in an Age of Hunger*, p. 21.
[23] *Ibid.*, p. 148; *cf.* J. V. Taylor, *Enough is Enough* (SCM Press, 1975).

11:17–32

19. Faith in hard times

1. Anticipating the promises (11:17–22)

This section resumes the exposition of faithful exploits, and four incidents are brought to the reader's attention. They illustrate the power of the promise and the role of faith, both in receiving God's promises and in anticipating them. Abraham, Isaac, Jacob and Joseph are summoned here as witnesses to the power of the promises of God.

a. Abraham's submission (11:17–19)

[17]*By faith Abraham, when he was tested, offered up Isaac, and he who had received the promises was ready to offer up his only son,* [18]*of whom it was said, 'Through Isaac shall your descendants be named.'*[19]*He considered that God was able to raise men even from the dead; hence, figuratively speaking, he did receive him back.*

In Jewish tradition Abraham was said to have been *tested* by God on ten different occasions. Here the letter focuses on the occasion when he was ordered to offer his son Isaac as a sacrifice.[1] At a time when Abraham must have been bewildered by God's command, he continued to believe and refused to act in any way other than the Lord had told him. It seemed ridiculous to *offer up his only son* when, after all, the child had been God's promised gift. The Lord had assured him that it would be through his child that the promised grace

[1] Gn. 22:1–14.

would begin to be established: *Through Isaac shall your descendants be named.* God now seemed to be going back on his word, but Abraham was determined to do what the Lord God required. He held on to the truth of God's promise, believing that if Isaac had to be killed as the sacrificial victim, then God would raise him from the dead to fulfil his ultimate purposes. Abraham refused to put limits to either his obedience or God's power. He maintained his faith in the creative power of God (11:3) and his word (4:12). The saving event was an eloquent parable. Isaac was received back from the verge of death, a sign of God's unfailing provision in the moment of man's desperate need.

b. Isaac's perception (11:20)

By faith Isaac invoked future blessings on Jacob and Esau.

The only incidents selected from the lives of Isaac and Jacob concern the blessings they bestowed on others. In the ancient world it was of the greatest possible importance to secure such parental blessing and receive the assurance of the future inheritance. What is astonishing about the blessing imparted to Jacob by Isaac is that in the biblical narrative it looks on a surface reading as though it owed more to Jacob's deceptive skill than Isaac's perceptive insight.[2] But the narrative is found in Scripture in order to impress upon us the infinite wisdom, overruling sovereignty and astonishing mercy of God.

God's wisdom is manifested in this event in that the natural and customary thing to do was to impart the blessing to the firstborn. Esau was naturally chosen by Isaac for this privilege, but God knew that the line must be continued through Jacob's family and therefore allowed Jacob to practice this deceit. Although he was so desperately unkind to his father, so pathetically misled by his mother, so astonishingly jealous of his brother, yet God helped him, used him and blessed him. God's blessings are given not because we deserve them, but because we need them.

Reflecting on these events, Isaac perceived the activity of his wise, sovereign and merciful God. But his perceptive faith

[2] Gn. 27.

is illustrated not only in the historical circumstances of the parental blessings, but in their remarkable content. It was only by 'faith' that a 'sojourner', a man who did not own land, could talk about the peoples who would serve his descendants and the nations who would ultimately honour them.

c. *Jacob's anticipation* (11:21)

By faith Jacob, when dying, blessed each of the sons of Joseph, bowing in worship over the head of his staff.

Similarly, old Jacob, blind and infirm, gave a blessing to his grandsons and, much to Joseph's annoyance, gave the younger son the blessing which was customarily awarded to the elder. But once again Jacob's faith is expressed in the content of the blessing. 'Let them grow into a multitude', 'a multitude of nations'.[3] Physically, the old man was weak and had to be supported by either his staff or the head of his bed (an alternative reading), but his faith was strong. He anticipated a time when his descendants would inherit their own land and prosper under God's merciful direction. His blessing expressed 'the assurance of things hoped for' and he knew that the God who had guided him would not fail them.[4]

d. *Joseph's conviction* (11:22)

By faith Joseph, at the end of his life, made mention of the exodus of the Israelites and gave directions concerning his burial.

When Joseph's sons were blessed by his father, Jacob told Joseph that God would be with him and bring him to the land of his fathers. Joseph believed that, and when he came to the end of his days was so sure that God would bring his people to the promised land that he left careful instructions about the conveyance of his embalmed body from Egypt to Canaan.[5] Calvin says that Joseph's request was not for selfish interest, but was intended as a stimulus to the Israelites: 'he wanted to sharpen the desire of his people so that they would

[3] Gn. 48:16, 19. [4] Gn. 48:15, 21. [5] Gn. 50:24–26.

look more earnestly for their redemption' and that they might 'hope with certainty that they would at length be liberated.'

Before we move on, it is important to see that two principles emerge here as issues of practical importance for Christians in the contemporary world. There is a message in these verses for those who are going through tough times.

First, when faith is tested, believe in God's word. Abraham went through dark days, but he held on to what God had promised. He refused to be daunted or discouraged. Even when he left his servants at the foot of Mount Moriah, he told the young men, 'I and the lad will go yonder . . . and come again to you.' When young Isaac was puzzled about the missing sacrificial animal, Abraham renewed his confidence in the Lord: 'God will provide himself the lamb for a burnt offering.' Abraham's greatest test provided the occasion for God's finest promise, but it was all because he had obeyed God's voice.[6]

Secondly, when faith is tested, rejoice in God's power. Abraham knew that the God who had provided for him thus far in life would not forsake him in the moment of his greatest emotional distress. God had said, 'Through Isaac shall your descendants be named', so he trusted God to bring that promise to fulfilment, if necessary by resurrection. He fervently maintained that nothing was impossible for God. In times of testing we need not only the confidence which accepts what God has said, but the ability to remember what God can do.

2. Moses and the believing multitude (11:23–29)

Abraham received the promise (6:13) and Moses received the law (10:28). Quite naturally, the exploits of two leading personalities are of particular interest to our writer. But, although Moses is important, the outstanding faith of the Hebrew leader is not allowed to minimize the effectual faith of the individual Israelite. The ordinary person in Israel begins now to emerge as a significant figure in the chapter. *By faith* the Israelites shared Moses' vision and kept the Passover (11:28). It was not only Moses who believed in God's word and rejoiced in his power.[7]

[6] Gn. 22:16–18. [7] Ex. 3:8, 19–20.

In these verses the writer emphasizes five aspects of faith. It conquers our fears, determines our options, sharpens our vision, recognizes our dependence and overcomes our difficulties.

a. Faith conquers our fears (11:23)

By faith Moses, when he was born, was hid for three months by his parents, because they saw that the child was beautiful; and they were not afraid of the king's edict.

Although Pharaoh had ordered the execution of all male infants, Moses' parents ignored *the king's edict* and were not afraid of the consequences. Motivated initially by purely natural considerations, the physical beauty of their child,[8] they hid the baby in their home, taking a great risk in order to do what they believed to be right. Their fearlessness is given special prominence here. Human fear is an important and recurrent pastoral problem, carefully expounded by our author in the course of his letter.[9]

What is important in this context is that by faith the people of God have overcome their worst fears. For many of these Christians in the Roman Empire their *king's edict* would naturally evoke deep fear. One did not need to be a prophet to realize that the days of initial toleration would soon be replaced by fierce hostility. The example of a believing husband and wife who took risks, even over their treasured child, would not be without its special appeal in the first-century world.

b. Faith determines our options (11:24–26)

24*By faith Moses, when he was grown up, refused to be called the son of Pharaoh's daughter,* 25*choosing rather to share ill-treatment with the people of God than to enjoy the fleeting pleasures of sin.* 26*He considered abuse suffered for the Christ greater wealth than the treasures of Egypt, for he looked to the reward.*

[8] Ex. 2:2.

[9] Heb. 2:15; 4:1; 5:7; 10:31; 12:21, 28; 13:6.

Life confronts everyone with alternatives and frequently the believer can make a responsible choice only *by faith*. By faith Moses took a series of important decisions by which he cast in his lot with the people of God. By faith Moses abandoned social honours, physical satisfaction and material gain.

Social honours had been heaped on Moses. He was the adopted son of Pharaoh's daughter;[10] life as an Egyptian prince gave him constant access to privilege and distinction. When he had to choose between the glories of an Egyptian court and the hazards of the desert, he decided on the latter. People can choose social deprivation of that kind only by faith.

Physical satisfaction was constantly available to Moses in the Egyptian palace, but he identified such pleasures as morally corrupt (*sin*) and only temporarily enjoyable (*fleeting*). He left all that in order to identify himself fully with God's people, the despised Jewish slaves.

Material gain was characteristic of Egypt. Its riches and treasures were proverbial, but Moses decided against them in favour of physical abuse in this world and God's approval in the next. We can make this kind of decisive choice only *by faith*. It is only *by faith* that a Christian can decide not on the things which please himself, but on that which pleases God, exalts Christ and helps others.

Most expositors point out that this choice made by Moses became a theme of pastoral urgency in the lives of these first-century Jewish Christians. Moses could have remained with a godless people, a nation without the true God, but by faith he came to realize that *abuse suffered for the Christ* was of greater value eternally than secular considerations. The author is thinking particularly of some of those Christians who may have been in serious danger of abandoning their membership of Christ's community, God's true people, in favour of the physical security and social acceptability of the synagogue. 'Be like Moses' he says. 'Decide by faith for the things which are imperishable. Be prepared to bear abuse for the sake of God's anointed.' The writer views the abuse which the people of God suffered at the exodus as a type of Christ's reproach at the new exodus. 'The stigma that rests on God's Anointed' (NEB) was for Moses a treasure of priceless worth.

[10] Ex. 2:10.

c. Faith sharpens our vision (11:27)

By faith he left Egypt, not being afraid of the anger of the king; for he endured as seeing him who is invisible.

Moses refused to look to the prestige, pleasures and treasures of Egypt. He was determined not to look into the angry face of Pharaoh; he focused his vision not on earth but on heaven. The verse gives expression to one of the delightful paradoxes of the Christian faith; he looked into the face of the God who could not be seen. When it says, 'he looked' (11:26), the word means 'his eyes were fixed' (NEB). The verb is used 'of keeping one's attention fixed on something, as an artist keeps his fixed on the object or model that he is reproducing in painting or sculpture' (Bruce). But the word also indicates determined choice. Westcott says that it is used by classical writers in the sense of 'looking away from one object to another'. We fix our eyes on the ultimate, not the immediate, on the eternal reward rather than our temporal gain.

All this happened, says our author, when Moses *left Egypt*. This may be a reference to his flight to Midian when his offence of manslaughter was made known to Pharaoh,[11] though it probably refers here to his second departure with the redeemed people of God. The main point in favour of the Midian event is that such an interpretation would leave the next 'by faith' reference (to the Passover) in correct historical order. If the Midian flight is intended here, it might be regarded as an encouragement to *passive endurance*. He could have used the taskmaster incident to stir up a revolt, and with their huge numbers and his patriotic leadership the Hebrew slaves would have had a good chance of success. But, as A. S. Peake observed, he 'had the insight to see that God's hour had not yet struck, and therefore he resolutely turned his back on the course he had begun to tread . . . For it was harder to live for his people than it was to die for them'.[12] When his people were in such desperate trouble, it required endurance to stay in Midian. In his commentary on this letter, Peake reminds us that the 'courage to abandon work on which

[11] Ex. 2:11–15.
[12] A. S. Peake, *The Heroes and Martyrs of Faith* (London, 1910), p. 121.

the whole heart is set, and to accept inaction cheerfully as the will of God, is of the rarest and highest kind, and can be created and sustained only by the clearest spiritual vision'.

If the reference to the flight of Moses is to the great exodus of the Israelite nation, it is an encouragement to *active endurance*. Pharaoh was angry and, although he had been brought low by the successive plagues, Moses knew only too well that if the Egyptians had their way they would not let the Hebrews go without bloodshed. The leader of God's people endured by meditating not on Pharaoh's anger, but on God's mercy. He looked to the invisible, living and faithful God and was given the strength to endure.

d. Faith recognizes our dependence (11:28)

By faith he kept the Passover and sprinkled the blood, so that the Destroyer of the first-born might not touch them.

Despite the numerical strength and patriotic leadership given to the Hebrew people, the exodus event could be achieved only by God's powerful intervention. In one dreadful night the angel of death (*the Destroyer*) visited the house of every Egyptian family and the *first-born* in each home perished. All the earlier attempts to convince Pharaoh of God's power seemed but to increase his arrogance. Then, the angel swept through the Egyptian territories on his mission of judgment and only those houses whose doorposts and lintel were sprinkled with blood were unharmed. Pharaoh and the Egyptians had consistently refused to obey God's voice, but that night every Hebrew made sure that the blood of the Passover lamb was seen on the entrance to his house. They brought their united and unqualified obedience to the Lord. The instructions were strange, the demands costly (a lamb without blemish) and the ritual unprecedented, but they did precisely as they were told. In simple faith they *kept the Passover*. They relied on the God who had spoken to them through his servant: 'Then the people of Israel went and did so; as the Lord had commanded Moses and Aaron, so they did.'[13]

[13] Ex. 12:1–3, 28.

e. *Faith overcomes our difficulties* (11:29)

By faith the people crossed the Red Sea as if on dry land; but the Egyptians, when they attempted to do the same, were drowned.

It was not only Moses' faith which responded to the word of God the deliverer. That *the people* were enabled to cross the Red Sea was an act of obedient faith. Once again their dependence on God is powerfully underlined. Moses told the distressed Israelites, 'The Lord will fight for you, and you have only to be still.' Once again Moses and the people obeyed God's word. Moses was ordered to stretch out his staff and he did as he was commanded.[14] By this event, these first-century Christians could be encouraged to believe in the God of the impossible.[15] All the might of the Roman Empire and all the powerful hostility of their Jewish opponents might be ranged against them, but by faith they would triumph over their difficulties and discover that each daunting obstacle was a further opportunity to prove the faithfulness of God's word and the immensity of God's power.

3. Life in the land of promise (11:30–32)

Our writer passes over the years in the wilderness and resumes his story at the first main difficulty which the Hebrews had to overcome once they reached Canaan, the impregnable city of Jericho. He then mentions the faith demonstrated by Rahab the harlot, before a brief reference, by name only, to six characters from the period of the Judges to the establishment of the Davidic monarchy. The faith which is exemplified in these verses is undaunted, adventurous and diversified.

a. *Undaunted faith* (11:30)

By faith the walls of Jericho fell down after they had been encircled for seven days.

Jericho stood as a symbol of Canaan's invincible might, but

[14] Ex. 14:10–31. [15] Gn. 18:14; Jb. 42:2; Mk. 10:27.

once again, in obedience to God's word, the Hebrews did exactly as they were commanded. Day after day the ark of the covenant was carried in solemn procession around the walls of the well-fortified city, until on the seventh day it was carried round seven times. The trumpets were blown, the people shouted, the walls fell and the city was taken. The writer may want to emphasize the believing persistence of the Hebrew people. It was after the walls *had been encircled for seven days* that they fell. Just as when they left Egypt, both at their first Passover and at the crossing of the Red Sea, they relied on God's word and his power, so now, as their children entered Canaan, they also trusted what he had said and witnessed what he could do.

b. Adventurous faith (11:31)

By faith Rahab the harlot did not perish with those who were disobedient, because she had given friendly welcome to the spies.

In case the letter's first readers had thoughtlessly imagined that exemplary faith is peculiar to specially virtuous believers, the author now demonstrates how even the most unlikely people can receive God's word and prove his power. Although she lacked the religious identity and moral integrity of so many of the heroes of this chapter, Rahab put her faith in their God and was delivered. She heard how God had enabled the Hebrew pilgrims to cross the Red Sea.[16] She knew that humanly speaking she had no right to claim salvation, but she did not wish to *perish with those who were disobedient*, so she cast herself boldly and directly upon the mercy of the spies: 'Give me a sure sign, and save . . .' She believed in God's power, so she expressed the validity of her faith through the hospitality of her home; she gave them a *friendly welcome*. To receive them into her house was a daring venture, for to shelter alien spies was to expose herself to danger. She believed that the God who had delivered them would save her, and such faith would certainly be rewarded.

[16] Jos. 2.

c. Diversified faith (11:32)

And what more shall I say? For time would fail me to tell of Gideon, Barak, Samson, Jephthah, of David and Samuel and the prophets.

But our writer knows that this impressive account of valiant men and women must not be extended. Time is running out. Six leading men are mentioned; the first four from the period of the Judges, when faith was at a premium. In those days, instead of obeying God's voice, or honouring a devoted leader, everyone did 'what was right in his own eyes'.[17] It was a period of backsliding and apostasy. The devout minority recalled the stories of God's power in days gone by to bring the people renewed confidence in the God who could deliver them.[18] Yet for the Judges as well as for David after them, faith was not stereotyped. God works as he pleases and uses whom he will.

All six men were vastly different in human personality, social circumstances and spiritual opportunity, yet in various ways God used them. He did not press them into an identical mould or demand the same response from each of them. Moreover, they were hardly without faults. Gideon was frightened, Barak was hesitant, Samson was flippant, Jephthah was rash, David was sensuous and Samuel was careless.[19] Calvin says:

> There was none of them whose faith did not falter . . . In every saint there is always to be found something reprehensible. Nevertheless although faith may be imperfect and incomplete it does not cease to be approved by God. There is no reason therefore why the fault from which we labour should break us or discourage us provided we go on by faith in the race of our calling.

If those who need his help will but seek God's face, they will not cry in vain. He delights in choosing those who seem most unsuitable and using those who seem most rebellious.

[17] Jdg. 6:10; 17:6. [18] Jdg. 6:13; 7:7.
[19] Jdg. 6:15; 4:8; 16:4–20; 11:30–31; 2 Sa. 11:2–5; 1 Sa. 8:1–3.

11:33–40

20. Unknown conquerors and sufficient strength

God's valiant host does not consist solely of outstanding leaders, patriarchs, judges, kings, prophets and martyrs. In the verses which close the chapter we are introduced to a vast company whose names we may never know, but whose heroic faith will be not only remembered but treasured. In many circumstances their faith inspired heroism. In other instances their faith encouraged fortitude. In all cases their faith awaited fulfilment.

1. A faith which inspired heroism (11:33–35a)

. . . [33]*who through faith conquered kingdoms, enforced justice, received promises, stopped the mouths of lions,* [34]*quenched raging fire, escaped the edge of the sword, won strength out of weakness, became mighty in war, put foreign armies to flight.* [35]*Women received their dead by resurrection.*

There is a clear recognition here that faith is often on the offensive. It refuses to accept the situation as inevitable and moves out on the attack. But it is not simply concerned with military qualities. Faith wins moral and spiritual victories too. By it God's justice is enforced, God's promises are received and God's power made manifest, even in resurrection. It is by such faith that weakness is exchanged for strength.

No less spectacular are its physical accomplishments. By faith people are enabled to cope with wild beasts, raging fire and aggressive warriors. In all these cases faith was a forceful, active ingredient, and always essential to life.

This record of faith's heroic deeds now turns to an important and necessary change of emphasis. In some of life's situations it is impossible to conquer, escape, become mighty or victorious. The powers are too great, the circumstances beyond our control. In these cases faith is a life-accepting quality, enabling a man or woman to face suffering and adversity with serenity, endurance and trust. The writer now turns to these virtues, which possibly require even greater faith.

2. A faith which encouraged fortitude (11:35b–38)

Some were tortured, refusing to accept release, that they might rise again to a better life. [36]*Others suffered mocking and scourging, and even chains and imprisonment.* [37]*They were stoned, they were sawn in two, they were killed with the sword; they went about in skins of sheep and goats, destitute, afflicted, ill-treated –* [38]*of whom the world was not worthy – wandering over deserts and mountains, and in dens and caves of the earth.*

In time of fierce hostility and cruel persecution, many were given the faith to cope heroically with torture (in 11:35b the word used explicitly refers to the rack), mockery and other sufferings. The world despised them, but was not worthy of them. As Calvin says, 'Although the world may reject the servants of God as rubbish, the fact that it cannot bear them is to be thought of as its penalty because along with them goes some blessing from God.' In their moments of crisis, faith was imparted to them, by which they could evaluate the present and anticipate the future. Presented with an opportunity for release, they realized that present liberty is of passing worth. They looked forward to a better resurrection, knowing that the joys of that better country had already been prepared by a God who is always faithful (11:16, 11). These valiant men and women were given the strength to suffer rather than to conquer. They turned agonizing distress into triumphant achievement.

3. A faith which awaited fulfilment (11:39–40)

[39]*And all these, though well attested by their faith, did not receive what was promised,* [40]*since God had foreseen something better for us, that apart from us they should not be made perfect.*

Rich as it was, all their faith was confined to the limits of the old covenant. It strained forward to *something better.* They anticipated the fulfilment of God's promise, the fuller revelation in Christ, but they did not witness its realization. They could be *made perfect* only as Christians are today, that is by Jesus himself and his sacrifice. Perfection or fulfilment would come through a new covenant, by an eternal legacy, made possible because of a better sacrifice. The household of God (3:2, 6) consists of the faithful participants in the old covenant and the members of the new. All alike are redeemed by Christ, the only perfecter of everyone's faith (12:2).

Conclusion

In this passage the reader is confronted with both the courageous achievements and the imperfect attainments of the Old Testament heroes. They were enabled to do so much, but it was limited and partial. They inherited, received, obtained and proved the promises. But in some cases it was mainly a sense of expectancy and lifelong anticipation which characterized their faith. Abraham, Isaac and Jacob did not receive all that was promised (11:13); the fulfilment was not theirs to see, but they endured. Similarly, Christians receive some promises and experience their blessings, whilst at the same time they trust other promises and await their fulfilment. But we have received far more than any believer could have hoped to experience under the old covenant. They could not hope to experience personally the inward purification, freedom from fear, immediate help, timely grace, present and eternal salvation, certain hope, clear conscience, assured pardon and constant access[1] which we have in Christ. The richer provision ought surely to inspire us to better faith and more costly

[1] Heb. 1:3; 2:15, 18; 4:15–16; 7:25; 5:9; 6:18–19; 9:14, 26; 10:19–22.

sacrifice. If these courageous and devout sufferers achieved so much when, comparatively speaking, they had so little, then there must be no limit to our service. The opportunities are innumerable and the resources are limitless.

12:1–3

21. Consider him

At this point in his exposition the author turns from the lives of Old Testament heroes to the sufferings and achievement of the greatest example of all, the Lord Jesus Christ. Christ had warned his disciples that some would be delivered to tribulation, put to death and 'hated by all nations' for his name's sake. And persecution would come not only from the political authorities but from religious ones. Jesus told them that they would be excluded from synagogues and anyone who killed them would imagine he was doing God a service.[1] The letter has already made it clear that it is immensely rewarding to be a believer (10:35), but it is not easy. Ours is a strenuous race demanding steady perseverance. We must surely be encouraged by the fact that we are surrounded by former contestants who are *witnesses* to us of the faithfulness of God. As John White says, 'the writer's point is to bring witnesses before us who will testify that faith is worth it'.[2] They have finished the race. Now it is our turn; we must run it. Yet, although they inspire us, they cannot strengthen us. For the necessary qualities of continuance and endurance we need to look away to Jesus who not only offers a perfect example, but imparts necessary help (2:18; 4:16). The description of the Christian life as a race is familiar to all readers of the New Testament.[3] Using this vivid athletic imagery, the author tells his readers what they must reject, how they must run and where they must look.

[1] Mt. 24:9; Jn. 16:2.
[2] John White, *The Fight* (IVP, 1977), p. 108.
[3] 1 Cor. 9:24; Gal. 2:2.

1. What we must reject (12:1a)

Therefore, since we are surrounded by so great a cloud of witnesses, let us also lay aside every weight, and sin which clings so closely . . .

These Christian readers cannot afford to be hindered in a race which has such eternal consequences. Two items could easily impede their progress. One will restrict their activity (weights), the other would mar their performance (sin). This word *weight* (*onkon*) is used in classical literature for excessive physical weight and also for a burdensome load. In this context it can also refer to superfluous clothes and anything which handicaps us. The spiritual athlete must also throw off the *sin which clings so closely* – though it must be admitted that the distinction between *weight* and *sin* is not easy to define, and some commentators prefer to see this second phrase simply as an explanatory expansion of the first. The sin which clings so closely all too easily entangles. Before we know where we are, we have been tripped up and hurled to the ground in a race which had all the possibilities of triumphant victory.

2. How we must run (12:1b)

. . . and let us run with perseverance the race that is set before us.

Believers are expected to *run with perseverance* (*hypomonēs*) or 'endurance', a word which appears several times in this letter.[4] Jesus 'endured' the cross and also, before his death, 'endured from sinners such hostility against himself' (12:2–3). The disciples of Christ must surely realize that to 'follow in his steps'[5] is to experience opposition, pain, suffering and rejection. Mature believers know that the life to which they are committed has incomparable compensations, but also makes rigorous demands. Running with perseverance is possible only whilst they are looking not to the encouraging witnesses, the present contestants, the ultimate goal, or even the promised reward; but to Christ alone, or they will either

[4] Heb. 10:32, 36; 12:7. [5] 1 Pet. 2:21.

drop out through distraction or collapse with exhaustion.

3. Where we must look (12:2–3)

. . . [2]*looking to Jesus the pioneer and perfecter of our faith, who for the joy that was set before him endured the cross, despising the shame, and is seated at the right hand of the throne of God.*

[3]*Consider him who endured from sinners such hostility against himself, so that you may not grow weary or fainthearted.*

In the course of the race the eyes of every Christian athlete must be directed firmly and continually on the Lord Jesus himself. The word used here (*aphorōntes*), translated *looking*, indicates the action of one who, aware of rival attractions, deliberately looks away from other things. This runner must keep his eyes 'fixed on Jesus' (NEB), not only at the first moment of the race, but constantly during the whole struggle, knowing that 'Christ is always near and in sight' (Westcott). Then, with superb theological skill, our author turns to a vivid description of the one to whom we must look.

We must look away to Jesus *the compassionate man*. Once again Christ's human name, Jesus, is given a place of special emphasis. The human Jesus has known our experiences of trial and fierce adversity. When we feel that we cannot summon another ounce of energy for 'the race that is set before us', we must think of the race that was set before him. He endured, though his course was incomparably more difficult than ours. Jesus triumphed and, in his strength, so can we.

Moreover, we must direct our gaze to Jesus *the victorious pioneer*. Christ is described here as the pathfinder or trailblazer of faith. He certainly initiated our faith as Christians and is used to bring many sons to glory (2:10), but he is also the pioneer of those Old Testament saints whose valiant deeds have just been described. He has 'led all the people of God, from earliest times, along the path of faith, although, since His incarnation and passion His personal example makes His leadership available to His people in a way that was impossible before' (Bruce). He did not fail them and he will not disappoint us.

Believers are required to fix their attention on Jesus *the only perfecter*. He brings the faith of the former saints (11:40) and ours to triumphant completion. He makes it all perfect and he alone. Our moral integrity is essential, but that cannot bring our faith to completion. Our devoted service is valuable, but that cannot perfect our faith. Our spiritual experiences can be inspiring and illuminating, but Jesus is faith's only consummator. Believers rely completely on him, for he ran the greatest race right to its finish, and we come to fullness of life only in him.[6]

Those who wish to run the race with perseverance must also look to Jesus *the devoted servant*. He came into the world, this letter reminds us, to do God's will (10:7, 9) as a lowly (2:14, 17) and obedient (5:8) servant. The 'joy that was set before him' may have been the joy of anticipating God's delight that his will had been done and his work accomplished,[7] or the joy of 'bringing many sons to glory' (2:10). Some expositors suggest that the words *for the joy* should be translated not as we have just done, 'because of', but 'in exchange for' or 'in the place of', so reading, 'Instead of the joy set before him he endured the cross.' In this case the joy that was set before him was the pre-existent bliss which he enjoyed with the Father in eternity. Jesus took 'the form of a servant' and 'did not count his equality with God a thing to be grasped'.[8]

Christians must look away to Jesus *the effective priest*. He is *seated* in the heavens. This recalls this letter's majestic introduction: 'When he had made purification for sins, he sat down' (1:3). The writer rejoiced that 'we have such a high priest, one who is seated at the right hand of the throne of the Majesty in heaven' (8:1). Obviously there will be occasions when the weights of life hinder our movements in the race and when the sin which clings so closely impedes our progress, troubles our fellow Christians, mars our witness and grieves our Lord. At such times we must look away to Christ and recall that he is seated in the heavens, his saving work complete. If we look in faith and penitence[9] we can receive the cleansing we need and the forgiveness he bes-

[6] Col. 2:10. [7] Jn. 17:4.
[8] Phil. 2:5–8. [9] 1 Jn. 1:9.

tows.[10] He is the only one who can effectively remove the impediments.

Moreover, believers must turn their eyes to Jesus *the enthroned Lord.* He is at the *throne of God.* His redemptive work complete, he waits for the consummation of the ages and for the great moment when every tongue shall confess his lordship. These first-century believers were about to be exposed to the cruel hazards of Caesar's lordship. As the social pressures gave way to physical assault, they would need this assurance of the enthroned Christ. They took heart from the assured fact that their destiny was not in the hands of Caesar, his provincial governors or their local magistrates. Their frail lives were in the strong hands of Jesus, the enthroned Lord.

Finally, Christians must look away to Jesus *the patient sufferer.* They must *consider him* lest they become exhausted. They might be mocked, assaulted, scourged, forsaken, handed over by informers, imprisoned, falsely accused and even killed – but so was he. In the last few days of his life especially, he had suffered all this. They must consider him and his endurance in the face of such bitter hostility, lest they become exhausted in the race. Our author uses two vivid words when he writes about the danger of growing *weary* and *fainthearted.* William Barclay points out that Aristotle uses these words 'of an athlete who flings himself on the ground in panting relaxation and collapse *after* he has surged past the winning post of the race. So the writer to the Hebrews is in effect saying: "Don't give up too soon; don't relax before the tape; don't collapse until the winning post is past; stay on your feet until you get to the end." ' No man or woman can hope to stay the course in such a hazardous contest without divine aid. But this letter and the rest of the New Testament assure us that the promised help is in Jesus. We must look away to him.

[10] Heb. 9:14, 26; 10:11–12, 17–18.

12:4–11

22. The correction we need

[4]*In your struggle against sin you have not yet resisted to the point of shedding your blood.*

The author has just emphasized the strenuous nature of true faith. It is like an adventurous pilgrimage (11:14–16), a hazardous conflict (11:32–38) and an exacting race (12:1–2). It seems that some of these first-century athletes were in danger of dropping out and they are exhorted to consider Jesus, who encountered bitter and relentless opposition during his earthly ministry. By looking away to him they will be saved from exhaustion and apostasy (12:3). It looks as though the author is here reminding his Christian friends that, although they have experienced some unpleasant hostility, they have not yet been required to pay for their faith by the surrender of their lives. Christ endured the contradiction of sinners and was ultimately brought to a cruel cross, but they had certainly not had to resist the enemy to the point of shedding their blood. They might well be imprisoned (13:3), attacked and made to suffer abuse for Christ (13:13), but they must not look on these experiences as pointless adversity. God may well be using these perilous events as a means of necessary correction and helpful, purposeful discipline. The author gives three reasons for accepting such experiences as divine correction or pruning[1] designed to increase our fruitfulness. In times of testing, those who believe in God must recall his word, his care and his purpose.

[1] Jn. 15:2.

1. Remember God's word (12:5–6)

5*And have you forgotten the exhortation which addresses you as sons? –*

'My son, do not regard lightly the discipline of the Lord,
nor lose courage when you are punished by him.
6*For the Lord disciplines him whom he loves,*
and chastises every son whom he receives.'

Have you forgotten the exhortation . . .? This epistle recognizes that not all who hear or read God's word give their total attention to it. At times the truth is quickly forgotten; we can easily drift away from its teaching (2:1). Once again the writer demonstrates his profound confidence in the teaching of the Old Testament Scriptures and this time he refers to a familiar saying from the book of Proverbs (3:11–12) to drive his point home. The quotation presents us with three important aspects of the theme. When the Lord disciplines his people some are indifferent to it, others become overwhelmed by it, but, as Christians, we ought to rejoice in it.

First, some are indifferent to it. *'My son, do not regard lightly the discipline of the Lord.'* Some Christians may well be in danger of ignoring or dismissing the fact that God's sovereign hand is at work as much through life's adversities as in its joys and pleasures. He may well be saying something extremely important to us through our troubles that we could not or would not easily receive if everything went well for us at all times. He may be calling us to renewed confidence in his providential care, to a fresh willingness to commit our entire life to him whatever the outcome of our immediate difficulties, to a desire for God's will and not our own wishes, to a readiness to go through any experience if only it will make us more Christlike in the end. People with spiritual values of this kind will certainly not want to *regard lightly the discipline of the Lord.*

Secondly, others become overwhelmed by it. Far from disregarding what the Lord is saying to them through suffering, some Christians *lose courage* when adversity overtakes them. Weighed down by their troubles, they become despondent and feel sure that the Lord must have forsaken them. It is a great mistake to react in this way to the discipline of the

Lord. The Christian who goes through severe trouble must remember therefore that the God who tests us is the Lord who helps us. He will certainly not test us beyond our strength,[2] and however serious our adversities, his grace will be sufficient.

Thirdly, Scripture teaches that we should rejoice in our sufferings. *For the Lord disciplines him whom he loves.* Adversity should not drive us to despair. Those who are not loved in this special way are not tested. The devil is content to leave most of his subjects in the superficial 'peace' of spiritual apathy and ignorance. Those who are in the Lord's company are sure to be wounded by the arrows which are constantly directed at Christ himself. Jesus told his disciples they should expect nothing less.[3] These sufferings prove that, through faith in Christ, we belong to God's family. He *chastises every son whom he receives.* The Lord's corrective ministry verifies our sonship.

2. Remember God's care (12:7–9)

[7]*It is for discipline that you have to endure. God is treating you as sons; for what son is there whom his father does not discipline?* [8]*If you are left without discipline, in which all have participated, then you are illegitimate children and not sons.* [9]*Besides this, we have had earthly fathers to discipline us and we respected them. Shall we not much more be subject to the Father of spirits and live?*

In the earlier verses of this chapter these persecuted Christians are urged to recall the example of Christ. Here the author directs his readers' attention to another highly important biblical doctrine which will fortify believers in time of severe testing: the fatherhood of God. Our tribulations can bring us a far deeper experience of the continuing and dependable love of God.

In these verses we are reminded, first of all, that the father treasures his children. *God is treating you as sons.* The person who has no experience of the Lord's discipline may well question whether he truly belongs to him. Our adoption into

[2] 1 Cor. 10:13. [3] Mt. 10:22.

the family of God will bring not only privilege and security, but adversity also.

Next, we notice here that the father corrects his children. *What son is there whom his father does not discipline?* A father who really loves his children is anxious that they should realize their potential and come to maturity. Without his discipline they will remain immature, childish and undeveloped.

Furthermore, these verses make it clear that the father equips his children. Fathers who love their children do not merely issue orders; they encourage our response by the quality of their love and do all within their power to help us. The author of this letter says, 'We respect our earthly fathers, but let us submit ourselves entirely to our heavenly Father.' The term *Father of spirits* is used as a way of expressing the contrast between an earthly parent and our spiritual Father, the eternal God. It is interesting to observe that if we submit, we shall *live*. The first man and woman were clearly told that if they disobeyed God's word, they would die. By refusing to *be subject to the Father of spirits*, they brought spiritual death upon themselves and their children.

3. Remember God's purpose (12:10–11)

This whole experience of hardship, suffering and discipline is essentially purposive. No matter how painful the experience may be, God will use it. In his sovereignty nothing is wasted or useless. When confronted by trials, believers must think of their immediate benefit, ultimate outcome and permanent effect.

a. Think of their immediate benefit (12:10)

For they disciplined us for a short time at their pleasure, but he disciplines us for our good, that we may share his holiness.

Family discipline is motivated by, and tends to be subject to, the personal whims or views of the parents. It is *at their pleasure* or 'as they choose'. The motives for parental discipline are not always commendable and, as Westcott observes, the human 'may fail as to the method, and his purpose may be selfish'. But all God's disciplinary processes are directed to *our good*. There is an immediate benefit. By his very nature as our loving and generous Father, he could not possibly introduce any form of discipline into our lives which would not be of real help to us. More than all else, he longs that we might *share his holiness*; our closeness to God in sanctification often becomes far more real to us in the grim and difficult episodes of life. Adversity sometimes helps us to enter more fully into our indebtedness to God, our partnership with Christ and our reliance on the Spirit. In this way we can the more fully *share his holiness*.

b. *Think of their ultimate outcome* (12:11a)

For the moment all discipline seems painful rather than pleasant; later it yields the peaceful fruit of righteousness . . .

At the time all discipline is *painful*. The believer, however, does not think solely of his present reaction, but considers its ultimate usefulness: *later it yields the peaceful fruit of righteousness*. It all takes time. Fruit does not appear immediately the tree is planted. If life's adversities, and God's use of them in discipline, produce in the end both inward peace and moral uprightness, we cannot possibly have suffered in vain.

c. *Think of their permanent effect* (12:11b)

Discipline produces the peaceful fruit of righteousness *to those who have been trained by it*. Divine correction provides the church with well-trained Christians. Our writer here leaves his horticultural illustration of the chastised believer's fruit and returns to the athletic imagery he has used at the beginning of the chapter. Those who are *trained* (*gegymnasmenois*) know that it all requires effort, but it is abundantly worth while.[4]

[4] 2 Tim. 2:5–6.

12:12–17
23. What to do next

The previous passage is largely concerned with the believer's passive acceptance of fatherly correction. The writer now addresses himself to the complementary and equally important truth, that of the Christian's active pursuit of spiritual ideals. In these verses he further illustrates his intense love for Old Testament Scripture. The paragraph is almost a mosaic of biblical ideas and images drawn from the prophetic tradition (12:12), the wisdom literature (12:13), psalmody (12:14), the law of Moses (12:15) and the story of the patriarchs (12:16). The earlier presentation of the Christian life as a strenuous race now gives place to the picture of a difficult journey. What is required here is not a sudden burst of energy, but steady and persistent exertion. In a group of important exhortations these Christians are urged to overcome despondency, maintain harmony, pursue holiness, seek grace and prevent defilement.

1. We must overcome despondency (12:12–13)

[12]*Therefore lift your drooping hands and strengthen your weak knees,* [13]*and make straight paths for your feet, so that what is lame may not be put out of joint but rather be healed.*

Making use of familiar language from the prophet Isaiah's description of the highway of holiness,[1] our writer urges his readers to lift up their *drooping hands* and make firm their

[1] Is. 35:3.

feeble knees. Motivated by this idea of the Christian life as the 'route march of the people of God' (Montefiore), the first exhortation is quite simply: 'Be strong and go straight. Cast away despondency and press on.' The reference to *drooping hands* and *weak knees* is familiar imagery in Jewish literature, often used to describe attitudes of discouragement and despair. Here the writer uses the Septuagint version of Proverbs 4:26 and urges these believers to press on to the goal so that those members of the church who have become despondent (*lame*) will notice their good example, receive fresh courage and begin to march again rather than fall even further behind. He knows that some members desperately need to *be healed*, for some of these vital limbs in the local church have been *put out of joint*. But if healing is to come, it is not simply the responsibility of the leaders, tireless pastors though they are (13:17), but of every single member.

2. We must maintain harmony (12:14a)

Strive for peace with all men . . .

A sense of rich corporate unity in the local congregation will do more to create the right atmosphere for healing than almost anything else. They must not only keep the peace; they must actively pursue it. Possibly this church's recent troubles with their Jewish persecutors had led to sharp differences of opinion within the congregation itself. What attitude should one take towards apostates, for example? Does a Jewish Christian have any spiritual responsibility to obey the cultic requirements of the old covenant? These issues could give rise to sharp division within the local church. These Christians must *strive for peace*, an adaptation of the psalmist's injunction to 'seek peace, and pursue it'.[2] It will not come automatically because people are Christians. The devil will try to disrupt the life of any group of believers; the 'roaring lion'[3] is not likely to leave them for long in harmonious peace.

[2] Ps. 34:14.   [3] 1 Pet. 5:8.

3. We must pursue holiness (12:14b)

Strive for . . . the holiness without which no one will see the Lord.

In this onward march believers must not only live in loving harmony with one another, but also in vital personal holiness before God. In Christ they have been sanctified (10:10); that is part of Christ's saving work. But here holiness, like peace, is also a quality for which one must earnestly *strive*. It is an ambition which must be pursued throughout the whole of life. Without it no-one will see the Lord. Possibly, as Nairne suggests, the reference to seeing the Lord is an anticipation of the coming of Christ (10:37) and the great concluding subject of this chapter (12:22–29). This is the writer's call to practical and personal holiness of life. Clearly in the teaching of Scripture, sanctification has both negative and positive aspects. Negatively, believers must keep themselves from defilement, a theme to be developed in the following verses. Like the sanctified vessels in the temple, or the best vessels in a house, they must be kept pure and clean.[4] But there is a positive side to all this as well: believers must not only be set apart *from* what is evil, but separated *to* God, consecrated and entirely given up to his service.

4. We must seek grace (12:15a)

See to it that no one fail to obtain the grace of God . . .

If these Christians are to follow after holiness, then they must rely upon God's grace. It cannot be pursued in their own energy. Possibly some of this church's membership had drawn back or fallen short of that grace. They began this life of faith only by God's saving grace[5] and only by grace can it be continued. The writer takes care, therefore, to issue a solemn warning: Make sure that you rely constantly on the promised grace. See to it that you do not fall behind by 'not keeping pace with the movement of divine grace' (Westcott).

[4] 2 Tim. 2:21. [5] Eph. 2:8.

5. We must prevent defilement (12:15b–17)

... that no 'root of bitterness' spring up and cause trouble, and by it the many become defiled; [16]*that no one be immoral or irreligious like Esau, who sold his birthright for a single meal.* [17]*For you know that afterward, when he desired to inherit the blessing, he was rejected, for he found no chance to repent, though he sought it with tears.*

If believers are to pursue holiness, then they must also shun evil. Sin, possibly in this context the frightening sin of apostasy, is like a contagious disease. It can quickly spread throughout a whole church. Once more, Scripture is used to drive the point home to these Jewish believers, so familiar with their Old Testament. The Mosaic law described the damage done by an idolator in the Israelite camp, a person 'whose heart turns away . . . from the Lord our God'. He is a root, bearing bitter and poisonous fruit. His sin is unpardonable because he is insincere. The words of the covenant are on his lips but not in his heart. His hypocrisy and apostasy are like a dangerous poison; the defilement spreads from the offender to his compatriots.[6]

Possibly in their case, however, the disease is caused not by apostasy (as the Deuteronomy quotation certainly implies), but by immorality. The peril is the same. In the Jewish tradition it was fervently believed that Esau was profane and corrupt, basically godless and *irreligious*. He sold his birthright to Jacob and once that was done it could not be recovered. He tried in vain to reverse the decision he had made in that moment when he was dominated by his sensual appetites. The sombre warning may refer to Esau's plea with his father. Though he cried to his father *with tears,*[7] there was no opportunity for change of mind (*repent*) on the part of Isaac. It was all too late; the blessing had been given to Jacob. The promises were not for Esau now but for his brother. Alternatively, the verse may refer to his cry to God. Similarly, it could not be reversed. He had despised the promises and forfeited the blessing. Physical appetites had meant more to him than spiritual privileges. It is a serious pastoral warning.

[6] Dt. 29:18–19. [7] Gn. 27:34.

The apostate who has deliberately turned his back on the divine blessing and persists in his stubborn rejection cannot be restored. The Esau illustration simply repeats in a more stark form the letter's earlier warning: 'Therefore, while the promise of entering his rest remains, let us fear lest any of you be judged to have failed to reach it' (4:1).

The rich, promised blessings may be forfeited by those who deliberately choose apostasy or immorality. Probably both sins are intended by the Esau illustration, though apostasy and religious infidelity are more likely in this context. Manson is probably right when he says, 'It was unbelief in the divine promise to his house, not mere sensuality, that led Esau to the irrevocable step of bartering away his birthright. No later repentance was able to undo that act.'[8] These readers must take care lest they too forfeit the promises of God and thereby expose themselves to the danger of losing their inheritance.

Conclusion

Two very practical responsibilities emerge here: we need to be careful about our own spiritual lives, and helpful to others in theirs.

a. We need to be careful

It is all too easy to become *defiled* by immorality or infidelity. There is no room here for a casual or superior attitude to the possibility of defilement. Believers can be seriously hindered by the bad example, low standards and corrupt teaching of others. Christians need to *see to it* that they are not defiled. This does not mean that we adopt a 'holier than thou' attitude; it is sheer realism in action. The devil will use all manner of means to waylay us in the march, or throw us out of the race. Believers are on the alert 'hating even the garment spotted by the flesh'.[9] It was in a similar religious and moral context to that found in this passage (idolatry and immorality) that Paul told the Corinthians: 'Let any one who thinks that he stands take heed lest he fall.'[10]

[8] Manson, p. 85. [9] Jude 23. [10] 1 Cor. 10:12.

b. We ought to be helpful

But the Christian life is something far more than simply keeping our own garments clean. That is only part of our responsibility. If, as seems likely, the members of this church were exposed to spiritual and moral hazards, then everybody is expected to do his best to help the rest. How do we help others?

Our basic attitude is important. *Drooping hands* and *weak knees* have a depressing effect on others. Despondency is the devil's tool, not only to hinder us, but to depress others. An elderly friend of mine had these words written in the front of her Bible: 'I absolutely refuse to gratify the devil by being downhearted.'

Our personal example is essential; the *straight paths* we make for our feet may ensure safe travel for others. We do not want those who are already *lame* to be further disabled. If we spend our time creating peaceful relationships and pursuing Christian holiness, our example will be a blessing to all.

Our loving correction is necessary. Remember that this pastoral appeal is addressed to *all* the members and not just to the leaders (13:17). If particular members are at fault, then the spiritual responsibility for putting the matter right rests on the whole congregation. Every Christian has some pastoral responsibility for his fellow Christians.[11] It needs to be given practical expression in warm encouragement, sensible advice, prayerful sympathy, supportive fellowship, and the regular sharing of spiritual truth, as well as in mutual correction.

[11] Gal. 6:1–2.

12:18–29
24. Then and now

This section brings our writer's main argument to an arresting conclusion. He comes now to his final contrast-picture:[1] Mount Sinai and Mount Zion, the awesome promulgation of the law and the joyful proclamation of the gospel. Old and new covenants are here presented in majestic contrast. Three aspects of the theme appear to dominate the exposition: through Christ we belong to a spiritual, eternal and unshakeable kingdom.

1. We belong to a spiritual kingdom (12:18–22a)

18*For you have not come to what may be touched, a blazing*
fire, and darkness, and gloom, and a tempest, 19*and the sound*
of a trumpet, and a voice whose words made the hearers
entreat that no further messages be spoken to them. 20*For they*
could not endure the order that was given, 'If even a beast
touches the mountain, it shall be stoned.' 21*Indeed, so terri-*
fying was the sight that Moses said, 'I tremble with fear.'
22*But you have come to Mount Zion . . .*

There is an implied, but unmistakable, contrast in these verses between the physical features of the old covenant and the spiritual aspects of the new. It is portrayed here as the difference between a physical mountain where the law was given, Sinai; and the spiritual mountain, Mount Zion, the heavenly

[1] *Cf.* 1:4–14; 2:1–4; 2:5–9; 3:1–6; 3:7 – 4:11; 5:1–10; 8:1–5; 9:1–5; 8:6–13; 9:6–14.

Jerusalem. Under the old covenant God's holiness and majesty were emphasized by those natural signs which accompanied his presence, sometimes *a blazing fire*, at other times deep *darkness* and *gloom*, and the piercing blast of the celestial trumpets. Under the old covenant the emphasis was on the infinite distance between God and man. Two things are given special mention.

First of all, *the divine voice was overwhelming*. They could not bear to hear God speaking and implored Moses to communicate the word to them.[2] But our writer contrasts this Israelite entreaty with the Christian revelation by which God speaks to his people *directly* in his word. 'See that you do not refuse him who is speaking' (12:25). It is no less serious a word than that spoken at Sinai. But though it makes exacting demands, it also offers enabling promises. At the people's request, the voice at Sinai warned on earth; it came through the lips of Moses. But this voice speaks directly from heaven. If they did not escape, how much less shall we?

Secondly, *the divine presence was unapproachable*. The Hebrew people were instructed to keep away. Even if a straying animal, let alone a responsible Israelite, touched the mountain, it had to die (12:20). But under the new covenant to go up is to live. It is by 'a new and living way' that believers come to God (10:25), not a way of death. When they traverse that living way they discover that a living priest is interceding for them (7:25). So when the law was given, people were under the penalty of death; under the gospel they rejoice in the promise of life. They have arrived, not at the foot of an unapproachable earthly mountain, but within the gates of a gloriously accessible and eternal city.

2. We belong to an eternal kingdom (12:22–24)

[22]*But you have come to Mount Zion and to the city of the living God, the heavenly Jerusalem, and to innumerable angels in festal gathering,* [23]*and to the assembly of the first-born who are enrolled in heaven, and to a judge who is God of all, and to the spirits of just men made perfect,* [24]*and to Jesus, the mediator of a new covenant, and to the sprinkled blood that*

[2] Ex. 20:18–19.

speaks more graciously than the blood of Abel.

We now come to a matchless one-sentence description of the Christian believer's destiny. The ceremonial provisions of the old covenant were temporary. It is apparent here that we have come to the rich provision of not only a new covenant, but an eternal one. It will last for ever, because it belongs to the realm of divine imperishable reality.

Perhaps these Jewish Christians had been taunted by their relatives, friends and neighbours, and their Christianity exposed to the criticism that they had abandoned all the great majestic features of the Jewish faith in favour of the man from Nazareth. Had they forgotten the land which God had given them, and Jerusalem, its holy city where God had been worshipped and his power acknowledged throughout the centuries? And what of the heavenly visitations this nation and people had experienced, and those celestial messengers who had served them throughout the dark and difficult centuries? Again, what about the great personalities of former years, Moses, David and the rest, who had obeyed this law and worshipped the God of Abraham, Isaac and Jacob, *the spirits of just men*? Could these Christians forsake such a noble heritage?

The author's teaching is rich in warm pastoral encouragement. Believers do not dismiss the past; they inherit its treasures and witness its fulfilment. The saints of former days were on pilgrimage. They stood on tiptoe, their eyes fixed on the distant horizon. In one sense Christians share their anticipation (13:14), knowing that the best is yet to be, but in another sense they have arrived, their feet have stood within the gates. They have come to the heavenly Jerusalem, the city of the living God. And having arrived, they realize that all the abiding blessings of God's earlier revelation are here. The angels are present in vast numbers, this company of *the first-born*, robed in festal attire, their presence indicating beyond doubt that God is in the midst. The righteous of days gone by are here too, *made perfect* through the work of Christ.

Although the scene describes a joyous festival, it is a serious theme to contemplate, for to enter the city is to meet the judge who is *God of all*, the Lord of both the earlier saints and the present believers, of Gentiles as well as Jews. He is the universal sovereign and all must prostrate themselves before him. But the mediator is present as well as the judge. Confronted with God as judge, Moses, the mediator of the old covenant, trembled with fear (12:21) but, through the ministry of Jesus, *the mediator of a new covenant*, we draw near with confidence. Christ's human name is introduced deliberately here. We have come to Jesus, the man like us, and the man for us, whose *sprinkled blood* is still eloquent. It *speaks* of grace and pardon, whilst Abel's blood cries for vengeance and retribution. Our author is saying, in effect, as Christian believers, all this is ours in Christ. The blessings are eternal. No persecuting Jewish neighbour could rob these believers of such rich assurance. Like the heavenly multitude, their names were *enrolled in heaven*. They are citizens of an eternal kingdom.

3. We belong to an unshakeable kingdom (12:25–29)

Yet all this confronts the privileged believer not only with deeper certainty, but also with greater responsibility. The account of this celestial assembly will inspire reflective contemplation, and that is all to the good. But in the mind of the writer it has a further purpose; it is intended to inspire an immediate and active response. For all Christian people earthly troubles, as well as celestial joys, were on the immediate horizon. Where everything around them was being shaken, these believers were not to be afraid, but to rejoice in the secure, immovable kingdom to which they most certainly belonged.

This indebtedness to Christ is to be given practical expression in obedience, confidence and reverence.

a. We must be obedient (12:25)

See that you do not refuse him who is speaking. For if they did not escape when they refused him who warned them on earth, much less shall we escape if we reject him who warns from heaven.

The word of this kingdom shares the imperishable quality of

the kingdom itself. It is an eternally relevant word and its injunctions are for all time. These Christians must not refuse to hear and obey *him who is speaking*. Membership of the permanent and abiding kingdom inspires not only diligent study of God's word, but an eager obedience and faithful witness to its truth.

b. We must be confident (12:26–27)

[26]*His voice then shook the earth; but now he has promised, 'Yet once more I will shake not only the earth but also the heaven.'* [27]*This phrase, 'Yet once more,' indicates the removal of what is shaken, as of what has been made, in order that what cannot be shaken may remain.*

The description of the events at Sinai is here linked to a prophetic account in Haggai 2:6 of the last days. In Moses' day the mountain shook, but in the coming great Day the entire earth, and also heaven, will be shaken and removed. Believers actually belong to the order of things that *cannot be shaken*. These things, like the Christ who controls them, *remain* (*cf.* 1:11–12). Christians are alert to what is happening in the world, but the news does not fill them with fear. Conscious as they are of political instability, social pressures, economic hazards, religious apostasy, physical hardship and moral decay, they do not despair. Their trust is in God and they are safe.

c. We must be reverent (12:28–29)

[28]*Therefore let us be grateful for receiving a kingdom that cannot be shaken, and thus let us offer to God acceptable worship, with reverence and awe;* [29]*for our God is a consuming fire.*

But the confidence does not lead to a form of cocksure arrogance. Believers are often in danger either of taking these great things for granted, or of trivializing them by flippant attitudes or inappropriate language. In the teaching of this passage, the Christian should live in the spirit of adoring gratitude, for he of all people has received *a kingdom that cannot be shaken*. Moreover, the believer is grateful that such an incomparably holy God has made himself known to sinful men. The fire on Sinai is a thing of the past (12:18), but the blazing fire of God's holy, jealous and righteous love[3] will never be extinguished. The believer knows that in the presence of that bright light all his sins are exposed.[4] He also rejoices that mercifully, in its refining flames, they can also be consumed.

[3] Dt. 4:24. [4] Is. 33:14.

13:1–16
25. Pastoral exhortations

This closing chapter comes almost as an abrupt intrusion. We are confronted with urgent pastoral instructions about love in the congregation and hospitality in the home, about prison visiting and the importance of marital loyalty, about man's greed for present possessions and his fear of an uncertain future. Why does the author suddenly turn to this apparently disconnected series of moral exhortations?

All these issues have immediate relevance in twentieth-century society. Those who are indifferent to them thereby prove that they have hardly grasped the letter's earlier teaching, for this Christian message has profound social and moral content. They are not merely implications which can be considered and ignored as an optional addendum to a more spiritual message. 'Therefore, if this truth be so, it demands the following changes in your life . . .'[1] In the teaching of these verses Christians are expected to be loving, pure, contented, loyal, bold and worshipful.

1. Be loving (13:1–3)

In the cultivation of this and every congregation's corporate life, love matters more than all else. Our writer identifies three aspects of brotherly love, and devotes the first sentences of this pastoral exhortation to stress the importance of love's necessary continuance, its generous expression in Christian hospitality, and its practical responsibility in caring for prisoners and the afflicted.

[1] Rom. 12:1; Eph. 4:1; Phil. 2:12.

a. Love's necessary continuance (13:1)

Let brotherly love continue.

It is called *brotherly love* (*philadelphia*), a term both used by the apostles Paul and Peter,[2] and specially meaningful in Hebrews. Christ is not ashamed to address believers as his 'brothers' (2:11–12) and our author is also delighted to use that name. They are to be not only holy brothers (3:1), but loving brothers also. If believers belong to the same family, then the Father's love must be expressed in their lives. This exhortation may have been particularly important if, as seems likely, this local church had been disrupted by divisions, rivalries and feuds (12:14; 13:9).

This *brotherly love* must *continue*. Christian love must not degenerate into a mere pious emotion. It must be expressed in continuing practical concern. Calvin reminds us here that 'nothing evaporates more easily than love when everybody looks after himself more than his wife and gives less consideration to others. Moreover many offences occur every day to separate us'.

b. Love's generous expression (13:2)

Do not neglect to show hospitality to strangers, for thereby some have entertained angels unawares.

Love is not content with words. It demonstrates its reality in compassionate deeds. The readers must open their homes to visitors and be generous with their possessions. First-century inns were notoriously immoral, unhygienic and expensive. Christian travellers had to know that they could count on a warm welcome at the home of a fellow believer. If love does not issue in a hospitable home, it has scarcely begun to work at all. In the course of this exhortation the author's love of Scripture emerges again. He reminds his readers of the generosity of Old Testament saints who, in entertaining angels, received the attendant blessing of God.[3] Of course, as Jesus said, when we welcome strangers we receive not only angels,

[2] Rom. 12:10; 1 Pet. 1:22.   [3] Gn. 18:19; Jdg. 13.

but Christ himself.[4]

One of the most encouraging features of contemporary church life is the way in which homes are being used, possibly as never before, in the work of evangelism, teaching and fellowship. Church Bible studies are held in the homes of Christian people and evangelistic house-groups are also being used as a way of reaching non-churchgoers with the good news of Christ. Many unbelievers find it extremely difficult to attend a church service. The informal meeting in the relaxed atmosphere of a Christian home can enable them to speak freely and openly about their doubts.

This verse is not only a challenge about the occasional use of the home for meetings, but also about the regular ministry of the home for hospitality. Students and nurses, especially those from overseas, or those denied the blessing of Christian parents, can be strengthened in the faith and helped to spiritual maturity by men and women who offer the warm encouragement of Christian hospitality. It is more necessary in these days than ever. With the serious breakdown of family life and the erosion of home stability, young converts particularly need 'parents' in the faith. Love which is merely vocal is in danger of becoming mainly sham.

c. *Love's practical responsibility* (13:3)

Remember those who are in prison, as though in prison with them; and those who are ill-treated, since you also are in the body.

What about those who, robbed of their freedom, cannot visit our homes, but long for us to visit them? The readers must think of the prisoners and feel for them sympathetically as though they were in prison alongside them. This means that they think carefully about the kind of help they would like if they were prisoners; a personal visit, some warm encouragement, a sustaining prayer, some useful provisions. It is most likely that *those who are in prison* were there because of their faith, but of that we cannot be certain. The reference to compassionate responsibility for *those who are ill-treated*

[4] Mt. 25:31–40.

does sound as though some believers had been physically assaulted. These too must be helped in love by those who can feel for those in trouble, remembering that they share the same human frailty and limitations.

This letter's concluding exhortations, for all their disjointed appearance, have a marked contemporary relevance. In an age like ours where political persecution is a sad feature in several nations and where thousands of people are devoting their energies to the battle for human rights, this letter's insistence that we 'remember those in prison as if you were their fellow prisoners' (NIV) is a salutary and necessary reminder of our spiritual, social and political responsibilites. In the Lausanne Covenant evangelical Christians all over the world have given expression to their concern about prisoners of conscience. They have not only promised to pray for the leaders of the nations, but have also appealed to such leaders to 'guarantee freedom of thought and conscience, and freedom to practice and propagate religion in accordance with the will of God and as set forth in The Universal Declaration of Human Rights'. The Covenant goes on to express 'deep concern for all who have been unjustly imprisoned, and especially for our brethren who are suffering for their testimony to the Lord Jesus. We promise to pray and work for their freedom.' Such expressions need to be not only embodied within an important covenant, but manifest also in practical concern and appropriate political action. Andrei Sakharov estimated that of the 10,000 prisoners of conscience in the USSR, about 2,000 are religious prisoners. If such believers belong to our family, we shall surely want to feel for their needs, pray intelligently for their spiritual support and campaign strenuously and sensitively for their release. Many Christians give time to meaningful intercession for prisoners of conscience with the aid of a prayer booklet which provides photographs, maps, terms of punishment and other important details of many people who share our faith but not our freedom.[5]

We also need to be reminded that some of our own neighbours may be suffering from other forms of 'imprisonment', less stark but no less distressing. Many elderly people are

[5] The booklet *Christian Prisoners in the USSR* is distributed by Keston College, Heathfield Road, Keston, Kent, BR2 6BA, UK.

desperately 'cut off'. A recent report publishes the words of an eighty-one-year-old widow:

> I am still terribly lonely. It's the evenings. The club closes at 4.30 p.m. and there's nothing but long, empty hours until bed-time . . . I've heard so many old people say 'There's nothing for us now'. You've got to eat to sort of keep alive. But there's nothing. The time is so long . . . the evenings . . . the weekends. I've heard several people say 'I don't care how soon the end comes for me' . . . I know lots of people. But that isn't the same as a close friend.[6]

Some patients in geriatric units would welcome regular visits from a Christian. Are not such 'isolated' people in greater need of the good news of Christ at the end of their lives than others who may often hear of him through everyday contacts with believers? But shut-in people will hear only if they are remembered and visited by Christians who discern this neglected area of work as their opportunity for pastoral service and compassionate witness.

2. Be pure (13:4)

Let marriage be held in honour among all, and let the marriage bed be undefiled; for God will judge the immoral and adulterous.

The political prisoner may seem remote from our immediate environment, but everyone is in touch with someone for whom marriage breakdown has become the most tragic aspect of his or her life. Our writer's exposition of 'brotherly love' leads naturally to marital love. This first-century letter insists that marriage should be honoured by all, calling us as it does to moral uprightness and eternal accountability. Although strikingly relevant for contemporary Christians, this is a slightly unexpected injunction in this first-century context, for if the letter was addressed to Jewish Christians, the moral code they had imbibed was clear and uncompromising about marriage loyalty. But more recent Jewish leaders were per-

[6] *Cry, and you Cry Alone* (Help the Aged, London), p. 19.

petrating some more 'acceptable' teaching about divorce.[7]

Some expositors have wondered whether this exhortation is directed to those who are in danger not of violating their marital vows, but of deprecating the institution of marriage. Ascetical groups, both Christian and Jewish, were well known in the early centuries, and some disdained marriage if they did not actually prohibit it.[8] They believed that all things to do with 'the flesh' were essentially corrupt since they concerned 'matter' rather than 'spirit'. It is possible that some readers of this letter had become enamoured of such teaching, causing the author to insist that marriage is honourable for *all* classes of people. It is immorality and adultery, not marriage itself, which will come under God's judgment.

The exhortation and warning found in this verse are strikingly relevant in our own day when such a high percentage of marriages end in divorce. Even the Christian marriage is at risk unless both partners recognize the importance of commitment to Christ and to each other. Some churches make excessive demands on married Christians. Loyal participation in weeknight activities, in addition to Sunday responsibilities, means that married couples with children are kept apart, family life is seriously endangered and essential leisure time reduced to a minimum. Church leaders need to pay more than lip-service to the spiritual importance of the family and the sanctity of marriage. It is tragic if the local church's claim on a member's time robs him or her of the opportunity to maintain a happy marriage and cultivate a healthy, attractive home and family life. Young people and older alike need to remember that a good marriage doesn't just 'happen'. In the rush and tear of modern life, when people have to cope with financial difficulties and anxiety over employment, it is all too easy for overworked and preoccupied husbands or wives to take their partners for granted.

3. Be content (13:5–6)

5*Keep your life free from love of money, and be content with what you have; for he has said, 'I will never fail you nor forsake you.'* 6*Hence we can confidently say,*

[7] Mt. 19:3. [8] 1 Tim. 4:3.

'The Lord is my helper,
I will not be afraid;
what can man do to me?'

A highly materialistic society like our own, with all the pressures of godless secularism, needs the exhortation of this early Christian writer that we should keep our lives *free from love of money* and *be content* with the possessions we already have. Covetousness, either of another man's wife,[9] or someone else's property, is a perilous snare. The Christian believes that in his providential goodness the Lord will give him what is good for him. He will work hard, be generous with his possessions, and leave the rest with God.[10] He certainly does not spend his precious time fretting about how he can collect more money, or acquire more valuable things. This is the way the godless behave.[11] The believer is grateful for those material necessities he already possesses and rejoices in far more satisfying spiritual possessions. His heart is set on those riches,[12] not on the perishable things which have no value beyond death. Covetousness is born of doubt; contentment is the child of faith. It does not come suddenly; it is a habit of mind and can best be acquired by constantly reminding ourselves of God's fatherly provision and his generous promises. Once more, Old Testament Scripture is used to support the argument.[13] God says something generously to us so that we can say something confidently to others; *for he has said, 'I will never fail you nor forsake you.' Hence we can confidently say, 'The Lord is my helper.'* Ultimately, contentment becomes vocal. It is given an opportunity to explain the reason for its astonishing calm, trust and satisfaction.

Possibly there is a hint here not only of the fear of poverty but also of the fear of persecution. The writer recalls not only the reassurance given to Joshua but also the peace which came to the afflicted psalmist. He quotes Psalm 118:6: *I will not be afraid; what can man do to me*? It is possible to covet popularity and be prepared to make almost any sacrifice to acquire it. Believers know that the fear of man is just as enslaving as the love of money. When the Lord is their *helper* they are

[9] Ex. 20:17. [10] 2 Thes. 3:10; 2 Cor. 9:6–11. [11] Mt. 6:32.
[12] 1 Tim. 6:17–19. [13] Dt. 31:6, 8; Jos. 1:5; Ps. 118:6.

released from such tyranny. Pleasure (13:4), possessions (13:5) and popularity (13:6) are all under the sovereign control of their holy, generous and loving God.

The appeal for 'contentment' in the New Testament is not intended to convey the idea that ambition of every kind is contrary to God's purpose. Every believer ought to bring his best to his job or profession, recognizing that whatever he does in life ought to be of such quality that it can be presented as a sacrificial offering to Christ. He does his utmost to be a first-rate worker, but he does not lust fretfully after promotion for its own sake. He is content to leave that in the hands of a providential God who knows what is best for him. Self-regarding ambition can be the most destructive force in the world. Dominated by greed, it pays little attention to the needs of others, the will of God, or even personal health. In a selfishly ambitious society Christian contentment is a quality of great evangelistic worth. It reminds others that there is more to life than transitory success.

4. Be loyal (13:7–12)

7Remember your leaders, those who spoke to you the word of God; consider the outcome of their life, and imitate their faith.
8Jesus Christ is the same yesterday and today and for ever.
9Do not be led away by diverse and strange teachings; for it is well that the heart be strengthened by grace, not by foods, which have not benefited their adherents. 10We have an altar from which those who serve the tent have no right to eat.
11For the bodies of those animals whose blood is brought into the sanctuary by the high priest as a sacrifice for sin are burned outside the camp. 12So Jesus also suffered outside the gate in order to sanctify the people through his own blood.

The reference to those who are unafraid, because the Lord is their helper, leads the writer to reflect on the heroism and faith of this church's former leaders. They were remembered in this church for their faithful preaching (*who spoke to you the word of God*) and their exemplary living. The readers are urged to examine or 'scan closely' the lives of such people, paying special attention to the *outcome* of their lives. That word (*ekbasis*) may refer to the issue of their testimony, its abiding fruits, the 'result of one's way of life'.[14] But it is probably far more natural here to see in this statement a reference to the death of these leaders, possibly even by martyrdom. Even if they did not pay that supreme price, the very way in which they had passed from this life serenely and unafraid was a radiant example in a world terrified by death and an unknown future. Christians of this kind have an abiding influence; the readers are encouraged to *imitate their faith*.

But though such leaders have gone, the eternal, living and changeless Christ is still alongside them. He is always their contemporary, *the same yesterday and today and for ever*. The letter closes as it began by reminding its readers of their unchanging Lord. He is always *the same* (1:11–12). In the great *yesterday* of world history he died for them as the unique sacrifice. *Today* he is the forerunner who has already entered heaven and is even now interceding at God's right hand. The future is known fully to him. He lives *for ever*, the Lord of history who will certainly return (10:37) for those 'who are eagerly waiting for him' (9:28).

This sentence (13:8) is probably the letter's most famous verse. We must not forget its context. It is set between the commendation of faithful leaders (13:7) and the condemnation of false ones (13:9). Some of these Christians may have taken their eyes off Christ (12:2), only to develop 'itching ears' by accumulating 'teachers to suit their own likings'.[15]

We live in a period when the warning and exhortation of verse 9 have special relevance. Many of our contemporaries are beginning to acknowledge some form of spiritual need in their lives and into this vacuum the perpetrators of various religious notions or Christian deviations press their unbiblical or distorted teaching. There has scarcely been any other time in this century when so many of these cults have been present and active. New ones seem to proliferate every year or so and it is hard to keep up with them. Some are particularly successful in reaching students and other young people away from home. We need to take seriously the teaching of this letter about the primacy of God's Word and the supremacy of God's Son, so that we are not blown about or led away by

[14] AG, p. 237. [15] 2 Tim. 4:3.

diverse and strange teachings of any group not firmly based on the teaching of Scripture. We need to pray for friends who may be involved in them, recognizing that many are genuinely seeking the truth and could discover peace, life and security if they came to Christ. Some young adherents of the sects are disillusioned with the church, and that should come as a rebuke to us all. Have we offered the warmth, friendship, acceptance, sense of community and 'certainty' which attract many people to these cults in the first place?

The reference in verse 9 to *foods* certainly implies that these first century 'blind guides' had perpetrated their *strange teachings* about dietary restrictions or food laws of one kind or another. Such things were popular enough in the first century among both Jews and Gentiles (9:10).[16] Those who have embraced this teaching have imbibed no lasting spiritual benefit from it. It is *grace* which strengthens the believer's heart, not subscription to rules and the avoidance of prohibited foods. There is no room now for material sacrifices, animal offerings, sacred meals and hallowed altars. All that is over and gone. Christians have determined to give central importance to one great aspect of their faith: Christ died for them. He was sacrificed for us and shed, not the blood of bulls, but *his own blood*. Those who stay within the narrow confines of Judaism and serve its *tent*, or tabernacle, can derive no benefit from the only sacrifice which really matters.

The sacrificial imagery recalls the sin offering and the annual Day of Atonement.[17] Under the old covenant the priests were entitled to use the sacrificial animals as food after they had been offered, but that did not apply to the sin offering, nor to the great Day of Atonement. On those occasions the sacrifice was burnt in its entirety (13:11). *All* the offering was presented to God; none was available for the ministering priest. The author is emphasizing here that those who wish to remain under the old covenant cannot share in the great sin offering of all time, the sacrifice of Christ. To *serve the tent* is to remain under the old covenant and such people have *no right to eat* the eternally satisfying provisions of the new.

[16] Col. 2:16, 20–23; 1 Tim. 4:3.   [17] Lv. 4:12; 16:27.

5. Be bold (13:13–14)

13*Therefore let us go forth to him outside the camp, and bear the abuse he endured.* 14*For here we have no lasting city, but we seek the city which is to come.*

The use of the sin-offering illustration suggests to the writer another truth of immediate practical relevance to his readers. The sacrifice was 'burned outside the camp' (13:11). In the same way, the Lord Jesus suffered 'outside the gate'; rejected by his own people, he died outside the walls of Jerusalem, abused and despised by his own nation. These Christians must now recognize that they too must go outside the secure confines of Judaism, which was a 'safe religion' officially recognized by the Roman authorities and usually left in peace. Believers in Christ must *go forth* as he went forth, *bearing the abuse he endured*, and so fully identifying themselves with his sufferings.[18] Let it be clearly noted that they must go *to him*, not 'for him', for that is where Jesus is, in the hostile Christ-rejecting world.

In his exposition of this letter, William Manson explores the possibility that the letter may have been written not to a company of Christians who were about to apostasize, but rather to an insular Jewish Christian group who had become exclusive and isolationist in their attitude, keeping the gospel to themselves. Afraid of drawing attention to their *distinctive* Christian message, they had minimized it, 'living too much in the Jewish part of their Christianity'.[19] In this way they had built secure walls around themselves, ignoring God's purpose that they should be a missionary people. It is an attractive interpretation and, if his thesis is correct, the exhortation to *go forth to him outside the camp* has even more striking appeal. In that case it is not addressed to heroic Christians who had been cast out of the synagogue, but to hesitant Christians who prefer to stay within it. This verse calls this group of reticent believers to heroism and courageous testimony. If they are to follow Christ, they must be prepared for hardship.

Manson also suggests that this group may have been feeling

[18] Phil. 3:10; Col. 1:24. [19] Manson, p. 24.

quite acutely the attraction, if not allurement, of the specially 'Jewish' aspects of their faith, 'its worship, sanctions, sacraments, holy prerogatives, and means of grace.'[20] The author seems to enter into their difficulty, pointing out the ineffectiveness of the old covenant, but not in any sense deriding them. He is sensitive about the things that are dear to his readers. His delicate portrayal of the tabernacle furnishings (9:1–5) betrays the mind of one for whom these things were of treasured significance. Even when the author is writing about the old covenant sacrifices he does not for a moment deny that they procured ceremonial purification, even if they did not reach man's disturbed conscience (9:13–14). It is possible that their sense of privation, which some of his readers may feel if they put organized corporate Judaism behind them, makes the writer all the more concerned not only to exalt Christianity's better things (12:22–24) but also to emphasize the elements of continuity which would be specially precious. After all, they worship the same God and the doctrine of God in this letter is wholly in keeping with the Old Testament revelation. Then again, they loved the same Scriptures. Throughout the letter we have noticed the author's intense love for the Old Testament and his brilliant use of it in exposition. The angels who visited God's people in former days continue to minister to the needs of the Christian community (1:14). In leaving the synagogue they have not turned their backs on the choice leaders and personalities of the old dispensation; the patriarchs and their successors are now part of the church triumphant, 'made perfect' by the work of Christ (11:40; 12:23).

6. Be worshipful (13:15–16)

[15]*Through him then let us continually offer up a sacrifice of praise to God, that is, the fruit of lips that acknowledge his name.* [16]*Do not neglect to do good and to share what you have, for such sacrifices are pleasing to God.*

When these great personalities of Old Testament times offered sacrifices, they did so anticipating a better sacrifice (9:23).

[20] *Ibid.*, p. 158.

But, says the writer, although the one perfect, complete, unrepeatable sacrifice has been made by our great high priest, other sacrifices ought to be presented to God day by day. These offerings are made not in order to secure redemption, but to please God. It may not be too fanciful to see in these verses four sacrifices which Christians need to offer *continually*.

The first is *the sacrifice of thankful praise. Through him*, that is through Christ who suffered for us and lives for ever, let us *offer up a sacrifice of praise to God*. The busy rush of modern life often robs us of time for quiet reflection about all that we owe to God. The godless do not 'give thanks to him'[21] but Christians should do so. Just to reflect on the teaching of this chapter alone surely inspires praise to God. Do we not want to praise him for the 'brotherly love' (13:1) which has been shown to us in our Christian lives and for the generous hospitality we have often received (13:2)? Have people not cared for us in our needs, and shown compassion when we were in trouble (13:3)? Some of us thank God especially for loyal and loving partners in marriage, or for the fine example of a happy relationship we have seen in our own parents (13:4). Do we not want to praise God that he has met our material needs (13:5a) and assured us of his providential and protective care (13:5b–6)? Many of us bless God for outstanding preachers, teachers, Bible class leaders, Sunday School teachers, Christian parents and friends, who shared with us 'the word of God' and we praise him not only for the imperishable things they proclaimed, but also for their radiant Christian example (13:7). Every believer wants to offer *a sacrifice of praise* for the gift of Jesus, the changeless Lord, for his saving death, his present help, and his future plan (13:8). Can we not praise him for the sound doctrine imparted to us in the past and available to us today in holy Scripture, and for the fact that so many times our hearts have been 'strengthened by grace' (13:9)? All this, and so much more, should inspire our adoration and prompt our thanksgiving so that, not occasionally, but *continually*, that is whenever these great facts cross our mind, we should offer *a sacrifice of praise to God*. Sacrifices of this kind were not

[21] Rom. 1:21.

unknown in Old Testament times[22] and ought to have a prominent place in our own lives.

Secondly, we can offer *the sacrifice of unashamed witness.* Such sacrifices are represented as *the fruit of lips that acknowledge his name.* Here is another aspect of our sacrificial worship. If the sacrifice is made by our lips and not only in our hearts, then it becomes vocal and public; other people are soon aware of it. Although the phrase obviously amplifies *the sacrifice of praise*, it does express another aspect of Christian gratitude, and one which might have been specially relevant to the first readers of this letter. They are to use their lips, literally 'to make confession' (*homologountōn*, the verbal form of the noun used in 4:15; 10:23). Possibly, as Manson suggests, they did not want to expose themselves to the kind of harassment which would inevitably come their way if they openly confessed their faith and acknowledged Christ's name. It is one thing to express one's indebtedness to God; it is quite another to allow other people to know how much he means to us. In a spiritually ignorant society, like our own, regular attendance at Christian worship presents the Christian with an opportunity to witness. As we too offer *the fruit of* our *lips*, people with no clear faith may become aware that we too *acknowledge his name.*

Thirdly, there is *the sacrifice of compassionate service.* Another offering 'which God approves' (NEB) is that of doing good to others: 'Never forget to show kindness' (NEB). Such loving ministry to the needs of others was characteristic of this church's past (10:33–34) and present (6:10) life. Here our writer pleads that this form of daily sacrifice must be offered devotedly and regularly. 'Doing good' is an important aspect of the New Testament doctrine of the Christian life. In their understandable fear of 'salvation by works', evangelicals have sometimes minimized this important feature of biblical Christianity. Jesus expected his disciples to do good works and the early Christian people were deeply influenced by this practical aspect of Christ's teaching.[23] The apostle Paul clearly taught that God has ordained that his people should practice good works.[24]

[22] Lv. 7:12; Ps. 50:12–14, 23.
[23] Mt. 5:16; Gal. 6:10; 1 Thes. 5:15.
[24] Eph. 2:10.

Finally, Christians are expected to offer continually *the sacrifice of generous giving*. They are to share what they have. The fact that this word *share* (*koinōnias*) is used may suggest that its author is thinking of those monetary offerings which were made in New Testament times on behalf of needy people. The term soon came to be employed in this technical sense, much as we might talk about a 'fellowship fund'. Our imaginative financial support of the Lord's work is a Christian sacrifice still to be offered, not only regularly, methodically and proportionately, but cheerfully[25] as well. It is not at all necessary or even wise, however, to restrict this form of sacrifice to 'the collection'. Christians have other opportunities to offer this sacrifice by sharing with others, believers and unbelievers, some of the good things that God has so generously given to them.

[25] 1 Cor. 16:2; 2 Cor. 9:7.

13:17–21

26. Honouring the church's leaders

An earlier verse in this chapter (13:7) referred appreciatively to this church's former leaders, and there are three references to local Christian leadership; these men are to be remembered (13:7), obeyed (13:17) and greeted (13:24). We have already had an opportunity to discern the pattern of leadership most approved by our author. Faithful leadership in the Christian congregation should be both didactic and exemplary. The leader must teach 'the word of God' and have a faith that is worth imitating (13:7). The writer now goes on to emphasize some additional qualities which he also considers to be of supreme importance. Those whose responsibility it is to have oversight in the local church, or in any group where Christians meet, need to recognize that their leadership is pastoral, accountable and dependent.

1. Pastoral leadership (13:17)

Obey your leaders and submit to them; for they are keeping watch over your souls, as men who will have to give account. Let them do this joyfully, and not sadly, for that would be of no advantage to you.

The leaders are here described as those who are *keeping watch* (*agrypneō*) over their souls. These men have to keep watch as shepherds caring for sheep, or as a sentry on military service. This word is used in the Septuagint to describe the activities of a watchman on duty in the city, rich imagery used by the Old Testament prophets.[1] The word might even be meant literally; in the recent troubles and divisions in this church these leaders have lost sleep over the congregation. They are diligent pastors, alert shepherds, with a God-given responsibility to care for the flock.[2] How are the members expected to react to such devoted pastoral leadership? They should offer responsive obedience, respectful submission and loving co-operation.

a. Responsive obedience

The teaching ministry of these leaders will be of limited value if local Christians merely listen to their words but do not put them into practice.[3] As we have frequently observed, there is repeated emphasis throughout this letter on the necessity of obedience to the revealed word of God. Naturally, the writer is not inculcating blind, unthinking obedience to everything a Christian teacher says, otherwise there would be little point in issuing the warning he has just given about 'diverse and strange' doctrines. In New Testament teaching there is clear recognition that discernment is obviously necessary[4] and also that obedience to the revealed word of God is essential.

b. Respectful submission

Similarly, they are exhorted to *submit* to their leaders. If obedience applies to the leaders' teaching, then submission relates to their leaders' function. The clear recognition of authoritative leadership is essential for the harmony and effective administration of any group. Just as the New Testament does not encourage undiscerning obedience, neither does it teach unintelligent submission. One of the markedly unhealthy aspects of some contemporary teaching is the current 'shepherding' fashion and the notion, popularized in some house churches and elsewhere, that every believer is meant to have a spiritual mentor to whom he is fully accountable for every aspect of his life. The spiritual 'elder' has to be consulted before making significant purchases, changing one's

[1] Is. 62:6; Ezk. 3:17; 33:1–9. [2] 1 Pet. 5:2.
[3] Jas. 1:22. [4] 1 Jn. 4:1.

job and accepting fresh responsibilities. The Scripture does not teach, encourage, or exemplify submission of this sort. It is bad for the one who practises it in that it discourages personal accountability to the Lord God, a mark of true Christian maturity. Furthermore, it minimizes the importance of other deep relationships, especially marriage, through which the will of God can be most naturally discerned.

More seriously, however, teaching of this kind places a highly dangerous power in the hands of those who either distort or manipulate biblical teaching in this way. It is a refined form of megalomania, out of keeping with the teaching and example of one who poured out water to wash the feet of his disciples and knelt in the presence of those he wished to help. The Christian is answerable to Christ alone. His desire to be an obedient, submissive member of a local church must not be exploited in the interests of the incongruously papal pretensions of either individual or collective leadership. Remember that the New Testament has something to say about *mutual* submission.[5] It is important to compare scripture with scripture and see New Testament teaching as a whole, and also to remember that a minister in the early church was not expected to be a dictator, but a 'model of good deeds' and of exemplary humility.[6]

c. *Loving co-operation*

It is possible that there had been a marked lack of obedience and submission in this church, for the writer urges that the members should respond eagerly to their leaders so that such people might derive happiness and pleasure from their ministry and not grief. The word *sadly* is a strong one; it can be translated 'groaning'. If spiritual leaders have to labour under grim and hostile conditions in the local church, then that does not work out to the members' immediate good and certainly not to their ultimate advantage. This leads us to the next feature of our writer's concept of Christian leadership; it has eschatological implications.

[5] Rom. 12:10; Gal. 5:13; Eph. 5:21; Phil. 2:3–4.
[6] 1 Tim. 5:1–2; Tit. 2:7; 1 Pet. 5:3–5.

2. Accountable leadership

Leadership in the local church does not operate merely from a this-worldly point of view. All good Christian service has an other-worldly perspective. These teachers know that in the great Day when the books are opened, they *will have to give account*. It may well be that the reference here to the leaders' joy may be not to their present satisfaction but to their ultimate destiny. It conveys strongly the future accountability not only of the ministers (*let them do this joyfully*) but also of the awkward members in the congregation (*that would be of no advantage to you*)! One thing is certain, these ministers knew that (like all other Christians) in the end they were not answerable to fellow church members for their leadership; their divinely ordained appointment made them responsible primarily to God. Because such work deals with eternal issues, it has eternal consequences.

3. Dependent leadership (13:18–21)

Some indication of the writer's own understanding of humble leadership can be discerned from the fact that he asks for the prayers of this congregation for himself and then prays for them in a concluding benediction. In the exercise of his own spiritual responsibility, he is depending on their prayers for him and they and he alike are dependent on *the great shepherd of the sheep*.

a. Their prayers for him (13:18–19)

18*Pray for us, for we are sure that we have a clear conscience, desiring to act honourably in all things.* 19*I urge you the more earnestly to do this in order that I may be restored to you the sooner.*

Conscious of the fact that no-one can work effectively for Christ unaided and unsupported, he asks them to continue to pray on his behalf. He has written this 'word of exhortation' (13:22) only out of a deep sense of pastoral concern. He does not want them to misunderstand his intention in sending the letter. His conscience is now clear on the matter, for he wants to act in this as in all things only in an honourable manner, worthy of his vocation and the Christ he serves. By way of special emphasis, his request for prayer is repeated. He *earnestly* urges them to go on praying, just as he urged them earlier to attend earnestly to the word (2:1 where the same term is used). Obeying the word, through which God speaks to us, and engaging in prayer, by which we speak to him, are inseparable spiritual responsibilities. The writer longs not only to communicate with his congregation by letter, but to see them face to face. He knows that in Christian work a leader has more to do than just declare truth, essential as that is. It is an equal privilege to enjoy the fellowship of Christ's people. Obedience to the word of God will issue in love for the people of God.

b. His prayer for them (13:20–21)

[20]*Now may the God of peace who brought again from the dead our Lord Jesus, the great shepherd of the sheep, by the blood of the eternal covenant,* [21]*equip you with everything good that you may do his will, working in you that which is pleasing in his sight, through Jesus Christ; to whom be glory for ever and ever. Amen.*

The author brings this inspiring letter to a majestic conclusion by praying for those who have listened to his words as they have been read in the Christian congregation. His great longing is that the Lord God will equip them *with everything good*. His confidence in the God to whom he prays is as important as the things he asks for as he prays.

Only *a saving God* can equip them with everything good. He is *the God of peace*. Peace in biblical thought is something far more than serenity; it denotes the quality of salvation God is able to give to his people. He has obtained peace for us through the work of Christ, who brought man's greatest warfare to an end by his victory over sin, death and the devil. By that triumphant conquest we have peace with God and peace with man.[7] It is also distinctly possible that our writer chooses to address the Lord in this way because he thereby

[7] Rom. 5:1; Eph. 2:14–17; Col. 1:20.

prays that any strife or disharmony in this local fellowship (12:14) will be removed by the God of peace, who is able to save his people not only from past transgressions, but also from present failure.

He knows too that because he has *a mighty God* they will be equipped with everything good. Their God brought the Lord Jesus up from the dead. Such an invincible God can surely answer their prayers. Are their difficulties greater than the problem of raising the dead to victorious life? Nothing is too hard for such a God.

On behalf of these believers, he beseeches the help of *a compassionate God*, the God who gave his Son, our Lord Jesus, *the great shepherd of the sheep*. Throughout his lifetime Christ exercised the caring, compassionate ministry of a 'good shepherd'. He loved the sheep so much that he gave his own life for them and, by his risen power, he continues to guard and protect them. As the 'chief Shepherd' he certainly cares for his under-shepherds and for the whole flock of God.[8] As the great shepherd nothing is impossible for him and no detail too insignificant for his attention.

The writer's prayer is also addressed to *a faithful God*, for his great redeeming work was accomplished through *the blood of the eternal covenant*. He has pledged himself in love to his people to pardon their sins (10:15–18) and meet their needs. This covenant God, who is bound to his people in such a strong and eternal relationship, is always true to his word.

Moreover, this pastoral prayer is addressed to *a resourceful God*. He knows what is good for them and has gifts with which he can *equip* them. The word used here (*katartisai*) literally means 'put into a proper condition' or 'make complete'. The readers may have become aware of those gifts of God they needed in their Christian lives in order to be put into a proper condition. Possibly they longed for renewed confidence in Christ's supremacy and sufficiency and the other great truths with which our author has sought to encourage them at this time of doubt and persecution. Whatever their needs, the God of peace would certainly *equip them with everything good*.

But this verb *equip* (*katartizō*) can also mean 'restore',

[8] Jn. 10:11, 15, 27–29; 1 Pet. 5:4.

'repair', or 'mend'. It is the word used in the gospels to describe the work of the disciples when they were 'mending' (*katartizontas*) their nets.[9] In equipping his people with everything good, our God is able not only to supply what is necessary, but also to repair what is broken. Some of the believers who first received this letter may well have felt that their compromise with Judaism had marred their distinctive Christian witness, that their inadequate view of Jesus had led to devastating effects, not only in their own Christian experience, but in the lives of others. Could they ever be restored to their former devotion? The writer urges them to believe that they can, because the God of peace is able to do this for them. Or there may be a hint here about the corporate difficulties within this local church. It had become torn and divided by strife; the limbs had been dislocated (12:13) and some were beginning to wonder whether they could ever be made whole again. The superb final prayer of this letter assures these believers that things can be different; the God of peace can mend that which is torn and repair that which is broken.

We have noticed the God who is addressed and the request that is made. We must also mention the ambition which is pursued. By his promised resources the God of peace will enable them to keep some important objectives paramount in their living and praying. Equipped *with everything good* they will do that which honours him (*do his will*), which pleases him (*that which is pleasing in his sight*) and which glorifies him (*to whom be glory*).

[9] Mt. 4:21; Mk. 1:19.

13:22–25
27. Closing salutations

The closing sentences of the letter bear all the marks of the pastoral compassion which has been dominant throughout its earlier chapters. Before the writer takes leave of his readers, he reminds them that throughout the Christian life there is instruction to heed, fellowship to cherish and grace to appropriate.

1. Instruction to heed (13:22)

I appeal to you, brethren, bear with my word of exhortation, for I have written to you briefly.

The writer refers to his letter as a brief *word of exhortation.* It took about one hour to read to the members of this local church, and is essentially an exhortation rather than a detached and remote doctrinal treatise. Repeatedly the author urges his friends to fresh endeavour or renewed dedication with the phrase, 'let us . . .'. Throughout the entire letter there has been recurrent emphasis on the importance of the word of God in the experience of the believer. The truth is not only a message to read, or a story to inspire, but an exhortation to heed and an instruction to be obeyed. We also need to face the same question: what practical difference has the study of this letter made to our own Christian lives?

2. Fellowship to cherish (13:23–24)

[23]You should understand that our brother Timothy has been released, with whom I shall see you if he comes soon. [24]Greet all your leaders and all the saints. Those who come from Italy send you greetings.

Even this letter's conventional greetings express its author's pastoral concern. He longs that *all* the members might know how deeply he feels for them. He is not content to restrict his message or his greetings to those who are 'keeping watch' (13:17) or hold office in the church. 'Greet *all* your leaders and *all* the saints.' Possibly some of this church's leaders and members had become estranged, but he is eager that his congregation's earlier unity should be regained and its fellowship restored. *Those who come from Italy* is most naturally interpreted not of people who, at the time of writing, are living in Italy, but of Italian people who are resident in some other part of the world. The personal references to Timothy, the author, the leaders and members of this local church, and the Italian Christians who wish to convey their greetings, all indicate the importance of fellowship. We owe an immense amount to the exhortation (3:13; 6:11; 10:24), encouragement (6:9–10; 10:25) and example (10:32, 35; 13:7) of other Christians. That kind of friendship is of rich immediate help and has unlimited spiritual potential. We need to ask ourselves whether we bring to other Christians the same quality of help as we have most certainly received from many of our fellow believers over the years.

3. Grace to appropriate (13:25)

Grace be with all of you. Amen.

Grace is a significant theme in this letter, and when the word occurs it is often in rather unusual but inspiring contexts. When he is expounding the work of Christ, the writer insists on the initiative of God as he explains that it was 'by the grace of God' that Christ tasted death for everyone (2:9). When he invites his readers to pray, he reminds them that they approach 'the throne of grace' and assures them that by praying they will receive all the available resources in the form of 'grace to help in time of need' (4:16). When he expounds the perils of apostasy, he describes the seriousness of those who have 'outraged the Spirit of grace' (10:29) and warns them to make sure 'that no one fail to obtain the grace of God' (12:15). When he recalls his readers to grateful thanksgiving, he uses this word again: 'Let us have *charis*' or 'Let us give thanks' (12:28). He also explains that the heart needs to be 'strengthened by grace' (13:9), not by ceremonial foods. In these seven earlier references to *grace*, the readers have had the opportunity to recognize that living the Christian life is exacting and demanding, but we are not left to our own slender and totally inadequate resources. A gracious God will meet all his people's needs. Because God is generous, his grace is certainly for *all*. The letter has contained passages of serious and necessary warning, but it closes on the note of radiant confidence. Whilst believers are depending on such grace, they cannot be shaken (12:28) and they will not be lost. The rich supplies of his unlimited grace are available to every believer (4:16) and they are ours for ever.